NEW
CHINESE
COOKING
SCHOOL

NEW CHINESE COOKING SCHOOL

Kenneth Lo

HPBooks®

新開辦中餐烹飪學校

ANOTHER BEST-SELLING VOLUME FROM HP Books®

Published by HP Books®, P.O. Box 5367, Tucson, AZ 85703
ISBN: Hardcover: 0-89586-406-1
Library of Congress Catalog Card Number: 85-80030

This book was designed and produced by
Quarto Publishing Ltd
The Old Brewery, 6 Blundell Street
London N7 9BH

Senior Editor Tessa Rose
Editors Barbara Croxford, Juliet Luiks (HP)

Art Editor Nick Clark
Design Penny Dawes
Photographers David Burch and Jon Wyand

Publisher Rick Bailey (HP)
Art Director Alastair Campbell
Editorial Directors Jim Miles, Elaine Woodard (HP)

- Special thanks to Scott Ewing and Hazel Edington
- Additional thanks to Cheong-Leen Supermarkets for
kindly loaning groceries, equipment and utensils

Typeset by Text Filmsetters Ltd, Orpington
Color origination by Universal Colour Scanning Ltd,
Hong Kong
Printed by Lee Fung Asco Printers Ltd, Hong Kong

CONTENTS

Introduction		6
Equipment for the Chinese Kitchen	Woks ● steamers ● pots and pans ● utensils	8
Ingredients for Cooking Chinese	Dried foods ● rice and noodles ● vegetables and fruit ● herbs and spices ● soy beans and bean-based products ● eggs ● sauces, oils, vinegars and wines ● nuts and seeds ● pickles	14
Basic Preparations	Cutting, slicing and shredding: vegetables ● garnishes ● meat and poultry ● fish and seafood	30
Methods and Techniques of Cooking	Stir-frying ● deep-frying ● reducing sauce ● making pancakes ● rice ● steaming ● flavor and texture blending	42

RECIPES

SOUPS		54
RICE, NOODLES AND VEGETABLES		66
BEAN CURD AND EGGS		98
FISH AND SEAFOOD		116
POULTRY		146
MEAT		180
DESSERTS		216
DIM SUM		224
REGIONAL CUISINE	Peking and the north ● Shanghai and the east Sichuan and the west ● Canton and the south	242

How to Choose and Order Chinese Food	276
Index and acknowledgements	282

★ ★ ★ ★ ★
Recipes have been graded according to ease of preparation and cooking, on a scale from ★ to ★ ★ ★ ★ ★.
★ denotes a dish that requires few and simple skills.
★ ★ ★ ★ denotes a dish for which mastery of certain techniques is required.

MSG
MSG is monosodium glutamate, white crystals which enhance the flavor of food. The use of MSG is optional.

INTRODUCTION

The speed at which the taste for Chinese food has spread throughout the Western world over the last 25 years is truly remarkable. Yet despite the enormous popularity of Chinese food, the practice of Chinese cooking is still regarded by many Westerners as being difficult and requiring some special talent of those who attempt it. This is mainly because the techniques used are so different from those of Western cuisines, but this does not mean that they are any more complex.

In Western cooking, individual foodstuffs are conditioned by heat until they are ready for consumption: meat is roasted or broiled; vegetables are boiled or fried. But, essentially, it is the nature of the initial ingredient that determines the character of the dish. Chinese cooking is dominated by compound dishes. Ingredients are mixed and cooked in different ways. It is this method – rather than the ingredients themselves – that determines the nature of the final dish. There is much more flavor- and texture-blending involved in Chinese cooking, which is where the fun starts.

Once you have grasped the implications of this radical new approach to cooking,

the rest is simple. Most of the techniques used in Chinese cooking are the same as those used in the West, and those that are different can be categorized into a few set patterns of using heat and marrying ingredients. The only completely new skill that needs to be mastered is stir-frying. Other techniques employed are quick, open steaming, steaming in a closed container and slow simmering. These methods are used when fresh, prime ingredients are not available, but the end result is often as tasty as if first-rate ingredients had been used. Red-cooking is simply slow-stewing in soy sauce. Each of these techniques is well known to cooks in the West.

The exotic ingredients required should present no problem either. Over 80 percent of Chinese dishes can be prepared with no more than a handful of specifically Chinese ingredients, which are easily obtained from foodstores everywhere. If you examine the recipes in this book, you will find that in a majority of cases the dishes can be easily prepared and cooked. The essential point is to regard Chinese cooking as fun-cooking. Once you have done that you will find that the techniques are soon mastered, leaving you free to fully enjoy and explore the creativity that Chinese cooking allows.

Equipment for the Chinese Kitchen

THE WOK WAS INVENTED about two thousand years ago and is definitely the most useful piece of equipment for Chinese cooking. Its thin metal and deep, curved sides and bottom make it perfect for frying: less oil is needed for deep-frying, and for stir-frying bite-sized ingredients can be quickly tossed without spilling out. Because wok–cooking is so quick, several dishes can be prepared one after another in the same wok which saves cooking space and washing up time.

The best woks are traditional ones made of iron or carbon steel, with one long or two wooden side handles. The first is excellent for stir-frying since the cook can hold the wok yet is far away from the very hot oil, using a long-handled spoon, chopsticks or wok scoop to toss the ingredients. The two-handled wok is better for deep-frying or for steaming food because it is steadier to move when full of liquid. When buying a wok the important thing is that yours has deep sides, is fairly large, about 14 inches in diameter, and the metal is not too thin or stir-fried food will burn easily. Make sure your wok has a good fitting domed lid to use when steaming.

SEASONING AND CLEANING A WOK

It is very important to season a wok before first cooking in it. Scrub it well to remove any protective coating, rinse, then dry it well. Place the wok over low heat, wipe it lightly with vegetable oil and let it heat for about 10 minutes. When cool, wipe the wok with paper towels to remove the dark film. Repeat the process until the paper wipes clean. Clean a seasoned wok in plain water without soap; never scrub it. Let the wok dry thoroughly over low heat before storing it. If the metal ever rusts, clean it with a scouring cream or fine sandpaper, rinse, dry and season it again.

OTHER EQUIPMENT

A **wok brush** is a stiff bundle of thin bamboo splints that is good for cleaning a wok. A **wok stand** is necessary for wok cooking when deep-frying and steaming as it provides a steady base for the pan. The stand is also used with a two-handled wok for stir-frying. If cooking over gas, be sure to use a solid wok stand that has ventilation holes. It gives the wok stability and prevents the flame from going out.

Bamboo steamers are placed on a metal or bamboo trivet over water. When the food is in place, the wok can be covered with its lid or with the steamer's own tight-fitting bamboo lid, which is necessary when more than one type of food, each in its own steamer, is stacked on top of the other. When new, wash then put the empty steamer over water and let it steam for 5 minutes.

Metal steamers can be placed directly on the heat, fit snugly and have a tight-fitting lid. To prevent food sticking, place it on cheesecloth or in a heatproof dish.

With able-bodied men and women engaged in food production in China, it's the old and the young who operate the food stalls. Here the old woman is cooking some stir-fry delicacy to accompany the soft-rice or congee cooking in the large pot. The picture was taken in a market in Sian, where the famous Terracotta Warriors were discovered.

中餐廚房設備

Left: double wooden–handled wok with wok brush; *right:* single–handled wok on wok stand with long–handled metal sieve and smaller perforated ladle; *below:* long wooden chopsticks for cooking on chopstick stand and soft brush for cleaning woks.

Above: base and lid of a metal steamer; *below:* Chinese bamboo steamer with lid and ornate wooden cooking chopsticks.

Left: Chinese earthenware cooking pot with basket ladle; *right:* Mongolian hot pot with long–handled wire baskets for cooking. (Recipe page 211.)

Resting on a chopping board, *above:* small chopper (cleaver); *below:* heavier, large chopper.

■ EATING CHINESE STYLE ■

A simple Chinese table setting including a soup bowl and spoon, a small shallow bowl for dip sauces, chopsticks and a small, deeper bowl for holding rice and elements added from the several communal main dishes.

Below left: to eat with chopsticks, hold the bowl close to the mouth to facilitate and grace the movements.

Below: to use chopsticks, hold one chopstick towards its base between your thumb and index finger and against the middle of the fourth finger at its tip. This chopstick remains stationary. Hold the second chopstick similarly against your index finger, supporting it with your thumb like a pencil. The two thinner tips should be kept level, with the first or lower chopstick kept steady while you manipulate the second or upper chopstick to pick up the food.

Top: metal ladle. *Left to right:* bamboo sieve, basket ladle; wok scoop; glazing brush; larger wok scoop; whisk.

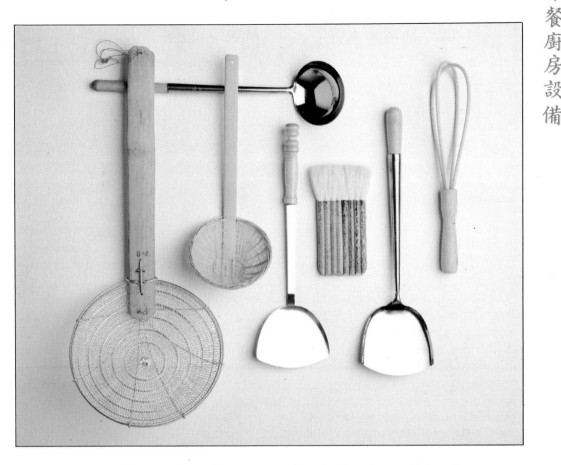

Electric rice cookers cook and keep rice warm during the meal, but they are not essential and may be expensive unless you cook a lot of rice.

Chinese earthenware cooking pots, also known as sand pots, come in a variety of shapes and sizes, all with unglazed exteriors and lids. They can be used over low heat, as in making soup, but not in the oven. Caution: they will crack if hot and put on a cold surface or an empty pot is heated. Any heavy casserole makes a satisfactory substitute.

Mongolian hot-pots, or fire-pots, heat stock or soup at the table from glowing charcoal under and in the middle of the pot. Small long-handled wire baskets or bamboo sieves or chopsticks are used to add and remove ingredients from liquid.

Long-handled sieves and perforated ladles are useful for lifting food from hot oil, when steaming or straining noodles. A **wok scoop** is a long-handled metal disc perfect for stirring and serving up stir-fried food. A long-handled wooden spoon or metal spatula can also be used.

Chinese choppers, or cleavers, come in two sizes: heavy ones for chopping through bones and tough ingredients and smaller, thinner and lighter ones for cutting vegetables and slicing meat.

Chopping boards should be fairly thick and either hard wood or white acrylic. A wooden board needs regular oiling. An acrylic board is easier to clean.

Miniature rolling pins are used for rolling out dough for making dim sum.

Chopsticks for cooking are wooden and long so they don't conduct heat and distance the cook from hot fat and steam. For eating, chopsticks can be wood, plastic or especially for special occasions, ivory. Chopstick stands are useful for resting chopsticks on and make a decorative addition to a Chinese meal.

Ingredients for Cooking Chinese

SOME INGREDIENTS IN Chinese cooking, like egg noodles, bell peppers, soy sauce and rice, will be familiar to the Western cook. Others may be new. It is these items, many of them imported dried or canned from China, which give the cuisine its distinctive character.

China is such a large country that sometimes these same ingredients are also bought dried and others, like hundred year old eggs, are prized because of the way they are preserved. Some can be kept almost indefinitely and will help you to try new oriental dishes in future.

On the other hand, if you do find fresh ingredients like water chestnuts when shopping, try them. Their superior flavor will be well worth any extra effort. Some Chinese ingredients are now sold at supermarkets, but nearly all of them are available from Chinese markets and grocery stores.

▦ DRIED FOODS ▦

Chinese mushrooms, known as shiitake in Japanese, add a smoky flavor and chewy texture to dishes. Whether the finer brown ones with blackish spots or the darker less expensive ones, they are always sold dried and must be reconstituted by soaking them in hot water for about 25 minutes.

Chinese wind-dried sausages are fatty, very highly flavored, slightly sweet sausages made of pork liver or pork and duck liver. They should be steamed for about 20 minutes before slicing and adding to dishes.

Cloud ears are a dried fungus smaller than wood ears which must also be soaked in hot water. They are used in stir-fried dishes to add texture and a delicate flavor.

Dried chilies are thin and reddish, and about ½ inch long. They are sold in Chinese supermarkets, usually in small plastic bags.

Dried shrimp are small to very small and are sold cleaned, shelled and whole, with or without heads and tails. They add a salty, savory seasoning to dishes.

Golden needles are the dried golden-brown buds of lily flowers. Soaked before use, they are added for their texture and unique flavor.

Hair seaweed is a hair-like, dried variety of black sea moss that is used mostly in vegetable dishes. Reconstitute in warm water before using.

Lotus leaves are soaked in lukewarm water, then used as an aromatic wrapping for steamed food.

Purple flat seaweed is sold dried. Rehydrated it is used in vegetable soups.

Red dates are the dried, prune-like fruit of the jujube tree. About the size of a kidney bean, they have a sweet taste and must be soaked before using.

Tangerine peel is the sun-dried peel of the fruit that, when soaked, has a tangy flavor. It is often used with Sichuan peppercorns and star anise.

烹
飪
材
料

In free markets in China
agricultural produce can
now be bought and sold.
This reversion to the
trading ways of the West
has accounted for a huge
expansion in food
production in recent years.
Famines are a thing of the
past and China is now self-
sufficient in food, despite
its one billion population.

Wood ears are a dried tree fungus exported from China. Reconstitute them in hot water, then wash repeatedly in cold water, picking over them to remove any grit.

■ RICE AND NOODLES ■

Cellophane noodles are fine, snowy-white, almost transparent dried noodles made from mung beans. They are soaked for 5 minutes and added to soups and braises.

Egg noodles are made from wheat flour, water and egg, and are used fresh or dried.

Glutinous rice is shorter and plumper than long-grain rice. It becomes very sticky when cooked and is used in both sweet and savory dishes.

Long grain rice has been hulled and polished, the basis of most Chinese meals.

Rice flour noodles are thin white, usually dried noodles made from rice flour. They come in a variety of shapes. Soak the dried ones for about 15 minutes in warm water until they are soft, then drain them to use in dishes.

Spring roll skins are fresh, very thin square or round sheets of flour and water dough. Different from egg roll skins, they come in packs of 10–25 skins. Store them sealed and covered in the refrigerator or freezer.

Wheat flour noodles are made from flour and water and used fresh or dried.

■ VEGETABLES AND FRUIT ■

Baby corn are miniature ears of corn used whole in meat and vegetable dishes. Rinse them before using.

Bamboo shoots are available canned, either whole or sliced. Used for their texture.

Bean sprouts are sprouted mung beans, highly nutritious and prized especially for their crunchy texture.

Chilies used in Chinese cooking are about two- to three-inches long and are sold fresh, both red and green, at Chinese grocers.

Chinese flowering cabbage is one of the favorite vegetables of the Chinese. It needs only brief boiling, steaming or stir-frying.

Chinese spinach has broad oval, rather than arrow-shaped leaves. Sometimes it has red markings. Cooked like western spinach, its taste is mild.

Chinese turnip, also called 'daikon radish', is a large, crisp and juicy vegetable with a slightly sharp flavor. It is eaten raw or cooked.

Chinese white cabbage has succulent, thick, long, white stalks and small green leaves. Both are delicious.

Fresh ginger root is an essential Chinese ingredient used to remove or cover objectionable flavors and odors in other ingredients. Choose pieces that are uniformly pale-skinned, firm and round.

Garlic is used to sweeten cooking oil and is removed before stir-frying.

Green onions are an essential ingredient in Chinese cooking. The green and white parts are often cooked separately in the same dish.

Green oriental radish is similar in flavor and texture to the Chinese turnip, or daikon, but pale green in color inside and out.

Kumquats are an orange-colored, juicy, acidic fruit, 1–1¾ inch in diameter, with few seeds and an edible sweet rind.

Lichees are a succulent, white-fleshed fruit which, when fresh, must be peeled before eating.

Longons, or 'dragons' eyes', are similar to lichees, but they have a smooth yellowish skin. Their season is short, but they are sold canned and dried.

Lotus roots are large and thick with naturally occurring holes. Sold canned in thick slices, they are used in stews and vegetable dishes.

continued page 26

Chinese wind-dried sausages,
whole and sliced, displayed on dried
lotus leaves. *Left:* pork and duck
sausages; *right:* pork liver sausages.
When steamed, the sliced sausages
add rich savoriness to blander dishes
like steamed or stir-fried vegetables.
Once soaked, the reconstituted
lotus leaves make an especially
flavorful parcel in which to steam
cooked rice mixtures.

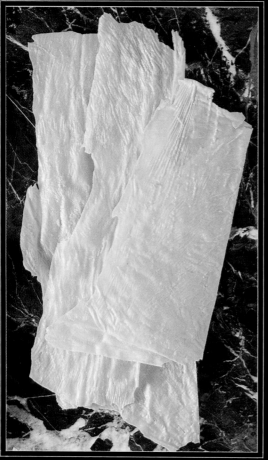

Above: dried bean curd skin. *Right, above from left to right:* wheat flour noodles; cellophane noodles; rice flour noodles; glutinous rice; *below, from left to right:* egg noodles; wonton skins; spring roll skins; long grain rice.

中
餐
烹
飪
材
料

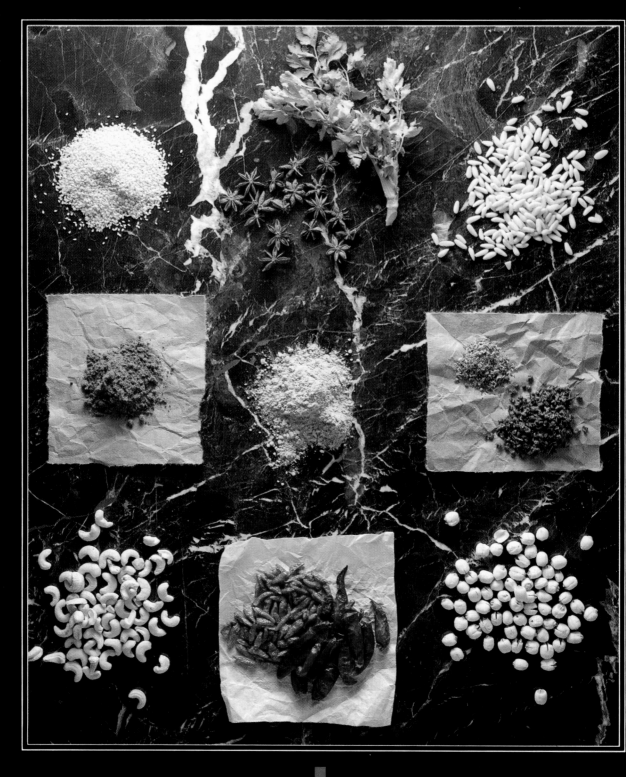

From the top, left: sesame seeds; star
anise; fresh cilantro or coriander;
pine nuts; *from the middle, left:* five

From the top, left: dried shrimp;
golden needles; hair seaweed; *from
the middle, left:* wood ears; tangerine
peel; purple flat seaweed; *from the
bottom, left:* red dates; chestnuts,
shelled and dried; Chinese
mushrooms.

中
餐
烹
飪
材
料

1, snow peas; 2, green onions; 3, bean sprouts; 4 garlic cloves and whole pods; 5, fresh ginger root, 6, Chinese flowering cabbage; 7, Chinese turnip (daikon radish); 8, longons, canned; 9, kumquats, preserved in syrup; 10, lichees, canned; 11, peppers; 12, lotus roots, dried.

中
餐
烹
飪
材
料

1, Chinese spinach; 2, chilies, fresh; 3, pickled mustard green, preserved in brine, has a tangy, bitter flavor prized in soups and in fresh vegetable dishes; 4, dried turnip; 5, water chestnuts, canned; 6, baby corn; 7, straw mushrooms, canned; 8, Chinese white cabbage; 9, bamboo shoots, canned.

Peppers, bell peppers or capsicums, are familiar to Westerners. They are a flavorful ingredient used in Chinese cooking.

Snow peas can be eaten in the pod. Choose young tender ones, trimming them to pull away the strings.

Straw mushrooms are grown on rice straw. They have a meaty texture and a savory, rich fragrance. When canned, drain and rinse them before using.

Water chestnuts are a crunchy root vegetable. Their black skin must be peeled off when they are fresh. The canned ones must be drained. Store them covered in water in the refrigerator, changing the water daily.

Water spinach tastes like a milder version of Western spinach and, when cooked, gives a much-prized contrast between its crunchy stems and limp leaves.

■ HERBS AND SPICES ■

Fresh cilantro, also called coriander, is a thin and flat-leaved plant sold in bunches. It is used as a garnish and seasoning, especially with fish.

Chili powder is made from dried pulverized chilies.

Dried ginger is dried pulverized ginger root.

Five spice powder is a sharp-smelling mixture of ground fennel seeds, star anise, Sichuan peppercorns, cloves and cinnamon. It is used sparingly.

Sichuan peppercorns are not as pungent as familiar black or white peppercorns. Often used with star anise, they have a slightly numbing effect on the tongue.

Star anise is a highly scented, licorice-tasting spice that should be ground or crushed just before using.

■ SOY BEANS AND BEAN-BASED PRODUCTS ■

Bean curd is made from the curdled liquid of soaked, pulverized and strained soy beans. Cut into squares, it is sold fresh covered in water. Store it in the refrigerator, covered in water. Change the water daily and the curd will keep for up to three days. It needs only brief cooking.

Bean curd cheese is made of fresh bean curd which is either 'white' – fermented with or without chili – or 'red' – fermented with rice wine and salt. Sold in small jars or cans, it tastes like salty cheese.

Bean curd skin is the thin skin which forms on top of freshly made bean curd. Preserved by drying, it must be soaked in water before use.

Salted black beans are cooked, salted and fermented whole soy beans. Mash them with other ingredients or mix into dishes for color and flavor.

Sichuan chili paste is yellow soy bean paste mixed with dried chilies and their seeds, sugar and garlic.

Soy bean paste is made of crushed soy beans mixed with sugar, salt and chili.

Sweet bean paste is made from cooked, puréed, sweetened red beans.

Yellow bean paste is made of fermented, salted puréed yellow beans with salt, flour and water.

■ EGGS ■

Hundred year old eggs are ducks' eggs 'pickled' by wrapping them in a straw, mud and lime compost. Shell before using them in dishes.

Marbled tea eggs are hen's or duck's eggs hard cooked, then finely cracked all over and simmered in a tea, anise and cinnamon mixture to marble them.

Quails' eggs are tiny eggs, usually hard cooked, sold fresh or preserved in liquid.

Salted eggs are ducks' eggs preserved in charcoal brine, so they have a salty flavor.

Above, from the left: quails' eggs surrounding a duck's egg; hundred year old eggs, halved, surrounding marbled tea eggs; soy eggs.

Left: fresh bean curd (tofu), drained.

Red chili oil

Chili sauce

Chinkiang vinegar

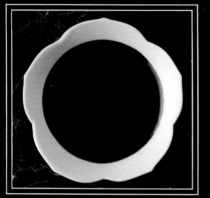

Dark (thick) soy sauce

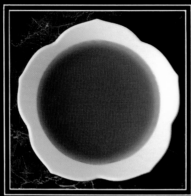

Fish sauce

Hoisin sauce

Light (thin) soy sauce

Oyster sauce

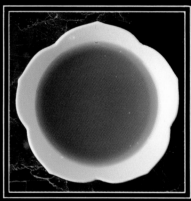

Sesame oil

Sesame paste

Shrimp sauce

Yellow bean paste

The yolk is solid, but the white remains liquid. Scrape off the black shell coating and cook the eggs before eating them.

Soy eggs are hard cooked eggs reboiled, in their shells, in soy sauce. They are brown in color and the salt in the soy helps them keep. The Chinese take them on picnics.

▨ SAUCES, OILS, VINEGARS AND WINES ▨

Chicken fat is slowly rendered (melted) and strained.

Chili oil is made by marinating or frying chopped red chilies in vegetable oil.

Chinkiang vinegar has a rather sweet flavor and is used in many Yangtze recipes. Add a little sugar to white or rice wine vinegar as a substitute.

Dark soy sauce has been aged longer so it is thicker, darker and heavier than light soy sauce. It is used to give a dark color and rich flavor to long-cooked dishes.

Fish sauce is a transparent, golden brown sauce made from fish, water and salt. It has a strong salty, savory flavor.

Hoisin sauce is a dark thick 'fruity' sauce made of puréed soy beans, sugar, salt, chili, vinegar and sesame oil.

Lard is rendered, strained pork fat which can be used instead of shortening in meat and vegetable recipes.

Light soy sauce is thin and salty and is the finest grade of soy sauce. Made from yeast-fermented soy beans, wheat, salt and sugar, it is used as a final seasoning in dishes and as a table condiment.

Mei Kwei Lu wine is a highly alcoholic, fragrant spirit flavored with rose petals. Gin or vodka are satisfactory substitutes.

Moutai wine is a clear spirit made from sorghum and wheat. Made in western China, it is drunk with food.

Oyster sauce is a slightly sweet, richly flavored oyster-based sauce.

Plum sauce is a sweet sauce used as a dip, especially for crispy or fatty foods.

Sesame oil is used in small quantities in many Chinese recipes to add an aromatic nutty flavor.

Sesame paste is thick and made from roasted, ground sesame seeds and sold in jars. Do not use tahini instead. Use peanut butter as a substitute.

Shrimp sauce is strongly flavored and made from shrimp. Use it sparingly.

Yellow rice wine, or Shaoshing wine, is made from glutinous rice fermented with yeast and is drunk with meals. In cooking, medium dry sherry can be substituted.

▨ NUTS AND SEEDS ▨

Cashew nuts are used especially in Cantonese stir-fried dishes.

Lotus seeds are candied for use in sweet dishes and are available canned.

Pine nuts are the soft white seeds of certain pine trees. The seeds' bland, slightly pine flavor improves when they are briefly broiled or fried.

Sesame seeds, both black and white, have the same distinctive nutty flavor. They are used whole or ground, often lightly toasted.

▨ PICKLES ▨

Salted, or pickled, cabbage is preserved in brine and canned. Rinse, drain before using.

Sichuan hot Ja Chai pickle is preserved in salt, then pickled with ground chili in cans. Rinse it before using.

Snow pickle is a salted, canned green pickle used especially in stir-fried dishes.

Winter pickle is a very savory, yellowish-brown pickle usually sold in jars.

Basic Preparations
Cutting, Slicing and Shredding

BECAUSE MOST CHINESE FOOD is eaten with chopsticks, it is cut into bite-sized pieces, usually before it is cooked. This is time-consuming, but it allows the ingredients to be cooked evenly and quickly so that they retain their natural flavor and texture, yet are enhanced by the oil and seasonings in the dish.

Visual appeal is another important part of Chinese cooking. Vegetables especially are cut so that their shapes as well as their colors appear in attractive contrast to other ingredients. Chinese slicing techniques are few and easily mastered with variations in style accomplished by subtle changes in the angle of the cutting blade. The Chinese always use a cleaver, or chopper, for slicing as its weight and sharpness make it a speedy and efficient tool though a sharp knife may be used instead.

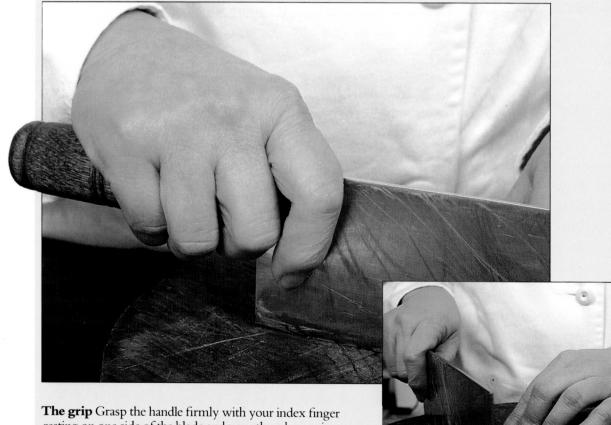

The grip Grasp the handle firmly with your index finger resting on one side of the blade and your thumb pressing against that finger on the other side (see inset).

For recipe see
Crispy 'Seaweed'
with Almonds,
p. 84

1 **Shredding cabbage** Cut the tough central vein out of each leaf, making a tapering slice on either side of the vein.

2 Fold half the leaf over lengthways then, starting at the bottom, roll up the leaf.

3 Resting the cleaver against the knuckles, cut the leaf into fine shreds or ribbons, never lifting the blade higher than the knuckles.

1 **Slicing mushrooms** Hold each mushroom by its springy cap, pressing it against the cutting board, and slice away the stem at the point it meets the cap.

2 For attractive horizontal slices, steady the mushroom with the free hand, hold the blade at an angle almost parallel to the cap and slice three or four times.

3 Always resting the blade against the knuckles, slice downwards on the cap. Regulate the thickness of the slices by adjusting the position of your knuckles.

基
本
準
備
：
切
、
薄
切
和
切
碎

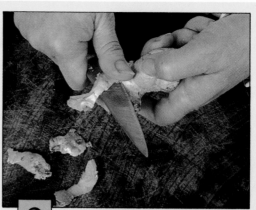

1 **Ginger root** Smash slices of fresh ginger root with the side of a chopper or heavy knife.

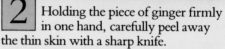

2 Holding the piece of ginger firmly in one hand, carefully peel away the thin skin with a sharp knife.

3 Slice the peeled ginger thinly, guarding and guiding the blade with the knuckles of the free hand.

4 Arrange the ginger slices on top of one another, then cut the stack into thin shreds.

5 Gather the ginger shreds into a bundle, then cut across them at short intervals to chop.

6 Top: sliced; smashed; chopped. Bottom: shredded.

1 **Bamboo shoot** Slice the bamboo shoot lengthways into several wedges.

2 Cut each wedge lengthways into thick slices.

3 Cut the slices across into cubes.

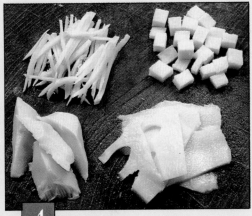

4 Top: shreds; cubes. Bottom: thick wedges; thin slices.

1 **Peppers** Carefully cut the seeds and white pith away from the pepper (*left*). Cut the pepper flesh into rectangles, then cut diagonally across them for triangles (*above*).

基本準備‥切、薄切和切碎

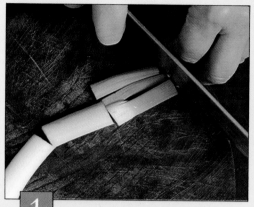

1 **Green onion** Cut the green onion across into 1–inch sections.

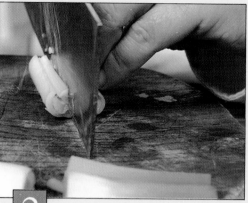

2 Cut each section in half lengthways.

3 Place each section cut-side down and slice it lengthways into fine shreds.

4 Roll cut thick green onions by firmly holding the green part, then cutting the white part diagonally.

5 Roll the green onion a quarter turn and make another diagonal cut.

6 Continue rolling and cutting until the green end is reached.

GARNISHES

To the Chinese, food is a foundation of life, for both physical and aesthetic sustenance. Attractive presentation of food is therefore very important, sometimes having symbolic significance. A dish's appearance should be given as much consideration as the freshness of the ingredients used in it.

Attractively sliced vegetables such as the carrot, radishes, cucumbers and lemon shown above are common garnishes, chosen for their color and flavor along with parsley and fresh cilantro (coriander), to complement the various dishes with which they may be served.

Though these garnishes may seem elaborate, all of them are made with a succession of simple, careful cuts and folding or a soaking in ice water to make the carrot and radish flowers open. With a sharp knife (or chopper), fresh crisp vegetables, a steady hand and a little practice, such decorations are available to everyone.

基本準備：：切、薄切和切碎

MEAT AND POULTRY

Chinese cooking involves a great deal of cutting and slicing because meat, poultry and other ingredients are usually cut into bite-sized pieces for rapid, even cooking. Chinese cooks deftly use a chopper, or cleaver, for this. A large knife can be used instead, but with a little practice you will find that the weight of the chopper and its sharp cutting edge makes the few Chinese slicing, cutting and chopping techniques even easier. Because the knuckles of your free hand are used to guide the chopper as you slice and cut, the chopper's size makes positioning the blade safer than if a knife were used.

Chicken, duck, pork, fish and shellfish and variety meats are so tender that it does not matter at which angle their flesh is sliced. Beef and lamb, on the other hand, should always be cut across the grain of the fibers to make the meat more tender when it is cooked. This is most important when quickly cooking as in stir-frying for which prime cuts are recommended.

When slicing meat very thinly, it is advisable to firm it up by freezing it for one to two hours beforehand.

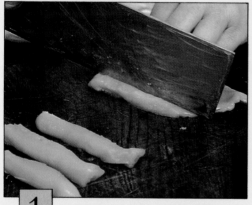

1 **Chicken** Guarding and guiding with one hand, cut the chicken breast lengthways into strips or more thinly into slivers.

2 Cut the strips across into cubes or more finely into dice.

3 Alternatively, hold the chopper blade at an angle to cut the breast lengthways into thin slices.

4 Top: cubed; Bottom: shreds; thin slices.

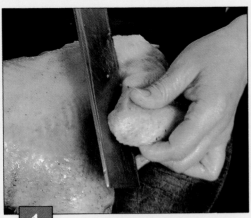

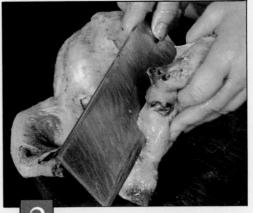

1 **Dismembering chicken and reassembling it for serving.** Pulling the wing gently from the body, cut through the joint where it attaches to the body.

2 Similarly, pull the thigh and leg away from the body and cut down through the thigh joint.

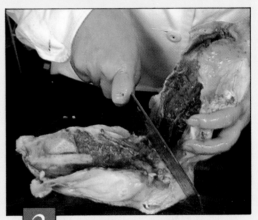

3 Holding the body with the tail-end upright, carefully and firmly cut down through the backbone.

Reassemble the meat pieces into a chicken shape, using the first wing joints for wings and the second wing joints for 'legs'.

4 Cut the boned breast sections across into pieces.

基本準備∷切、薄切和切碎

1 **Beef** Cutting across the grain while guarding and guiding with the other hand, cut the beef into slices about ¼-inch wide.

2 Lay each slice flat and cut the meat into double-size matchstick shreds.

3 Cut shredded meat into small pieces, then chop them finely, repeatedly gathering them into a pile and turning it over as you chop.

4 Top: slices; chopped. Bottom: shreds.

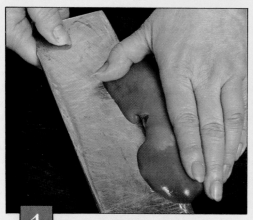

1 **Kidneys** Gently pressing the kidney with one hand, slice the kidney in two horizontally. (Cut each slice in half again if necessary.)

2 Cut away the core and connecting fat.

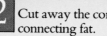

For recipe see Stir-fried Diced Beef with Kidneys, Shrimp and Mushrooms, p. 198

38

肉
類
與
鷄
鴨
類

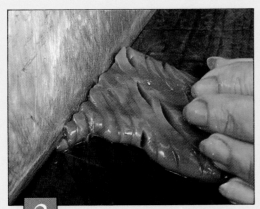

3 Make diagonal cuts or score half-way through the kidney, about ¼-inch apart, holding the chopper blade at a slight angle. Repeat on the opposite diagonal.

4 Cut the scored kidney into bite-sized pieces.

5 Left: poached; right: raw.

Duck Secure the deep-fried duck with chopsticks or a fork and tear the meat with a fork into shreds.

For recipe see Sweet and Sour Pork, p. 197

Pork Cutting thick, boneless slices of the meat into large bite-sized pieces.

基本準備：切、薄切和切碎

FISH AND SEAFOOD

Fish and shellfish are always eaten in China as fresh as possible – almost alive – and cooked lightly to preserve their natural flavor and delicate texture. Freshness and rapid cooking should also be your prime considerations when preparing these delightful foods. Unlike meat, fish does not improve with keeping and shellfish perishes extremely quickly. Though the prime aspect of freshness will be lost, frozen fish and shellfish, cooked as soon as it defrosts, is far better than fish and shellfish which has been kept too long so that its flesh has deteriorated.

Fish and shellfish need little cooking because their flesh is so tender, and everything for quick-cooked dishes must be prepared beforehand. The fish, shellfish, vegetables, noodles, rice and any condiments should be cut and measured, ready for a lightning stir-fry and hungry mouths poised to eat. Steaming is another technique the Chinese use for quickly cooking fish and shellfish. They are especially fond of it because a whole fish can be cooked at one time, usually on a heatproof dish from which the fish is served in its own juices, decoratively garnished.

Shrimp are a joy to the Chinese, who cook shrimp ever so briefly to protect their succulent sweetness and tenderness. In China often only the legs are torn off before cooking and people at the table expertly remove the shell in their mouth, then discard the shell.

For recipe see Quick-fried Crystal Shrimp, p. 143

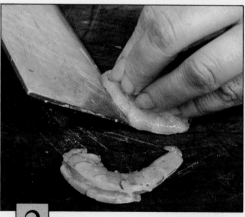

1 Peel the shell away from the body, then pull away the legs.

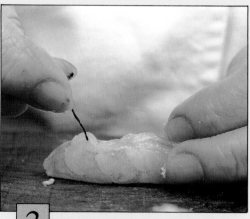

2 Holding the tail, make a shallow cut ¾-way down along the center of the shrimp's back.

3 Pull out or scrape and discard the black vein from the shallow cut.

Preparing fish Once fish is scaled, gutted, washed and dried, it is often cooked whole to preserve as much of its natural goodness as possible. The tender flesh absorbs flavor quickly from marinades and/or seasonings which can enhance its flavor. A common way of doing this is by making cuts in whole fish *(see above)* so that the marinade or condiments reach the flesh more easily and the fish is ready to eat that much sooner.

Alternatively, make 5–6 diagonal cuts in the top of the gutted, cleaned fish to allow more seasoning flavors to reach the flesh.

For recipe see **Quick Fry of Three Sea Flavors,** p. 260

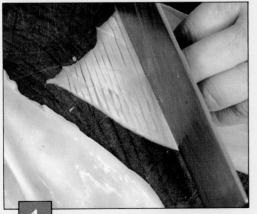

1 **Squid** Make light diagonal cuts or score part-way through the raw cleaned squid, guarding and guiding with the other hand.

2 Make similar diagonal cuts in the opposite direction.

Methods and Techniques of Cooking

STIR-FRYING IS THE MOST popular Chinese cooking technique as it cooks ingredients very quickly in only a small amount of oil so they retain much of their natural flavor, texture and color. Though not essential, a wok is best for stir-frying as its metal body, preferably carbon steel, gets hot very quickly, when the heat is lowered. The wok's very shape facilitates using little oil as well as the vigorous stirring and tossing needed to ensure even, rapid cooking.

It is important to heat the wok or skillet until it is very hot before adding the oil in order to prevent meat, fish and other ingredients from sticking when stir-frying. Experienced cooks can feel when the empty wok is hot enough by holding the palm of one hand above the heating metal. Another way is to wait until you see a wisp of smoke rising from the bottom of the empty wok. When it is hot enough, pour in the oil carefully and gently tip the wok or pan to spread the oil evenly before adding the ingredients. (Remember, if using a skillet, choose a large one.)

Large woks are easier to use than small ones, provided they have deep sides so they hold more food and allow more room for tossing and stirring. Woks can also be used for more gently shallow frying and for deep-frying, provided they are placed on steady wok stands and watched carefully.

One method of testing the temperature of a wok is by holding the palm of one hand over it and feeling the heat rising – for experienced cooks only

Sweet and sour pork is an excellent example of wok cooking, using it for deep- and stir-frying. The battered pork is first submerged in hot deep oil to fry it crisply. The pineapple and pepper pieces are stir-fried in a separate wok or skillet, then the sweet and sour sauce is stirred in. When the sauce thickens, the fried pork is added, to turn and toss in the sauce.

1 Roll the pieces of pork in cornstarch on all sides.

2 Coat the pieces well in a smooth egg and cornstarch batter.

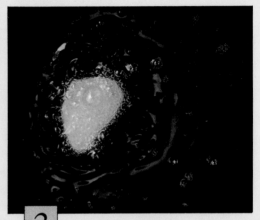

3 To test if the oil is hot enough, drop in a slice of peeled ginger – Chinese style. It should bubble instantly. Or see deep-frying on page 45.

4 Lower the battered pork into the oil with a slotted spoon and deep-fry. When cooked, remove, drain them on paper towels and keep warm.

5 Stir-fry the vegetables quickly.

6 Stir the sweet and sour sauce into the vegetables.

7 Add the battered, deep–fried pork to the sweet and sour sauce. Turn and stir for 1 minute.

For recipe see **Sweet and Sour Pork, p. 197**

44

Deep-frying For deep-frying, food is totally immersed in hot oil or fat. To obtain best results, the correct temperature is vital. Oil should just 'move' when hot enough; if it begins to smoke it is too hot. A thermometer is the best way to check the temperature – add to the wok or other deep-fryer, half-filled with oil, and heat until the thermometer registers the required temperature. If you have no thermometer, use a bread cube to test the temperature. The oil will be at 180°C (350°F) when the bread browns in about 60 seconds. Dry food thoroughly before deep-frying to prevent splattering. Carefully lower the food into the oil using a spatula, strainer, tongs or chopsticks. When cooked, remove food with a slotted spoon or strainer, drain over

Approximate deep-frying temperatures

	°C	°F
Meat	180–185	360–370
Poultry	170	350
Fish	185	370
Vegetables	180–185	360–370
Spring rolls	185	370

the wok and place on paper towels.

Deep-frying, properly carried out, seals the surface of the food and prevents the flavors of the food escaping into the oil; the cooked food itself will be crisp and non-greasy.

For recipe see **Aromatic and Crispy Duck,** p. 174

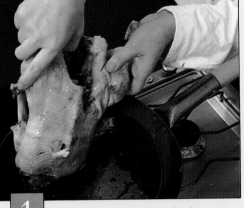

1 **Aromatic and Crispy duck.** Carefully lower the steamed duck into the hot oil.

2 Ladle hot oil repeatedly over the part submerged duck to ensure even crisping.

1 **Blanched noodles stir-fried in seasoned oil.** Add the cooked, drained noodles to the oil in the wok.

2 Turn the noodles frequently to ensure even cooking.

烹
飪
方
法
與
技
巧

Reducing sauce Concentrating the flavor in a Chinese dish is often achieved by reducing the marinade or cooking liquid into a thick sauce to pour over the ingredients. Sometimes this is done as they cook, sometimes after they are cooked and removed.

1 Soy sauce and the other marinade ingredients are poured over the spareribs.

2 The sauce reduces and concentrates as it simmers.

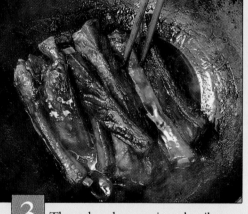

3 The reduced sauce gives the ribs a rich glaze.

For recipe see
**Barbecue
Spareribs, p. 193**

Onion pancakes Popular in Peking, these pancakes from northern China, shown here made as one large pancake, have a strong green onion flavor with an occasional sharpness of salt crystals in the fried crispy dough. Easy to make, they are a good example of Chinese pastry making and a tasty alternative to plain boiled rice (see also p.250 for special regional version).

1 Folding up the salt and green onion sprinkled pastry.

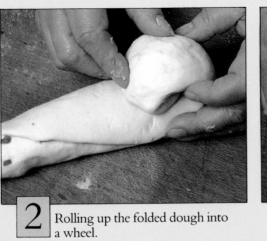

2 Rolling up the folded dough into a wheel.

3 Forming the wheel into a smooth mound.

4 Rolling out the dough again into a pancake.

5 Dusting the pancake with flour.

6 Above: frying the pancake. Left: the finished pancake.

烹飪方法與技巧

Rice is a staple food throughout China, especially in the south and west. White, long grain rice is preferred to short or glutinous varieties for most meals as long, properly cooked, fragrant grains are a perfect complement to other dishes served. To enjoy it at its best, be sure to use ordinary long grain rice that needs to be washed before cooking in preference to instant or pre-cooked varieties which lack flavor.

The Chinese are adept at estimating the proportions of water and rice for proper boiling. They do this by adding water to the first knuckle – or about 1 inch – above the rice level in a cooking pot. To cook smaller amounts of rice, measure the rice and water according to recipe instructions on page 68.

1 **Egg-fried rice** Frying in the beaten eggs until barely set.

2 Adding plain boiled rice to the egg.

3 Adding green onions and other ingredients to the mixture.

4 Seasoning with soy sauce.

5 Turn and mix over low heat to serve.

STEAMING

Steaming food is popular throughout China because it brings out a delicate quality in ingredients, especially if they are very fresh, and steam is readily available in Chinese kitchens. The steam's moist heat circulates freely around the food, cooking it quickly and, provided the food is not over-steamed, enhancing the ingredients' subtle blend of flavors. Steaming can be done with or without a wok.

When using a wok as a steamer, the base of a bamboo steamer is usually used as a stand for food placed on a heatproof cooking dish. Water is added to below the dish. The wok is covered with a lid or foil and the simmering water replenished as necessary. An appropriate-sized bamboo steamer with one or more stacked baskets and topped with its bamboo lid can also be used in a wok to steam one or more dishes at a time.

Metal steamers are used without a wok, but be sure to cook meat, poultry, seafood or fish or mixtures containing them on a heatproof dish, or wrap them in cheesecloth to prevent them sticking to the metal.

Steaming fish The Chinese steam almost all types of food including bread and dim sum (hors d'oeuvres), but they prize whole steamed fish above all. Served on its cooking dish, the fish juices blend with the seasonings and any marinade flavorings.

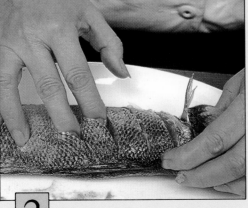

1 Sprinkle the seasoning mixture inside the fish and rub in.

For recipe see Steamed Fish with Garnish, p. 126

2 Make sure the seasoning gets well inside the slits, and leave for the flavor to develop.

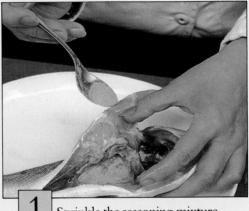

3 Season the outside of the fish.

烹
飪
方
法
與
技
巧

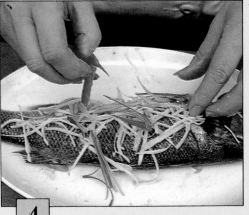

4 Spread the green onion and ginger garnish over the steamed fish.

5 Pour soy sauce along the length of the fish. Repeat the process with dry wine or sherry. Finally, pour smoking hot oil over the fish to finish cooking.

Poultry is another food the Chinese like to steam. Because of the relative speed of the process and the resulting delicacy of flavor, fresh, cleaned and not previously frozen poultry, either whole or in pieces, should be used. Often the meat is marinated or seasoned in some other way before steaming so that the cooking juices will be deliciously flavored to serve either on their own or with the meat.

1 Once cleaned and patted dry, a variety of seasonings can be used to enhance the flavor of steamed poultry.

For recipe see Melon Chicken, p. 165

2 The seasonings are sprinkled liberally inside the cavity of whole birds. Then the seasonings are sprinkled over the skin and rubbed in.

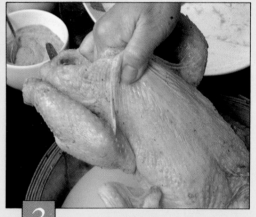

3 The seasoned bird is placed on a heatproof dish inside a bamboo or metal steamer to cook.

烹
飪
方
法
與
技
巧

The Chinese use many distinctive techniques for modifying and enhancing the flavor and texture of foods. A grasp of these will help you identify what you may expect from each recipe.

■ TECHNIQUE FOR CONTROLLING TEXTURE ■

TECHNIQUE	SUBJECT	OBJECT	EXAMPLE
Air-drying	Chicken or duck	Drying skin to make it crisp.	Peking Duck. (See page 178.)
Blanching	Vegetables	To fix the color and set the texture. Follow by rinsing in cold water and draining.	Madam Fei's Spinach and Radish Salad. (See page 89.)
Cutting across the grain	Beef	To make slices more tender.	Stir-fry sliced meat dishes.
Marinating in dry salt or sugar	Poultry, meat, vegetables	To extract water and improve crunchiness of vegetables or crispness of skin.	Salt-Buried Baked Chicken. (See page 156.)
Removal of skin and bones	Poultry	To prevent clash of textures.	Kou Shoa Deep-Fried Boneless Duck. (See page 171.)
Removal of tendons, membranes, ligaments and sheaths	Fish, poultry, pork, beef	To give homogeneity and smoothness of texture.	All chicken, pork, shrimp dishes.
Slicing with the grain	Chicken, pork	To minimize reduction in cooking and preserve appearance.	Sliced meats with vegetables or noodle dishes.
Soaking in salt and wine	Kidneys, other variety meats	To extract juices that would otherwise form scum. To improve firmness of texture.	Most dishes using cooked variety meats.
Trimming fat	Beef, pork	To remove membranes and keep stock clear.	Recipes where only tender, lean meat is required. Stir-fried sliced meat dishes.

■ INGREDIENTS USED TO ENHANCE TEXTURE ■

INGREDIENT	ADDED TO	OBJECT	EXAMPLE
Cornstarch	Beef, pork, chicken	To add smoothness to meat dishes and bind juices of meat with seasonings.	Most fried and sliced chicken and meat stir-fry dishes.
Cornstarch and egg white (1 egg white plus 1 level tablespoon cornstarch)	Seafood, chicken, lamb	To protect the meat from hot oil to preserve texture.	Stir-fry fish/shrimp.
Water or stock	Ground meat, seafood, vegetables	To keep dish moist and light.	Lion's Head Meat Balls. (See page 186.)
Water chestnut powder	Ground chicken, soups, sauces	To thicken. Similar to cornstarch but with smoother texture.	Use in place of cornstarch in most recipes.

■ INGREDIENTS USED TO MODIFY FLAVOR ■

INGREDIENT	ADDED TO	OBJECT	EXAMPLE
Black pepper	Tripe, seafood, pork, pig's hock, variety meats	To accentuate zest and spiciness in dishes.	Salt and Pepper Pork Chops. (See page 192.)
Hoisin sauce	Meat	To impart richness of taste.	Capital Spareribs. (See page 196.)
Chicken, duck or pork fat	Ground chicken or shrimp, meat balls	To add richness.	Lion's Head Meat Balls. (See page 186.)
Ginger, onions	Soups, stews, meat, seafood	To suppress or dissolve unwanted flavors. Brings out quality of blended flavors.	Marinated Lamb with Onions and Ginger. (See page 208.)
Monosodium glutamate	All ingredients except sweets and fruit	To intensify flavor. Use sparingly as if it were salt or pepper or not at all.	Mainly soups and vegetable dishes; Sichuan Braised Eggplant. (See page 96.)
Oyster sauce	Meat, vegetables, seafood, variety meats	To impart seafood savoriness.	Cantonese Stir-Fried Beef in Oyster Sauce. (See page 203.)
Salt black beans	Seafood, meat, vegetables	To add rich, earthy piquant flavor.	Sliced Beef in Black Bean Sauce. (See page 201.)
Sesame oil	Lamb, soups, sauces, jelly-fish, marinated vegetables	Added after cooking to compound aromatic flavor.	Quick Stir-Fried Lamb in Garlic Sauce. (See page 206.)
Sesame oil	Seafood, soups	To improve aroma. Added during concluding stages of cooking.	Most soups.
Soy sauce	Meats, soups, stir-fry sauces	To improve meaty taste and add color/flavor.	Most meat dishes.
Sugar	Fish, shrimp, vegetables, mushrooms, poultry	To accentuate sweetness of fresh foods. Used in moderation.	All soy-braised red-cooked dishes; Red-Cooked Chicken. (See page 148.)
Vinegar	Hot, red peppers	To intensify hot taste.	Sichuan Hot Crispy Fried Shredded Beef. (See page 203.)
Wine	Seafood, poultry, meat	To suppress rank flavors and bring out aromatic qualities.	Long-Steamed Wine-Soaked Lamb with Tangerine Peel and Turnips. (See page 214.)

■ TECHNIQUES FOR ALTERING FLAVOR ■

TECHNIQUE	SUBJECT	OBJECT	EXAMPLE
Blanching	Seafood, poultry, pig's feet	To cook lightly, to preserve fresh flavor.	Cantonese Poached Shrimp. (See page 136.)
Breaking of marrow bones followed by –	Spareribs, pork, duck, chicken bones	To expose marrow and enrich stock.	Duck Carcass Soup and Peking Duck. (See pages 178 and 179.)
Rapid boiling in water or stock	Fish head, marrow	To isolate fat deposits.	All dishes involved in rapid reduction of sauce; Shanghai Quick-Braised Chicken on the Bone. (See page 164.)
Sautéing	Ginger, green onions, garlic, hot pepper	To season oil.	Sautéed Fish Steaks with Garnish. (See page 123.)
Steaming	Fish, poultry	To preserve sweetness and freshness of ingredients.	Steamed Fish with Garnish. (See page 126.)

SOUPS

Wonton Soup (*left*); see page 231.
Yellow Fish Soup (*above*); recipe page 62.

SOUPS

Soups are mainly drunk as a savory beverage during a Chinese meal. Hence the majority of Chinese soups are clear, although they sometimes contain fairly large pieces of meat, seafood and vegetables. There are however a number of thick soups in the Chinese repertoire. During a multi-dish Chinese meal, these soups are treated more or less as another savory dish to be consumed with rice. There may be several soups included in a large Chinese meal, which add to the variety of dishes – an integral part and purpose of a Chinese meal.

3–4 chicken (stewing, if available) or duck carcass or spareribs

8¼ cups water

3–4 slices fresh ginger root

■ GOOD STOCK ■

★ ★ ★

Cooking time: about 2 hours

Serves: about 12

Cooking method: long simmer

Time–consuming but useful part of many dishes, especially soups

Good clear stock is the basis of all Chinese soups. The making of good stock is sometimes an elaborate affair, but it can be made relatively simply in the following manner:

Remove the breast meat and the 2 legs from a 3–4 lb chicken, stewing if available (a duck carcass or spareribs may also be used for this stock). Boil the remaining carcass of the chicken in 7½ cups water for 20 minutes. Remove from the heat and add ⅔ cup cold water. (The cold water causes the fat and impurities to cling together, making them easier to remove.) Skim the surface of all scum which rises to the top. Add 3–4 slices fresh ginger root and continue to simmer gently for about 1½ hours. After about an hour of simmering, remove the chicken carcass from the stock. Grind the leg meat and the breast meat separately. Add the leg meat to the stock at this stage. Simmer for 10 minutes, then add the breast meat and simmer for about 5 minutes. Strain the stock through a fine sieve or cheesecloth. The resulting stock will be both rich and clear, and can be made into many kinds of Chinese soup.

★★
Cooking time:
about 2¼ hours

Serves: about 12

Cooking method:
long simmer

**Time-consuming
but worth it**

BEEF STOCK

Beef stock or broth is considered a strong nourishing soup in China. Although not used as extensively as a good chicken stock, it forms the basis of a number of soups. Good beef stock is made in much the same way as chicken stock.

Cut about 2 lb beef shank into small cubes. Place beef in a pan containing 8 cups water and a few thin slices of fresh ginger root. Simmer gently for about 1½ hours to extract the richness from the beef. Add 1½ lb more lean beef and a little more ginger and simmer gently for 30 minutes to further enrich the stock. Finally, add another 1½ lb beef shank to stock and simmer for 15 minutes only to add an element of freshness to the stock.

To season stock, add salt and pepper just before using. Once a good beef stock is obtained, the making of a beef soup becomes easy. Strain before using.

5 lb beef shank
8 cups water
3–4 slices fresh ginger root
Salt and pepper to taste

★★★
Cooking time:
about 5 minutes

Serves: 4–6

Cooking method:
simmer

Quick to prepare

**Useful
accompaniment to
fish and seafood
dishes**

BEEF BROTH TOMATO SOUP

This is a tasty but light soup which is a suitable accompaniment to both spicy and plain cooked (boiled or steamed) dishes.

▮ PREPARATION ▮

Finely slice beef if necessary. Rub with salt and cornstarch, then toss in egg white. Heat vegetable oil in wok or skillet. When moderately hot, gently fry beef for 30 seconds, then drain. Cut each tomato into 6 pieces. Cut green onions into ½-inch sections.

▮ COOKING ▮

Bring stock to boil in wok or saucepan. Add ginger, crumbled bouillon cube, beef, soy sauce, pepper, green onions and tomatoes. Simmer for 2 minutes and then pour beaten egg into soup in thin stream. Finally, add sesame oil. Stir and serve immediately.

½ cup finely sliced lean beef
1½ teaspoons salt
1½ tablespoons cornstarch
½ egg white
¼ cup vegetable oil
6 firm medium tomatoes
2 green onions
5 cups good beef stock
3–4 slices fresh ginger root
1 chicken bouillon cube
1½ tablespoons light soy sauce
Pepper to taste
1 egg, beaten
1 teaspoon sesame oil

Hot and Sour Soup (*left*), a
popular soup especially in
winter; recipe page 63.
Egg-flower Soup (*above*),
garnish this light soup
with chopped green onion;
recipe page 63.

1 boneless chicken breast

4 canned asparagus stalks

8-10 canned straw mushrooms

1 egg white

½ tablespoon cornstarch

Vegetable oil for frying, about 1¼ cups

5 cups chicken stock (see page 56)

½ teaspoon salt

¼ teaspoon MSG (optional)

¼ teaspoon sesame oil

CHICKEN AND STRAW MUSHROOM SOUP

■ PREPARATION ■

Cut chicken into thin slices. Slice asparagus into 1-inch sections. Cut straw mushrooms in half. Beat egg white with cornstarch in a bowl. Add chicken to egg and cornstarch mixture and toss together.

■ COOKING ■

Heat enough oil in wok or deep-fryer to cover chicken. When hot, cook chicken over medium heat for ½ minute. Remove from heat, drain chicken and save oil for other uses. Bring stock to boil in wok or saucepan. Add chicken, asparagus and straw mushrooms. Bring back to boil, add salt, monosodium glutamate, if using, and sesame oil. Simmer for 2 minutes and serve.

★★★

Cooking time: about 8 minutes

Serves: 4-6

Cooking methods: deep-fry p.45 and simmer

Quick to prepare

4-5 lb chicken (capon or duck)

1 Chinese white cabbage, 2-3 lb

3 green onions

4 slices fresh ginger root

3 teaspoons salt

2 chicken bouillon cubes

2 tablespoons light soy sauce

¼ cup dry sherry

WHOLE CHICKEN OR DUCK SOUP

This soup is frequently served in China partly because it is so easy and can be made with a minimum of preparation. For a family dinner or informal party there is sufficient soup to serve up to 12 people. For smaller groups, leftovers can be reheated for another meal. When reheating, add more Chinese white cabbage and 2 tablespoons light soy sauce, which will liven up the soup. Although a simple and straightforward soup to cook, it is important to bear in mind that in the majority of Chinese dishes the aim is to marry the rich, mature and seasoned flavors to the fresh. In this case, the richness of the chicken or duck with the freshness of the cabbage.

■ PREPARATION ■

Place bird in large heavy metal pot, casserole or earthenware pot, as in the past in China, with 2½-3 quarts water. Bring to boil and simmer for 20 minutes. Skim away scum and impurities together with about 1 cup of stock. Meanwhile, cut cabbage into 10 sections and green onions into 1-inch sections.

■ COOKING ■

Add ginger and salt to simmering stock and reduce heat to very low. Simmer gently for 1½ hours, turning bird carefully every 30 minutes. Add crumbled bouillon

★★

Cooking time: 2-2½ hours

Serves: 6-12

Cooking method: slow simmer

Easy to prepare

Substantial centerpiece for family or party dinner

cubes, soy sauce, sherry and green onions. Lift out bird, place cabbage in pot and place bird back on top. Bring back to boil, reduce heat and simmer very gently for further 20 minutes.

■ SERVING ■

Serve in a very large serving bowl or bring the casserole to the table. The meat of the bird will be tender enough to remove pieces with a pair of chopsticks. Ladle soup, chicken meat and cabbage into individual rice bowls to consume with rice, each mouthful pepped-up by a little good quality soy sauce or one or two dip sauces.

CRACKLING CREAM OF GROUND FISH SOUP

Thick soups are called Kengs in China and are often eaten as warming savory dishes.

■ PREPARATION ■

Place fish in saucepan of boiling water and simmer for 5-6 minutes. Drain and chop fish into paste or puree in a blender. Soak dried mushrooms in hot water to cover for 25 minutes. Drain and discard tough stalks. Dice mushroom caps. Cut tomatoes into similar sized pieces. Dice bread into small cubes. Blend chicken fat with sesame oil. Roughly chop ginger.

■ COOKING ■

Bring stock to boil in wok or saucepan. Add ginger, salt and fish paste, then the monosodium glutamate, if using, pepper, mushrooms, peas and tomatoes. Simmer for 2-3 minutes, then add blended cornstarch, half and half, blended chicken fat and finally white wine. Continue stirring over medium heat for another 1-2 minutes until soup begins to thicken. Keep soup hot over low heat. Meanwhile, heat oil in wok or deep-fryer. When hot, fry cubes of bread until crisp. Transfer cubes to bottom of heated tureen, which should then be taken to the table. Pour soup into the tureen at the table; the soup will make a crackling noise. Serve immediately.

★★★★

Cooking time: 8-10 minutes

Serves: 4-6

Cooking methods: simmer and deep-fry, p.45

Needs care to prepare

Serve with meat and/or vegetable dishes

---

5 oz white fish steak, eg flounder, cod, haddock, sea bass etc, any skins and bone discarded

4 large dried Chinese mushrooms

3 firm tomatoes

1½ slices of bread

1 tablespoon melted chicken fat

1 teaspoon sesame oil

3 slices fresh ginger root

4 cups good stock

2 teaspoons salt

¼ teaspoon MSG (optional)

Pepper to taste

2 tablespoons peas or petits pois

1½ tablespoons cornstarch blended with ¼ cup cold good stock (see page 56)

2 tablespoons half and half

3 tablespoons white wine

Vegetable oil for deep-frying

1 trout (sea bass or bream etc), about 1½ lb

2 teaspoons salt

1 teaspoon ground ginger

1 teaspoon pepper

5 oz leeks

4 slices fresh ginger root

Vegetable oil for deep-frying

5 cups good stock (see page 56)

2 oz canned bamboo shoots

1 tablespoon drained, chopped canned snow pickles

2 tablespoons light soy sauce

3 tablespoons wine vinegar

YELLOW FISH SOUP (OR WHOLE FISH SOUP)

Called Yellow Fish Soup because this fish is most often used in China, being cheap and plentiful. Here in the West, fish such as trout, sea bass, bream, carp or herring may be used. The fish is first seasoned and fried until golden and crispy, then simmered in good stock with vegetables.

■ PREPARATION ■

Clean fish thoroughly. Rub inside and outside with salt, ground ginger and pepper. Leave to season for 20 minutes. Clean leeks and shred. Shred ginger and bamboo shoots.

■ COOKING ■

Heat oil in wok or deep-fryer. When hot, fry fish for about 7–8 minutes until beginning to brown and become crispy. Remove and drain on absorbent kitchen paper. Heat stock in oval-shaped flameproof casserole, wok or similar pan. Lower fish into stock. Bring to boil, add leeks, ginger, bamboo shoots and pickles and simmer for 5–6 minutes. Sprinkle on soy sauce and vinegar, continue to simmer for further 5–6 minutes.

■ SERVING ■

Ladle the soup and vegetables from the casserole into the individual rice bowls and consume with rice and the fish.

★★★

Cooking time: about 20 minutes

Serves: 4–6

Cooking methods: deep-fry p.45 and simmer

Quick to prepare

Serve with meat or vegetarian dishes

Illustrated on p.55

---

8 oz lean spareribs of pork

1 bunch watercress

2 medium tomatoes

4 cups chicken stock (see page 56)

2 slices fresh ginger root

¼ teaspoon MSG (optional)

Salt and pepper to taste

1 teaspoon sesame oil

WATERCRESS AND SPARERIB SOUP

■ PREPARATION ■

Cut spareribs into 1½-inch sections. Trim watercress leaves and attached tender stems into about 1½-inch lengths, discarding rest. Cut tomatoes into eighths.

■ COOKING ■

Bring stock to boil in wok or saucepan. Add spareribs and ginger and simmer for 35–40 minutes. Skim off any scum which rises to surface. Add tomatoes, watercress, monosodium glutamate, if using, salt and pepper to taste. Bring back to boil for 1 minute. Add sesame oil and serve.

★

Cooking time: 35–45 minutes

Serves: 4–6

Cooking method: simmer

Easy to prepare

EGG-FLOWER SOUP

★★

Cooking time: about 6–8 minutes

Serves: 4–6

Cooking method: simmer

A simple, light soup

Illustrated on p.59

■ PREPARATION ■

Finally chop garlic, ginger and green onions. Lightly beat egg with fork for ½ minute, then sprinkle with dash of salt and pepper.

■ COOKING ■

Heat stock in wok or saucepan. Add garlic, ginger and crumbled bouillon cube. Bring to boil and simmer for 3 minutes. Pour beaten egg in very thin stream, along prongs of fork, and trail it over surface of soup. When egg has set, sprinkle soup with green onion, remaining salt and pepper and sesame oil.

1 garlic clove
2 slices fresh ginger root
3 green onions
1 egg
1 teaspoon salt
¼ teaspoon pepper
4¼ cups good stock (see page 56)
1 chicken bouillon cube
1 teaspoon sesame oil

HOT AND SOUR SOUP

★★★★

Cooking time: about 15 minutes

Serves: 4–6

Cooking method: simmer

Needs a fair amount of preparation

A substantial soup which need not be accompanied by many courses

Illustrated on p.58

This is a popular soup especially in the winter. As the soup can be made from any leftover bits and pieces of meat and vegetables, I sometimes call it the 'Chinese Junk Soup' although it can be served in quite respectable company. An ingredient you need in order to produce the traditional version is bean curd (tofu).

■ PREPARATION ■

Shred pork and bamboo shoot into 1-inch strips if necessary. Soak dried mushrooms and dried shrimp separately in hot water to cover for 25 minutes. Drain reserving soaking water. Discard tough stalks from mushrooms, then cut caps into slices a similar size to the pork. Add soaking water to stock. Cut bean curd into ½-inch cubes. Beat egg lightly with fork for 15 seconds. Roughly chop green onions. Mix hot and sour mixture together in bowl.

■ COOKING ■

Bring stock to boil in wok or saucepan. Add pork, dried shrimp and mushrooms and simmer for 10 minutes. Add shrimp, bean curd, bamboo shoots, salt, crumbled bouillon cubes, monosodium glutamate, if using, peas and green onions. Continue to cook for 3–4 minutes, then stir in hot and sour mixture which will thicken soup. Gently pour beaten egg over surface of soup in a thin stream. Sprinkle soup with sesame oil and serve immediately.

2–4 oz lean pork
1–2 oz canned bamboo shoots
4 medium dried Chinese mushrooms
1 tablespoon dried shrimp
1–2 cakes bean curd
1 egg
2 green onions
5 cups good stock (see page 56)
¼ cup fresh or frozen shrimp
1 teaspoon salt
2 bouillon cubes
¼ teaspoon MSG (optional)
2 tablespoons peas
1 teaspoon sesame oil
Hot and sour mixture:
2 tablespoons soy sauce
3 tablespoons vinegar
2 tablespoons cornstarch
¼ cup water
Pepper to taste

6 oz frozen spinach, thoroughly defrosted

4 medium dried Chinese mushrooms

½ cup shredded ham

1 cup button mushrooms

2 tablespoons cornstarch

2 cakes bean curd

4 cups good stock (see page 56)

1½ teaspoons salt

Pepper to taste

1 chicken bouillon cube

1 tablespoon light soy sauce

1 teaspoon sesame oil

BEAN CURD, HAM, MUSHROOM AND SPINACH SOUP

★ ★

Cooking time: 6–7 minutes

Serves: 4–6

Cooking method: simmer

Quick to prepare

A substantial soup which need not be accompanied by many courses

▮ PREPARATION ▮

Roughly chop spinach. Soak dried mushrooms in hot water to cover for 25 minutes. Drain, reserving soaking liquid. Discard tough stalks and cut mushroom caps into shreds. Shred ham, if necessary, and fresh mushrooms. Blend cornstarch with soaking water from mushroom. Cut bean curd into 1½-inch cubes.

▮ COOKING ▮

Bring stock to boil in wok or saucepan. Add fresh and dried mushrooms, bean curd, salt, pepper and crumbled bouillon cube. Bring back to boil and add spinach, ham, soy sauce and blended cornstarch. Cook over gentle heat for 3–4 minutes. Sprinkle with sesame oil and serve.

6 medium dried Chinese mushrooms

1½ tablespoons dried shrimp

4 oz fine rice noodles

5 cups good stock (see page 56)

2 tablespoons minced or finely chopped chicken breast meat

1½ tablespoons drained, chopped canned snow pickles

1½ tablespoons drained, chopped canned Sichuan hot Ja Chai pickles

2 tablespoons chopped fresh ginger root

1½ tablespoons chopped green onions

2 teaspoons salt

1½ chicken bouillon cubes

1 cup finely shredded Chinese white cabbage

3 tablespoons vegetable oil

1 teaspoon sesame oil

2 teaspoons red chili oil or chili sauce

1 teaspoon chopped garlic

¼ teaspoon MSG (optional)

THE 'YUNNAN OVER THE BRIDGE' NOODLE SOUP

★ ★ ★

Cooking time: 5–6 minutes, plus standing time

Serves: 5–6

Cooking method: poach

Quick to prepare

Serve with any combination of dishes

Yunnan is one of China's far western provinces, where this light soup is often served. One curious thing about this soup is that the ingredients are not actually cooked, they only have a very hot stock poured over them; and in the very last stage a small quantity of hot oil is added as a 'hot lid' to seal them.

▮ PREPARATION ▮

Soak dried mushrooms and dried shrimp separately for 25 minutes in hot water to cover. Drain, discarding tough mushroom stalks. Roughly mince or chop mushrooms and shrimp. Soak rice noodles for 3–4 minutes in hot water to cover. Drain.

▮ COOKING ▮

Place shrimp, mushrooms, chicken, pickles, 1½ table-spoons chopped ginger and green onions at the bottom of large heatproof soup bowl, together with salt and crumbled bouillon cubes. Bring stock to boil in saucepan and pour immediately into bowl on top of ingredients. Leave contents to stand in hot stock for 5 minutes, stirring once or twice. Add noodles and cabbage and submerge in the soup. Heat vegetable oil, sesame oil and red oil in small saucepan, together with remaining chopped ginger, garlic and monosodium glutamate, if using, until boiling. Pour mixture immediately over soup; the oil will spread over entire surface, acting as a hot lid which imparts more heat to the soup. Leave to stand for an extra 5 minutes, then stir well and serve immediately.

PEKING SLICED FISH PEPPER POT SOUP

★★★
Cooking time: about 10 minutes

Serves: 4–6

Cooking methods: deep-fry p.45 and simmer

8 oz white fish fillets
1½ teaspoons salt
1 tablespoon cornstarch
1 egg white
2 slices fresh ginger root
1 garlic clove
2 green onions
Vegetable oil for deep-frying
4 cups chicken stock (see page 56)
½ teaspoon salt
¼ teaspoon MSG (optional)
3 tablespoons wine vinegar
½ teaspoon pepper

PREPARATION

Cut fish into 1½×1-inch slices. Dust with 1½ teaspoons salt and cornstarch, and wet with egg white. Finely chop ginger and garlic. Coarsely chop green onions.

COOKING

Heat oil in wok or deep-fryer. When hot, lightly fry coated fish for 1 minute. Remove and drain, pour away oil for other uses. Bring stock to boil in wok or saucepan. Add ginger, garlic, remaining salt and monosodium glutamate, if using, and bring back to boil for 1 minute. Add fish, vinegar and pepper and simmer for 3–4 minutes. Pour into heated tureen, sprinkle with the green onions and serve.

VELVET OF CHICKEN, HAM AND CORN SOUP

★★
Cooking time: 5–6 minutes

Serves: 4–6

Cooking method: quick simmer

Quick to prepare

Quite a substantial soup that goes well with any combination of dishes

½ boneless chicken breast
2 egg whites
3 tablespoons half and half
1 tablespoon cornstarch
5 cups good stock (see page 56)
8 oz canned creamed corn
2 teaspoons salt
Pepper to taste
¼ teaspoon MSG (optional)
½ cup chopped lean ham
1 tablespoon finely chopped green onion

PREPARATION

Coarsely mince chicken. Beat egg whites in small bowl until frothy. Add half and half and cornstarch and beat again. Blend minced chicken into the mixture.

COOKING

Bring stock to boil in wok or saucepan. Add corn, salt, pepper and monosodium glutamate, if using, and bring back to boil. Stir in egg white and minced chicken mixture. Finally, sprinkle on chopped ham and green onion. Stir gently and serve immediately. A few tablespoons of fresh shrimp may be added with the ham to enhance the color and taste of the dish.

RICE, NOODLES AND VEGETABLES

Colorful stir-fried selection of vegetables with Sweet and Sour Sauce; recipe page 197.

飯、麵與蔬菜

RICE AND NOODLES

Rice is not considered a dish in China, but is usually served as the bulk food to accompany the savory dishes on the table. Noodles are served and eaten as snacks, albeit often large snacks, between meals but occasionally they are included as an item to bulk up the meal. When they are served as such, they are usually fairly plainly cooked, perhaps with one or two vegetables and a minimum amount of shredded meat added, for the sake of variation in texture.

Rice is normally eaten plain in China (boiled or steamed) and is only very occasionally made savory (as in 'fried rice'), usually when there is a shortage of savory dishes and there is an abundance of scraps available. Plain rice is ideal for absorbing the numerous flavors and ingredients to be found on the Chinese dinner table.

There are three main types of noodle, made from wheat flour, rice flour and pea-starch. These are eaten in every part of China, but the various regions do have their favorites: wheat flour noodles predominate in the North while in the South rice flour noodles are more popular. Pea-starch or cellophane noodles are seldom cooked into bulk-food dishes, but more usually are used in soups or cooked with meats and seafoods in savory dishes to consume with rice.

1 cup or bowl long grain white rice
1¼ cups or bowls water

PLAIN BOILED RICE

■ PREPARATION ■
Wash and rinse rice, drain well. Place in saucepan and add water.

■ COOKING ■
Cover and bring to boil. Reduce heat and simmer gently for 9-10 minutes. Remove from heat and leave rice to continue to cook and dry in its own heat for a further 10 minutes.

★

Cooking time: 10 minutes plus standing time

Serves: 2-4

Cooking method: simmer

Easy to prepare

Serve with all savory dishes

★★

Cooking time:
6–7 minutes

Serves: 4

Cooking method:
stir-fry, p.42

Easy to prepare

Serve in conjunction with other dishes

BASIC FRIED RICE

■ PREPARATION ■

Peel and thinly slice onions. Cut bacon across the lean and fat into strips. Cut green onions into ¼-inch shreds. Lightly beat eggs.

■ COOKING ■

Heat 2½ tablespoons of oil in wok or skillet. When hot, stir-fry onion and bacon over medium heat for 1 minute. Add peas and continue to stir-fry for 45 seconds. Add cooked rice and turn and toss for 45 seconds. Remove from heat. Heat remaining oil in separate small wok or pan. When hot, add half green onions and stir over medium heat for 30 seconds. Pour in beaten egg. Tilt pan, so that egg flows evenly over bottom of pan. After 1 minute, when eggs have nearly set, sprinkle with salt and remainder of green onions. Stir and lightly scramble eggs. When set, transfer egg mixture to rice. Stir and turn over medium heat for 1 minute.

Note: A suitable convenience food to eat with fried rice is, surprisingly, a can of sardines.

2 medium onions
2–3 slices of bacon
2 green onions
3 eggs
5 tablespoons vegetable oil
3 tablespoons green peas
2 bowls cooked rice (see page 68)
1 teaspoon salt

★

Cooking time:
1½ hours

Serves: 4–6

Cooking method:
simmer

Easy, but takes time to prepare

Serve with pickled or salted foods for breakfast or late supper

PLAIN COOKED RICE GRUEL OR CONGEE

Rice eaten at breakfast time in China is cooked with much greater quantity of water and for a much longer period of time. It is when this rice porridge or congee is cooked in the Chinese kitchen that the most steam is generated; this steam is largely utilized in producing China's numerous steamed dishes.

■ PREPARATION ■

Wash and rinse rice, drain well. Place in deep heavy pot or pan and add water. Bring to boil, reduce heat and simmer very gently, uncovered, for 1½ hours, stirring occasionally. By this time, rice will be fairly thick suitable for serving for breakfast or late supper.

■ SERVING ■
Serve accompanied by pickled or salted foods.

2 cups or bowls long grain white rice
10 cups or bowls water

1 recipe Basic Fried Rice (see page 69)

1 medium-sized red pepper

1–1½ cups bean sprouts

½ cup jumbo shrimp, fresh or frozen

½–¾ cup canned straw mushrooms or 1 cup button mushrooms

1 medium sized zucchini

2½ tablespoons vegetable oil

2 tablespoons corn kernels

½ cup shrimp, fresh or frozen

1½ tablespoons shortening, lard or butter

1½ tablespoons light soy sauce

YANGCHOW FRIED RICE

★★
Cooking time: about 10 minutes

Serves: 5–6

Cooking method: stir-fry, p.42

Easy to prepare

Complements and provides bulk to a multi-dish meal

Illustrated on p.74

This is the best known of all fried rice dishes, the only one permissible to be served at a party table.
Yangchow Fried Rice is cooked in precisely the same manner as Basic Fried Rice, except that a few extra ingredients are added. (Yangchow is a famous river port on the Yangtze river.) The extra ingredients are all foods which abound in the Lower Yangtze regions: namely, mushrooms, straw mushrooms (normally available canned), lotus seeds, red peppers, pimientos, bean sprouts, tomatoes, string beans and fresh water shrimp. We will endeavor to use some of these in the following recipe.

■ PREPARATION ■

Repeat Basic Fried Rice recipe. Cut red pepper into ¼-inch pieces. Wash and dry bean sprouts. Cut each jumbo shrimp into 2–3 pieces. If using button mushrooms, quarter them. Cut zucchini into 8 sections, then further divide in quarters.

■ COOKING ■

Heat oil in wok or skillet. When hot, stir-fry pepper, mushrooms, bean sprouts, zucchini, corn, shrimp and jumbo shrimp over high heat for 1½ minutes. Add shortening or lard and light soy sauce and continue to stir-fry over medium heat for 1½ minutes. Turn contents into pan containing fried rice. Reduce the heat to low, turn and stir together for 30 seconds.

2 large sheets lotus leaf

1 cup long grain rice

¾ cup glutinous rice

2 teaspoons dried shrimp

1½ tablespoons soy sauce

½ teaspoon salt

1½ teaspoons sesame oil

¼ teaspoon pepper

⅔ cup shrimp, fresh or frozen, shelled

¾ cup chopped roast duck meat

½ cup flaked crab meat

½ cup chopped ham

LOTUS LEAF SAVORY RICE

★★★★
Cooking time: 15 minutes

Serves: 6–7

Cooking methods: simmer and steam, p.49

Lotus leaf packages take time to prepare, but cooking is straightforward

Interesting dish to serve as a dim sum

Illustrated on p.225

This large savory rice dish can be made into small individual packages, simply by dividing the rice mixture into smaller portions, and wrapping and steaming in ¼-sized piece of lotus leaf.

■ PREPARATION ■

Soak dried lotus leaves in warm water for 5–6 minutes to soften. Drain and wipe dry. Place and mix the two types of rice in saucepan. Wash, drain and just cover with water. Bring to boil and simmer for 6 minutes over very low heat until all water has been absorbed. Soak dried shrimp in ⅔ cup hot water to cover for 10 minutes. Pour soaked shrimp and soaking water into pan containing rice. Place pan over low heat to simmer gently for 5 minutes.

Remove from heat, cover and leave rice and shrimp to stand for 5 minutes to absorb water. Add soy sauce, salt, sesame oil and pepper and turn them over a few times. Add duck meat, shelled shrimp, crab meat and chopped ham to mixture; blend evenly. Wrap savory rice mixture in double layer of lotus leaves, tying them firmly with string to make a secure package.

■ COOKING ■

Place lotus leaf package in steamer and steam vigorously for 15 minutes.

■ SERVING ■

Bring package to table, open it and allow the diners to serve themselves.

GOLD AND SILVER RICE GRUEL (CONGEE)

■ PREPARATION ■

Chop duck and chicken into 12 equal pieces each.

■ COOKING ■

Pour congee into a heavy pan or casserole. Add 2 cups or bowls of water, ginger, duck and chicken pieces. Bring slowly to boil. Sprinkle with crumbled bouillon cube and stir in. Reduce heat to very low and simmer gently for 30 minutes, stirring every 10 minutes.

■ SERVING ■

Ladle congee mixture into 4 bowls, dividing the pieces of duck and chicken equally. Sprinkle top of each bowl with about 1 teaspoon soy sauce, chopped green onion and a drop or two of sesame oil.

★ ★

Cooking time: 35 minutes

Serves: 4–5

Cooking method: simmer

Easy to prepare

Serve on its own as a light meal

Illustrated on p.74

¼ roast duck

¼ boiled chicken

4 cups or bowls cooked rice gruel or congee (see page 69)

3 slices fresh ginger root

1 chicken bouillon cube

2 tablespoons soy sauce

2 tablespoons finely chopped green onion

1 tablespoon sesame oil

2 cups long grain rice

1 lb green cabbage or spring greens

1½ tablespoons dried shrimp

About ½ lb Chinese sausages

2 tablespoons vegetable oil

1½ tablespoons shortening or lard

1½ teaspoons salt

SHANGHAI VEGETABLE RICE

Surprisingly, this simple dish comes from Shanghai, the most populous and sophisticated of all Chinese cities. Without the sausage, it is a dish useful to serve with long-cooked meat dishes, such as Soy-Braised Pork (see page 196).

■ PREPARATION ■

Wash and measure rice. Simmer in same volume of water for 6 minutes. Remove from heat and leave to stand, covered, for 7–8 minutes. Wash and dry cabbage. Chop into 1½ × 3-inch pieces, removing tougher stalks. Soak dried shrimp in hot water to cover for 7–8 minutes, then drain. Cut sausages slantwise into 1-inch sections.

■ COOKING ■

Heat oil and shortening or lard in deep saucepan. When hot, stir-fry shrimp for 30 seconds. Add cabbage and toss and turn for 1½ minutes until well coated with oil. Sprinkle cabbage with salt. Pack in rice. Push pieces of sausage into rice. Add 4–5 tablespoons water down side of pan. Cover and simmer very gently for about 15 minutes. Transfer to heated serving dish.

★★★

Cooking time: about 15–18 minutes

Serves: 5–6

Cooking methods: stir-fry p.42 and simmer

Easy to prepare

Omitting sausages, a useful accompaniment to meat dishes

Illustrated on p.75

---

3 green onions

3 tablespoons soy sauce

3 tablespoons wine vinegar

1 lb wheat flour noodles, flat or Ho Fen noodles, spaghetti

Garnish:

Radish rose

Sauce:

3 tablespoons peanut butter

2 tablespoons sesame paste

3 teaspoons sesame oil

BEGGARS' NOODLES

Although this is an extremely simple and inexpensive dish of noodles, it is surprising how appetizing and satisfying it can be.

■ PREPARATION ■

Coarsely chop or shred green onions. Mix soy sauce and vinegar together. Mix all sauce ingredients together.

■ COOKING ■

Place noodles in saucepan of boiling water and simmer for 6–10 minutes, or spaghetti for 10–12 minutes. Drain.

■ SERVING ■

Divide hot noodles into 6 heated, large rice bowls. Sprinkle evenly with green onion. Add large spoonful peanut butter and sesame mixture to each bowl of noodles. Pour 1 tablespoon of soy sauce and vinegar mixture over contents of each bowl.

★

Cooking time: 10 minutes

Serves: 6

Cooking method: simmer

Easy to prepare

Inexpensive, tasty snack

Illustrated on p.78

★ ★ ★ ★

**Cooking time:
about 15 minutes**

Serves: 6–8

**Cooking methods:
stir-fry p.42 and
simmer**

**Good dish to serve
alone or as part of a
multi-dish meal**

FUKIEN
CRAB RICE

■ PREPARATION ■

Place bowl of glutinous rice in a saucepan with 1½ bowls of water. Bring to boil and simmer very gently for 15 minutes. Add this rice to cooked long grain rice and mix together. Clean and cut leeks slantwise into 2-inch sections. Shred ginger. Coarsely chop garlic. Chop each crab through shell into 12 pieces, cracking claws with side of chopper. Discard dead men's fingers.

■ COOKING ■

Heat oil in wok or large skillet. When very hot, add crab pieces and turn them around in hot oil for 3 minutes. Drain. Pour away oil to use for other purposes, leaving 2 tablespoons. Add shortening or lard and reheat wok or pan. When hot, stir-fry ginger and garlic over medium heat for 15 seconds. Add leeks and salt and stir-fry for 1 minute. Pour in stock and sprinkle in crumbled bouillon cube, then add tomato paste, paprika, soy sauce and sherry. Bring to boil, stirring, and return crab pieces to pan. Cook over medium heat for 3 minutes. Add blended cornstarch; turn and stir a few times until thickened.

■ SERVING ■

Place mixed rice into a medium-size 2 handled wok with lid, or a large flameproof casserole. Pour crab and leek mixture over rice. Place wok or casserole over a low heat, cover and cook gently for 5 minutes. Bring container to table for serving.

---

1 bowl cooked glutinous
  rice (see page 16)

2 bowls cooked long grain
  rice (see page 68)

½–¾lb young leeks

3 slices fresh ginger root

2 garlic cloves

2 medium crabs, about 3lb

⅔ cup vegetable oil

2 tablespoons shortening or
  lard

1 teaspoon salt

⅞ cup good stock (see page
  56)

1 chicken bouillon cube

2 tablespoons tomato paste

1 teaspoon paprika

1 tablespoon light soy sauce

⅔ cup dry sherry

1 tablespoon cornstarch
  blended with 2
  tablespoons water

Gold and Silver Rice Gruel (Congee) (*above*), a substantial dish with roast duck and boiled chicken; recipe page 71.
Yangchow Fried Rice (*left*), most famous fried rice dish; recipe page 70.
Shanghai Vegetable Rice (*right*), can be cooked without the sausages; recipe page 72.

¾–1 lb wheat flour or rice flour noodles

½ lb lean pork

½ teaspoon salt

4½ tablespoons vegetable oil

2 oz snow pickles

4 cups bean sprouts

2 green onions

1½ tablespoons shortening or lard

2 tablespoons soy sauce

1 tablespoon sesame oil

BASIC CHOW MEIN

★★

Cooking time: about 10 minutes

Serves: 4–6

Cooking methods: parboil and stir-fry, p.42

Quick and easy to prepare

Good snack or adds bulk to a multi-course meal

'Chow' in Chinese means 'to stir-fry', and 'Mein' means noodles, hence, 'stir-fried noodles'. Serve as a snack or add to a multi-course Chinese meal.

■ PREPARATION ■

Parboil noodles in saucepan of boiling water for 5 minutes, or 3 minutes for rice flour noodles. Drain. Cut pork into matchstick-sized shreds. Sprinkle with salt. Rub with 1 teaspoon of oil. Coarsely chop pickles. Wash and drain bean sprouts. Cut green onions into 1-inch sections.

■ COOKING ■

Heat vegetable oil in wok or large skillet. When hot, stir-fry pork and pickles for 2½ minutes. Remove half contents and put aside. Pour all noodles into pan; turn and stir for 2½ minutes. Transfer to heated serving dish. Add shortening or lard to wok and return reserved pork and pickles. Add green onions and stir-fry for 30 seconds over high heat. Add bean sprouts, soy sauce and sesame oil. Continue to stir-fry for 1½ minutes.

■ SERVING ■

Spoon stir-fried ingredients over noodles. Toss before serving.

¾ lb packet wheat flour noodles or egg noodles

¾ lb steak, eg tenderloin, rump or sirloin

2 tablespoons soy sauce

Pepper to taste

3 slices fresh ginger root

2 green onions

¼ cup vegetable oil

1½ tablespoons shortening or lard

1 tablespoon hoisin sauce

2 tablespoons good stock (see page 56)

1½ tablespoons dry sherry

1 tablespoon cornstarch blended with 2 tablespoons water

BEEF CHOW MEIN

★★★

Cooking time: about 10 minutes

Serves: 4–6

Cooking methods: simmer and stir-fry, p.42

Fairly quick and easy

Serve as a single snack or as part of a multi-dish meal

This noodle dish has a strong beef and ginger flavor.

■ PREPARATION ■

Place noodles in saucepan of boiling water and simmer for 5 minutes. Drain. Cut beef into 2 × 1-inch very thin slices. Rub with soy sauce and pepper to taste. Shred ginger. Cut green onions into 2-inch sections, separating white from green parts.

■ COOKING ■

Heat 3 tablespoons oil in wok or skillet. When hot, stir-fry ginger and white parts of green onion for 30 seconds. Add beef slices, spread them over wok or skillet, and stir-fry over high heat for 1½ minutes. Remove from pan. Add shortening or lard, hoisin sauce, remaining soy sauce and stock to wok. Bring to boil, stirring. Pour noodles into pan, toss and stir until heated through. Spread out on heated serving dish. Add remaining oil, green parts of green onions, sherry and beef to wok or pan. When mixture boils, pour over blended cornstarch and turn beef over several times. Spoon beef mixture evenly over noodles.

SINGAPORE CHOW MEIN

★ ★ ★

Cooking time: about 10 minutes

Serves: 5-6

Cooking method: stir-fry, p.42

Fairly easy to prepare

Serve as Beef Chow Mein

Illustrated on p.79

PREPARATION

Soak dried shrimp in hot water to cover for 8 minutes. Drain. Thinly slice onions. Cut bacon into matchstick sized shreds. Cut pork into 1-inch lean and fat pieces. Cut green onions into 1½-inch sections. Place noodles in saucepan of boiling water and blanch for 3 minutes. Drain.

COOKING

Heat oil in large wok or skillet. When hot, stir-fry dried shrimp, onion and bacon for 1 minute. Add salt and curry powder and continue to stir-fry for 2 minutes. Stir in stock. Add noodles, turn and toss. Remove from heat. Heat shortening in separate wok or skillet. When hot, stir-fry roast pork, cooked shrimp and green onions over high heat for 1 minute. Sprinkle with soy sauce, and stir few times. Add bean sprouts, turn and stir for 1 minute.

SERVING

Add freshly stir-fried ingredients to noodles and return to medium heat. Stir and turn ingredients together for 1½ minutes. Sprinkle with sesame oil.

3 tablespoons dried shrimp

2 medium onions

2 slices of bacon

½ lb Cha Siu roast pork (see page 274)

2 green onions

¾ lb packet rice flour noodles

¼ cup vegetable oil

1½ teaspoons salt

1½ tablespoons curry powder

¼ cup good stock (see page 56)

1½ tablespoons shortening or lard

⅔ cup shelled shrimp

1½ tablespoons soy sauce

1½ cups bean sprouts

1 teaspoon sesame oil

Beggars' Noodles (*left*), a
simple dish garnished with
a radish rose; recipe page
72.
Singapore Chow Mein
(*above*), a colorful dish
using Cha Siu roast pork;
recipe page 77.

2 tablespoons dried shrimp

3 tablespoons dry sherry

3 tablespoons light soy sauce

2 tablespoons wine vinegar

1½ teaspoons red chili oil

2 green onions

1 lb freshly-made noodles or ¾ lb wheat flour noodles

2½ tablespoons Sichuan hot Ja Chai pickles, coarsely chopped

2 tablespoons snow pickles, coarsely chopped

1½ tablespoons winter pickles, coarsely chopped

1½ teaspoons sesame oil

SHANGHAI COLD-TOSSED NOODLES

Cold-tossed noodles are a favorite summer dish.

■ PREPARATION ■

Soak dried shrimp in hot water to cover for 5 minutes. Drain and coarsely chop. Add shrimp to sherry and leave to soak for 15 minutes. Mix soy sauce, vinegar and red chili oil together. Cut green onions into ½-inch shreds.

■ COOKING ■

Place freshly-made noodles in saucepan of boiling water and blanch for 3 minutes; if using wheat noodles, simmer for 5–6 minutes. Remove from heat and leave to soak in hot water for further 5–6 minutes. Drain and cool.

■ SERVING ■

Spread noodles on a large serving dish. Sprinkle them evenly with chopped pickles, shrimp and sherry, then soy sauce mixture. Finally, add green onion shreds and sesame oil.

To serve Chinese way, each diner mixes and tosses noodles he requires and transfers it to his own bowl, adjusting any additional seasonings of soy sauce, red chili oil or vinegar.

★★

Cooking time: about 3–6 minutes

Serves: 3–4

No cooking except for initial blanching or boiling of noodles

A good starter or summer snack

---

1 lb leg of lamb

2 slices fresh ginger root

1½ tablespoons cornstarch

¼ cup vegetable oil

1½ lb mutton

3 medium onions

3 garlic cloves

¾ lb young leeks

1 chicken bouillon cube

1 teaspoon salt

¾ lb wheat flour noodles

1 tablespoon shortening or lard

2 tablespoons soy sauce

½ tablespoon yellow bean paste

1 tablespoon red chili oil

1 tablespoon prepared English mustard

MANCHURIAN BOILED AND BRAISED LAMB NOODLES

■ PREPARATION ■

Cut lamb into 1½ × 1-inch thin slices. Finely chop ginger. Dust and rub lamb with ginger, cornstarch and 1 tablespoon vegetable oil. Cut mutton into 1-inch cubes. Slice onions. Coarsely chop garlic. Clean and cut leeks into 1-inch sections.

■ COOKING ■

Parboil mutton in saucepan of boiling water for 5 minutes. Drain. Place mutton in flameproof casserole and add 3¾ cups water, crumbled bouillon cube, salt and onion. Bring to boil and simmer gently for 1¼ hours or until stock is reduced by a quarter. Place noodles in

★★★

Cooking time: about 1½ hours

Serves: 6–8

Cooking methods: long simmer and stir-fry, p.42

Fairly easy to prepare

A substantial snack or useful addition to a multi-dish meal for hearty appetites saucepan of boiling water and blanch for 3 minutes. Drain and add to mutton. Cook for 10 minutes. Meanwhile, heat remaining oil in wok or skillet. When hot, stir-fry leeks for 2 minutes, then push to sides of pan. Add shortening or lard to center of wok or pan. When hot, stir-fry lamb and garlic over high heat for 1 minute. Add soy sauce and yellow bean paste and stir-fry with lamb for 1 minute. Mix leeks with lamb and stir-fry for 1 minute.

■ SERVING ■

Pour noodles and mutton into deep-sided heated serving dish. Pour lamb and leeks over them. Trickle red chili oil and mustard in crisscross pattern over dish.

SICHUAN DAN DAN NOODLES

■ PREPARATION ■

Place noodles in saucepan of boiling water and blanch for 3 minutes. Divide noodles into 5-6 heated individual bowls. Heat stock in saucepan, add salt and crumbled bouillon cube. Stir in peanut butter, red chili oil and sesame paste. Stir and slowly bring to boil. Put aside. Cut green onions into 1/2-inch shreds. Soak dried mushrooms in hot water to cover for 25 minutes. Drain and discard tough stalks. Coarsely chop mushroom caps. Soak dried shrimp in hot water to cover for 15 minutes. Drain and coarsely chop. Seed and finely chop chili. Coarsely chop onions and pickles.

■ COOKING ■

Heat vegetable oil in wok or skillet. When hot, stir-fry dried mushrooms, dried shrimp, chili and onion over high heat for 1 1/2 minutes. Add pork and stir-fry for 2 minutes. Add soy sauce, yellow bean paste and chili sauce and continue to stir-fry for further 1 1/2 minutes. Add blended cornstarch and cook, stirring, for 1 minute until thickened.

■ SERVING ■

Reheat flavored stock. When boiling, pour equal amount of stock into 5-6 bowls of noodles. Sprinkle bowls with green onion and sesame oil. Pour an equal amount of sauce over each bowl of noodles.

★★★

Cooking time: about 15 minutes

Serves: 5-6

Cooking methods: simmer and stir-fry, p.42

Very versatile dish. Can be served as a starter, a final soup or just a spicy snack

---

1/2–3/4 lb package rice flour noodles

3 cups good stock (see page 56)

1 teaspoon salt

1 chicken bouillon cube

2 tablespoons peanut butter

2 teaspoons red chili oil

1 tablespoon sesame paste

2 green onions

2 1/2 tablespoons vegetable oil

Meat sauce:

6 medium dried Chinese mushrooms

2 tablespoons dried shrimp

2 dried red chilies

2 medium onions

2 tablespoons Sichuan hot Ja Chai pickles

1 cup ground pork

1 1/2 tablespoons soy sauce

1 1/2 tablespoons yellow bean paste

2 teaspoons chili sauce

1 tablespoon cornstarch blended with 3 tablespoons water

1 tablespoon sesame oil

1 medium onion

2 slices fresh ginger root

2 garlic cloves

4 green onions

6-inch section cucumber

1 lb wheat flour noodles (like spaghetti)

¼ cup vegetable oil

1 cup ground pork

½ teaspoon salt

1 tablespoon yellow bean paste

1 tablespoon soy sauce

¼ cup good stock (see page 56)

1 tablespoon cornstarch blended with 3 tablespoons water

PEKING JA CHIANG MEIN NOODLES

■ PREPARATION ■

Coarsely chop onion, ginger and garlic. Cut green onions into 2½-inch sections (dividing larger stalks in half or quarters). Cut cucumber into shreds. Place noodles in saucepan of boiling water and simmer for 8–10 minutes. Drain. Rinse noodles under running cold water to keep separate.

■ COOKING ■

Heat oil in wok or large skillet. When hot, stir-fry onion and ginger for 1 minute. Add garlic and pork and stir-fry over medium heat for 3 minutes. Add salt, yellow bean paste and soy sauce. Stir and cook for 3 minutes. Mix in stock and continue to cook for further 3 minutes. Pour in blended cornstarch, stirring until thickened.

■ SERVING ■

Reheat noodles by dipping them in boiling water for 15 seconds, then drain thoroughly. Arrange them on large heated serving dish. Pour sauce into center of noodles. Arrange shredded cucumber and green onion sections on either side of sauce.

★★★

Cooking time: about 15 minutes

Serves: 4–6

Cooking methods: simmer and stir-fry, p.42

Fairly easy to prepare

Serve alone or as an accompaniment

---

5 large dried Chinese mushrooms

3 slices fresh ginger root

3 green onions

4 oz cellophane noodles

2 tablespoons dried shrimp

⅔ cup lean diced pork

2 tablespoons vegetable oil

1½ cups good stock (see page 56)

1 chicken bouillon cube

2 tablespoons light soy sauce

1½ tablespoons vinegar

½ teaspoon salt

½ teaspoon pepper

BRAISED CELLOPHANE NOODLES

■ PREPARATION ■

Soak dried mushrooms in hot water to cover for 25 minutes. Drain and discard tough stalks. Cut mushroom caps into shreds. Soak noodles in hot water to cover for 3 minutes, then drain. Soak dried shrimp in hot water to cover for 5 minutes. Cut ginger and green onions into similar-sized shreds as mushrooms.

■ COOKING ■

Heat oil in wok or skillet. When hot, stir-fry shrimp, ginger, pork and mushrooms over medium heat for 1½ minutes. Add green onions, stock, crumbled bouillon cube and soy sauce. Bring to boil and simmer gently for 4–5 minutes. Add noodles, vinegar, salt and pepper. Stir and mix contents·evenly. Continue to simmer for another 4–5 minutes.

★★★

Cooking time: 10–12 minutes

Serves: 4–6

Cooking method: stir-fry, p.42

Fairly easy to prepare

Good addition to meat or vegetable dish accompanied with rice

Illustrated on p.90

'TEN TREASURE' TAPESTRY NOODLES

This classic noodle dish, called in Chinese 'Shih Jing Chow Mein', is popular and widely cooked, partly because you can use odds and ends of ingredients already in the kitchen – well, at least in a Chinese kitchen. These 'bits and pieces' are the 'Ten Treasures'!

■ PREPARATION ■

Shred bacon. Cut pork, beef and chicken into similar matchstick-sized shreds. Rub meats with salt. Dust with cornstarch. Coat with egg white. Cut bamboo shoots and celery into similar matchstick-sized shreds. Cut green onions into 1-inch sections, separating white parts from green. Trim green beans and parboil in boiling water for 2 minutes. Drain. Soak dried mushrooms in hot water to cover for 25 minutes. Drain and discard tough stalks. Cut mushroom caps into shreds. Blend remainder of cornstarch with stock and 1 tablespoon soy sauce. Place noodles in saucepan of boiling water and simmer for 4 minutes. Drain.

■ COOKING ■

Heat oil in wok or large skillet. When hot, stir-fry pork, chicken, beef, bacon and white parts of green onion over high heat for 2½ minutes. Remove two-thirds of contents and put aside. Add all vegetables and 1 tablespoon shortening or lard to wok or skillet and stir-fry for 2 minutes. Stir in 2 tablespoons soy sauce and half blended cornstarch mixture. Cook for 1 minute. Pour in noodles; turn and mix for 1½ minutes until noodles are heated through. Heat remaining shortening or lard in a separate wok or skillet. When hot, add green parts of green onion and reserved two-thirds meat mixture. Stir-fry over high heat for 1 minute. Pour in remainder of soy sauce and stir-fry for 30 seconds. Add remainder of blended cornstarch mixture, sherry and sesame oil. Continue to stir and mix for 30 seconds.

■ SERVING ■

Spread noodle mixture on to large heated serving dish. Pour over meat mixture from second pan.

2 slices of bacon
2-3 oz pork
2 oz beef or lamb
2 oz chicken
1 teaspoon salt
2 tablespoons cornstarch
1 egg white
2 oz canned bamboo shoots
2 stalks celery
2 green onions
2-3 oz green beans
4 dried Chinese mushrooms
5 tablespoons good stock (see page 56)
¼ cup soy sauce
½-¾ lb package egg noodles or wheat flour noodles
¼ cup vegetable oil
3 tablespoons shortening or lard
1 tablespoon dry sherry
1 teaspoon sesame oil

VEGETABLES

The Chinese are at least partially vegetarian. The majority of Chinese families only eat meat about a couple of times a month, and most of these meat dishes are constituted of two-thirds vegetable. Quick stir-frying, which is one of the primary methods used in Chinese cooking, is particularly suitable for cooking vegetable dishes. Among the seasonings used there is likely to be some soy sauce and other soy bean derivatives, such as soy bean 'cheese', soy paste and hoisin sauce.

What the Chinese endeavor to do with their vegetables is to both inject and draw out flavor, by adding meat stock or gravy, oil and fat impregnated with the flavor of strong-tasting vegetables such as garlic, ginger, onion, various dried food and pickles. The aroma is then enhanced by adding some sesame oil and freshly cut green onions at the last minute. Such treatment seems to have a beneficial effect on both short-cooked and long-cooked vegetable dishes. The latter are cooked over a very low heat and the vegetables sweated in their own juices to bring out their flavor.

2lb collards or other greens
1½ tablespoons finely chopped dried shrimp
Vegetable oil for deep-frying
6 tablespoons blanched almonds
¾ teaspoon salt
1½ teaspoons sugar
¼ teaspoon MSG (optional)

CRISPY 'SEAWEED' WITH ALMONDS

■ PREPARATION ■

Remove stalks from greens and, with a sharp knife, cut leaves into very fine shreds. Spread them out on paper towels to dry. Soak dried shrimp in hot water to cover for 15 minutes. Drain and finely chop.

■ COOKING ■

Heat oil in a wok or deep-fryer. When hot, fry the almonds until crisp, then drain well. Reheat oil. When beginning to smoke, fry greens for 3 minutes, turning and stirring occasionally. Remove with long-handled metal sieve and drain well on paper towels.

■ SERVING ■

Pile crispy 'seaweed' on heated serving plate. Sprinkle on salt, sugar, monosodium glutamate, if using, and dried shrimp. Surprisingly, this 'seaweed' tastes like the real thing.

★★★
Cooking time: about 10 minutes
Serves: 4–6
Cooking method: deep-fry, p.45
A good starter dish
To shred greens, p.31

COLD TOSSED CUCUMBER SALAD

★
Preparation time: about 40 minutes, including seasoning time

No cooking

Serves: 4–6

Quick and easy to prepare

Complements rich savory dishes

Illustrated on p.90

1 medium cucumber
2 teaspoons salt
2 tablespoons sugar
3 tablespoons vinegar
1 tablespoon vegetable oil
¾ tablespoon sesame oil
¼ teaspoon MSG (optional)

■ PREPARATION ■

Cut cucumber slantwise into ⅛-inch slices or cut into 2-inch shreds. Place in large bowl and sprinkle evenly with salt. Leave to season for 30 minutes. Pour away any water from cucumber. Sprinkle cucumber with sugar and vinegar and toss together. Just before serving, add oils and monosodium glutamate, if using. Toss well and sprinkle with presoaked, chopped dried shrimp, if liked.

QUICK-FRIED SNOW PEAS

★
Cooking time: about 8 minutes

Serves: 4–6

Cooking method: stir-fry, p.42

Quick to prepare

Ideal accompaniment to meat dishes

4 cups snow peas
2 garlic cloves
¾ cup vegetable oil for frying
¼ teaspoon MSG (optional)
1 tablespoon light soy sauce
1 tablespoon oyster sauce
2 tablespoons good stock (see page 56)

This bright green vegetable dish is very attractive to serve with all meat dishes.

■ PREPARATION ■

Clean and trim ends from snow peas. Crush garlic.

■ COOKING ■

Heat oil in wok or skillet. When hot, stir-fry snow peas over high heat for 1 minute. Reduce heat to low and continue to stir-fry for further minute. Drain off excess oil. Sprinkle snow peas with garlic, monosodium glutamate, if using, soy sauce, oyster sauce and stock. Simmer gently for 1½ minutes.

YANGTZE STIR-FRIED LIMA BEANS

★
Cooking time: 10 minutes

Serves: 4–6

Cooking methods: stir-fry p.42 and simmer

Easy to prepare

Complements meat dishes

1 lb lima beans, defrosted if frozen
2 green onions
¼ cup vegetable oil
2 teaspoons salt
3 teaspoons sugar
Pinch of MSG (optional)
¼ cup good stock (see page 56)
1 tablespoon shortening or lard

■ PREPARATION ■

If using fresh beans, blanch in boiling water for 3 minutes, then drain. Cut green onions into ½-inch shreds.

■ COOKING ■

Heat oil in wok or skillet. When hot, stir-fry beans and green onions over medium heat for 1 minute. Add salt, sugar, monosodium glutamate and stock. Stir together a few times. Cover, reduce heat to low and cook gently for 5 minutes. Add fat and stir gently a few times.

1 medium Chinese white or Savoy cabbage, about 3½ lb

¼ cup vegetable oil

1 tablespoon shortening or lard

¼ cup soy sauce

1 tablespoon sugar

Pepper to taste

5 tablespoons good stock (see page 56)

1 chicken bouillon cube

RED-COOKED CABBAGE

■ PREPARATION ■

Remove cabbage stalk and discolored leaves. Cut cabbage into 2½ × 2-inch pieces.

■ COOKING ■

Heat oil and shortening in wok or large saucepan. When hot, add all cabbage and toss for 1 minute. Add soy sauce, sugar, pepper, stock and crumbled bouillon cube and continue to stir and turn for further minute. Reduce heat to low, cover and cook for 10 minutes, turning occasionally.

★

Cooking time: 15 minutes

Serves: 6–7

Cooking methods: stir-fry p.42 and simmer

Easy to prepare

Serve with savory dishes and rice accompaniment

---

1 lb Chinese white cabbage

6 dried Chinese mushrooms

1 tablespoon dried shrimp

¼ cup vegetable oil

1 tablespoon shortening or lard

1 teaspoon salt

1 tablespoon sugar

2 teaspoons light soy sauce

¼ cup good stock (see page 56)

1 teaspoon sesame oil

STIR-FRIED CHINESE CABBAGE

WITH CHINESE MUSHROOMS AND DRIED SHRIMP

■ PREPARATION ■

Cut cabbage into 2½ × 2-inch slices. Soak dried mushrooms and shrimp separately in hot water to cover for 25 minutes. Drain and discard tough mushroom stalks. Cut mushroom caps into quarters.

■ COOKING ■

Heat vegetable oil and fat in wok or skillet. When hot, stir-fry dried mushrooms and shrimp for 30 seconds. Add cabbage and stir-fry for another 1 minute. Add salt, sugar, soy sauce and stock and continue to stir-fry for a further minute. Reduce heat to low; cover and cook for a further 1 minute. Sprinkle on sesame oil and toss. Serve hot.

★

Cooking time: about 10 minutes

Serves: 4–6

Cooking method: stir-fry, p.42

Quick and easy to prepare

Complements meat and savory dishes

---

2 bunches watercress

10 medium drained, canned water chestnuts

½ teaspoon salt

2 teaspoons sugar

1 teaspoon red chili oil

2 teaspoons vegetable oil

2 teaspoons sesame oil

1 tablespoon light soy sauce

WATERCRESS AND WATER CHESTNUT SALAD

■ PREPARATION ■

Cut away tough stalks of watercress. Clean thoroughly and blanch in pan of boiling water for 1 minute. Drain and rinse in cold water. Dry thoroughly and chop finely. Place watercress and water chestnuts in bowl. Add salt, sugar, oils and soy sauce. Toss well and serve.

★

Preparation time: 15 minutes

Serves: 4–6

Quick and easy to prepare

Serve with meat and savory dishes

WHITE CABBAGE SALAD

★
Preparation time: about 10 minutes

Serves: 5-6

Quick to prepare

Ideal with rich and/or meaty dishes

■ PREPARATION ■

Cut cabbage into $3 \times \frac{1}{2}$-inch strips. Blanch in pan of boiling water for 2 minutes, then drain. Dry well and place cabbage in large bowl. Add salt, sugar, soy sauce and oils; toss well and serve.

½ Chinese white cabbage, about 2 lb
1 teaspoon salt
2 teaspoons sugar
2 tablespoons light soy sauce
1 tablespoon vegetable oil
½ tablespoon sesame oil

CHINESE WHITE CABBAGE WITH CHILIES

★
Preparation time: 20 minutes plus 2-3 days seasoning

Serves: 5-6

Easy and quick to prepare except time required to season

Good accompaniment to rich and meaty dishes

Illustrated on p.91

■ PREPARATION ■

Chop cabbage coarsely, discarding tougher parts. Coarsely chop chilies and discard seeds. Pound pepper lightly. Place cabbage in a large bowl; sprinkle evenly with salt, chilies and peppercorns. Toss to mix. Refrigerate for 2-3 days before serving. Sprinkle cabbage with the oils; toss well and serve.

Chinese white cabbage, about 3½ lb
3 small, fresh red chilies
2 small, red dried chilies
2 teaspoons salt
1½ teaspoons Sichuan peppercorns
½ tablespoon sesame oil
1 tablespoon vegetable oil

WHITE-COOKED CABBAGE

★ ★
Cooking time: 15 minutes

Serves: 6-7

Cooking methods: stir-fry p.42 and simmer

Easy to prepare

Serve with meat and savory dishes with rice

■ PREPARATION ■

Soak dried shrimp in hot water to cover for 15 minutes. Drain. Remove cabbage stalk and discolored leaves. Cut cabbage into $2\frac{1}{2} \times 2$-inch pieces. Finely shred ginger.

■ COOKING ■

Heat vegetable oil and butter in wok or large saucepan. When hot, stir-fry ginger and shrimp for 15 seconds. Add cabbage and sprinkle with salt, pepper, stock and crumbled bouillon cubes. Bring to boil. Toss a few times and reduce heat to low. Cover and simmer gently for 10 minutes, turning occasionally. Sprinkle with sesame oil before serving.

1½ tablespoons dried shrimp
1 medium Chinese white or Savoy cabbage, about 3½ lb
2 slices fresh ginger root
¼ cup vegetable oil
1½ tablespoons butter
½ teaspoon salt
Pepper to taste
½ cup good stock (see page 56)
1½ chicken bouillon cubes
1 teaspoon sesame oil

2 oz 'hair' seaweed

6–8 dried Chinese mushroooms

1/3 lb Chinese white cabbage

2 oz bean curd skins, if available

Vegetable oil for deep-frying

6 water chestnuts

2–3 oz canned bamboo shoots

2–3 tablespoons pine nuts

1 1/4 cups good stock (see page 56)

1 teaspoon salt

1 1/2 tablespoons light soy sauce

1/2 teaspoon MSG (optional)

2 tablespoons vegetable oil

1 teaspoon sesame oil

1 tablespoon cornstarch blended with 3 tablespoons water

THE BUDDHIST'S DELIGHT

This dish is eaten by all Chinese on the first day of the New Year. It is meant to cleanse the body. Among the older Chinese, meat is not eaten on New Year's Day.

■ PREPARATION ■

Soak seaweed in warm water for 15 minutes. Drain. Soak dried mushrooms in hot water to cover for 25 minutes. Drain and discard tough stalks. Quarter mushroom caps. Tear cabbage into 2–3-inch pieces. Soak bean curd skins in boiling water for 15 minutes. Drain. Deep-fry for 2 minutes. Cut each water chestnut into eighths. Cut bamboo shoots same size as water chestnuts.

■ COOKING ■

Place seaweed, mushrooms, cabbage, bean curd skins, water chestnuts, bamboo shoots and pine nuts in wok or saucepan. Add stock, salt, soy sauce, monosodium glutamate, if using, and 2 tablespoons vegetable oil. Bring to boil and simmer gently for 5 minutes. Add sesame oil and blended cornstarch, bring to boil again and simmer for 2 minutes, stirring. Serve in large bowl or deep-sided serving dish.

★★★

Cooking time: 12–15 minutes

Serves: 6–8

Cooking methods: deep-fry p.45 and simmer

Good accompaniment to meat dishes

---

1 lb young spinach

2 garlic cloves

1/4 cup vegetable oil

1 tablespoon shortening or lard

1 1/2 teaspoons bean curd cheese

1/2 teaspoon salt

3/4 teaspoon sugar

1/4 teaspoon MSG (optional)

QUICK-FRIED SPINACH WITH BEAN CURD CHEESE

Unlike bean curd, which is bland and somewhat tasteless, bean curd cheese, called Fu Yu in Chinese, comes in jars and small cans and is highly salty. Only a small quantity should be used at a time.

■ PREPARATION ■

Remove tough stalks from spinach. Cut leaves into 3-inch slices. Wash thoroughly and drain well. Finely chop garlic.

■ COOKING ■

Heat oil and fat in wok or skillet. When hot, stir in garlic and cheese until mixed. Add spinach and stir-fry over high heat for about 1 1/2 minutes. Sprinkle spinach with salt, sugar and monosodium glutamate, if using. Continue to stir-fry for another 30 seconds.

★

Cooking time: about 5 minutes

Serves: 4–6

Cooking method: stir-fry, p.42

Quick and easy to prepare

Serve as an accompaniment to meat and savory dishes

MADAM FEI'S SPINACH AND RADISH SALAD

This dish makes an extremely good starter.

★★

Preparation time: 15 minutes

Serves: 4–6

Quite easy to prepare

Ideal starter or accompaniment to meat dishes

Illustrated on p.95

1 bunch of large or medium-sized red radishes
2 teaspoons salt
2 lb young tender spinach, with small leaves
2 teaspoons light soy sauce
1½ teaspoons sugar
3 teaspoons sesame oil
Pinch of pepper
¼ teaspoon MSG (optional)
Garnish:
Radish roses

■ PREPARATION ■

Clean and trim radishes. Flatten with side of a cleaver or with a rolling pin. Sprinkle with 1 teaspoon of the salt and reserve. Clean spinach, remove all tough stalks and discolored leaves. Place leaves in saucepan and pour a kettleful of boiling water over leaves. Strain immediately and rinse with cold water. Strain away all water and dry thoroughly. Chop spinach. Sprinkle remaining salt, soy sauce, sugar, oil, pepper and monosodium glutamate, if using, over spinach. Toss to combine seasonings. Arrange on large platter and place salted radish on top.

STIR-FRIED SPINACH IN SHRIMP SAUCE

WITH BEAN CURD CHEESE

★★

Cooking time: about 8 minutes

Serves: 5–7

Cooking method: stir-fry, p.42

Quick and easy to prepare

Good with meat and savory dishes

1 tablespoon dried shrimp
1½ lb spinach
3 garlic cloves
5 tablespoons vegetable oil
½ tablespoon bean curd cheese
1½ tablespoons good stock (see page 56)
1½ tablespoons shrimp sauce
½ teaspoon salt
3 tablespoons shortening or lard

■ PREPARATION ■

Soak dried shrimp in hot water to cover for 25 minutes. Drain. Wash and trim spinach. Finely chop garlic.

■ COOKING ■

Heat oil in wok or skillet. When hot, stir-fry shrimp for 15 seconds. Add spinach and turn around quickly for 1 minute until well coated with oil. Push spinach to side of wok. Add garlic, bean curd cheese and stock to center of wok or skillet. Stir them around for a few seconds, then stir in spinach. Sprinkle evenly with shrimp sauce and salt. Turn and stir for 1 minute. Add shortening. Continue to stir and turn. By this time spinach will be glistening and full of flavor. Transfer spinach mixture to heated dish and serve.

Cold Tossed Cucumber Salad (*above left*), a simple vegetable accompaniment garnished with chopped dried shrimp; recipe page 85.

Quick Fried Green Beans with Dried Shrimp and Pork (*center left*), a substantial vegetable dish; recipe page 97.

Braised Cellophane Noodles (*below left*), good accompaniment to meat or vegetable dish and boiled rice; recipe page 82.

Chinese White Cabbage with Chilies (*right*), an excellent accompaniment to rice gruel or congee; recipe page 86.

1 lb celery

Mustard dressing:

2 tablespoons prepared
  English mustard

½ teaspoon salt

1 tablespoon warm water

6 tablespoons water

1 tablespoon light soy sauce

½ teaspoon sugar

¼ teaspoon MSG (optional)

2 teaspoons cornstarch
  blended with
  2 tablespoons water

COLD TOSSED CELERY IN MUSTARD SAUCE

■ PREPARATION ■

To make dressing, mix mustard with salt and warm water; set aside. Bring 6 tablespoons water to boil in small pan and add soy sauce, sugar, monosodium glutamate, if using, and blended cornstarch. Stir until liquid thickens, add mustard mixture and leave to cool. Wash the celery well and chop off leaves and tough ends. Cut stalks and place in bowl. Pour cooled sauce over celery.

★
Preparation time:
30 minutes,
including cooling
time

Serves: 4–5

Easy to prepare

Complements
meat dishes

1 lb broccoli

¼ cup vegetable oil

2 tablespoons oyster sauce

3 tablespoons crab meat

2 tablespoons dry sherry

3 tablespoons good stock
  (see page 56)

1 tablespoon shortening or
  lard

2 teaspoons cornstarch
  blended with
  2 tablespoons water

QUICK-FRIED BROCCOLI IN OYSTER SAUCE WITH CRAB

■ PREPARATION ■

Break broccoli into florets, removing tough stalks.

■ COOKING ■

Heat oil in wok or skillet. When hot, stir-fry broccoli over high heat for 1 minute. Add oyster sauce and stir-fry for further minute. Break up crab meat and sprinkle with sherry, stock and chopped fat. Add to pan and turn together for 30 seconds. Sprinkle with blended cornstarch and stir until sauce thickens.

★
Cooking time:
about 10 minutes

Serves: 4–6

Cooking method:
stir-fry, p.42

Quick and easy to
prepare

Serve as
accompaniment to
meat dishes

¼ lb snow peas

3 oz canned bamboo shoots

3 oz asparagus

3 oz carrots

3 oz cooked cured ham

Vegetable oil for deep-
  frying

3 slices fresh ginger root

1½ tablespoons light soy
  sauce

1½ tablespoons good stock
  (see page 56)

1 tablespoon dry sherry

1½ tablespoons shortening
  or lard

½ teaspoon sesame oil

SAUTE OF FOUR VEGETABLES

■ PREPARATION ■

Cut snow peas, bamboo shoots, asparagus, carrot and ham into double-size matchstick shreds.

■ COOKING ■

Heat vegetable oil in wok or deep-fryer. When hot, fry vegetables for 2½ minutes. Drain. Reserve oil to use for all purposes, leaving 3 tablespoons. Reheat wok or skillet with oil. When hot, stir-fry ginger for 1 minute. Remove and discard. Add ham, then vegetables to wok or skillet and stir-fry for 1 minute. Stir in soy sauce, stock and sherry. Sauté for 1½ minutes. Add and melt shortening until vegetables are glossy. Sprinkle over sesame oil, turn and serve.

★★
Cooking time:
about 5–10 minutes

Serves: 4

Cooking methods:
deep-fry p.45 and
stir-fry p.42

Illustrated on p.95

BEAN SPROUTS WITH GARLIC AND GREEN ONIONS

★

Cooking time:
about 5 minutes

Serves: 5–6

Cooking method:
stir-fry, p.42

Quick to prepare

**Serve as
accompaniment to
meat and poultry
dishes**

1 lb bean sprouts

3 garlic cloves

2 green onions

¼ cup vegetable oil

1 tablespoon shortening or lard

2 teaspoons drained, canned finely chopped Sichuan Ja Chai hot pickles

1½ teaspoons salt

¼ teaspoon MSG (optional)

2 tablespoons good stock (see page 56)

2 teaspoons cornstarch blended with 2 tablespoons water

■ PREPARATION ■

Remove discolored bean sprouts, rinse under cold running water, drain and dry. Finely chop garlic. Cut green onions into 1-inch shreds.

■ COOKING ■

Heat oil and fat in wok or skillet. When hot, stir-fry garlic and pickles for 30 seconds. Add green onions, bean sprouts and sprinkle with the salt. Stir-fry over medium heat for 1½ minutes. Add monosodium glutamate, if using, and stock and stir-fry quickly for 30 seconds. Stir in blended cornstarch to thicken sauce.

DEEP-FRIED EGGPLANT CAKES

★★★★

Cooking time:
about 15 minutes

Serves: 4–6

Cooking method:
deep-fry, p.45

**Requires time and
care to prepare**

**Good starter for
multi-dish dinner**

1½ tablespoons dried shrimp

3 medium eggplants

2 green onions

2 slices fresh ginger root

¼ cup finely chopped fresh pork sides or pork shoulder

½ teaspoon salt

1 tablespoon soy sauce

1 tablespoon sesame oil

Vegetable oil for deep-frying

Batter:

1¼ cups all-purpose flour

2½ tablespoons cornstarch

3 tablespoons water

1 egg

Salt and pepper dip:

2 tablespoons sea salt

2 tablespoons pounded Sichuan peppercorns

■ PREPARATION ■

Soak dried shrimp in hot water to cover for 15 minutes. Drain and finely chop. Remove eggplant stalks. Without peeling, cut flesh diagonally into ¼-inch slices, cutting one slice right through, but leaving every second slice connected at base, making a pocket for stuffing. Finely chop green onions and ginger. For the stuffing, mix together pork, shrimp, salt, green onions, soy sauce, ginger and sesame oil. Place equal amounts of filling in space between each 2 hinged slices of eggplant. Combine batter ingredients together and use to coat stuffed eggplant slices.

■ COOKING ■

Heat oil in wok or deep-fryer. When very hot, fry coated eggplant slices for about 4 minutes. Drain. Meanwhile, make dip. Fry salt and pepper in dry skillet over low heat for about 30 seconds.

■ SERVING ■

Arrange eggplant cakes on heated plate. Surround plate with a few saucers of salt and pepper dip. Dip the eggplant cakes into lightly aromatic dip before eating.

Fu-Yung Cauliflower (*left*), a light vegetable dish with chicken; recipe page 97.

Madam Fei's Spinach and Radish Salad (*above right*), a good starter with attractive radish garnish; recipe page 89.

Sauté of Four Vegetables (*below left*), a colorful dish garnished with carrot flowers; recipe page 92.

¾ lb Chinese white cabbage

3 tablespoons shortening

Salt and pepper to taste

5 tablespoons good stock
(see page 56)

3 tablespoons vegetable oil

2 slices fresh ginger root

1 tablespoon chopped white
part of green onion

5–6oz crab meat

1 tablespoon dry sherry or
white wine

CRAB MEAT WITH CREAM OF CHINESE CABBAGE

★★

Cooking time:
5–6 minutes

Serves: 4–6

Cooking method:
stir-fry, p.42

Illustrated on p.258

■ PREPARATION ■

Cut cabbage into ½-inch sections.

■ COOKING ■

Heat shortening in wok or skillet. When hot, stir-fry cabbage for 1 minute. Sprinkle with salt and pepper to taste and add 3 tablespoons of stock. Stir-fry for 1½ minutes. Transfer to heated dish.

Reheat wok or skillet with oil. When hot, stir-fry ginger and white part of green onion over medium heat for 30 seconds. Add crab meat, stir and mix. Sprinkle with salt and pepper and add remaining stock and sherry or white wine. Stir-fry over high heat for 30 seconds. Spoon over cabbage in dish.

4 medium firm eggplants

3 slices fresh ginger root

3 garlic cloves

3 green onions

6 tablespoons vegetable oil

1½ tablespoons Sichuan hot
Tou Pan paste

2 tablespoons soy sauce

1 tablespoon sugar

½ teaspoon salt

½ cup good stock (see page
56)

¼ teaspoon MSG (optional)

1 tablespoon vinegar

1 teaspoon sesame oil

SICHUAN BRAISED EGGPLANT

★★

Cooking time:
12 minutes

Serves: 4–6

Cooking method:
stir-fry p.42 and
simmer

Easy to prepare

**A rich dish, good
with rice**

■ PREPARATION ■

Remove eggplant stalks and, without peeling, cut slantwise into approximately 2½ × 1½-inch pieces. Finely chop ginger and garlic. Cut green onions into fine shreds.

■ COOKING ■

Heat vegetable oil in wok or skillet. When hot, add eggplant pieces and stir and turn a few times. Reduce heat to low and stir-fry for about 5 minutes until eggplant pieces are soft. Press eggplant to squeeze out excess water or oil. Remove and set aside. Add garlic, ginger and bean paste to pan. Stir them a few times, then add soy sauce, sugar, salt, stock and monosodium glutamate, if using. Bring to boil, return eggplant to pan and cook until sauce reduces to a glaze. Sprinkle eggplant with vinegar, sesame oil and green onions. Turn mixture once more before serving.

QUICK FRIED GREEN BEANS WITH DRIED SHRIMP AND PORK

★★

Cooking time:
about 8–10 minutes

Serves: 4–6

Cooking methods:
deep-fry p.45 and
stir-fry p.42

Illustrated on p.90

■ PREPARATION ■

Trim green beans. Soak dried shrimp in hot water to cover for 20 minutes. Drain and chop. Finely chop pickle.

■ COOKING ■

Heat oil in wok or deep-fryer. When hot, fry beans for 2 minutes. Remove and put aside. Pour away oil to use for other purposes. Heat shortening in wok or skillet. When hot, add garlic and stir a few times. Add pork, shrimp, stock and pickle and stir fry for 2 minutes. Stir in soy sauce, sugar salt and water. Add green beans and turn and toss until liquid in pan has nearly all evaporated. Sprinkle with sesame oil, vinegar and green onions. Turn and stir once more, then serve.

- 1½ lb green beans
- 2 tablespoons dried shrimp
- 1 tablespoon chopped Sichuan Ja Chai hot pickle
- Vegetable oil for deep-frying
- 3 teaspoons chopped garlic
- 1½ tablespoons shortening or lard
- ⅓ cup ground pork
- 3 tablespoons good stock (see page 56)
- 1 tablespoon soy sauce
- ½ tablespoon sugar
- 2 teaspoons salt
- 3 tablespoons water
- 1 teaspoon sesame oil
- 2 teaspoons vinegar
- 2 tablespoons chopped green onions (optional)

FU-YUNG CAULIFLOWER

★★

Cooking time:
about 11 minutes

Serves: 4–6

Cooking method:
simmer

Illustrated on p.94

■ PREPARATION ■

Remove cauliflower stalk. Cut cauliflower into florets. Beat egg whites until nearly stiff. Mix in all remaining ingredients thoroughly. Lightly beat together.

■ COOKING ■

Place cauliflower florets in saucepan of boiling water and simmer for 7–8 minutes. Drain. Put cauliflower in wok or pan. Add egg white and chicken mixture. Bring to boil, reduce heat and gently simmer for 3 minutes, stirring and turning gently.

■ SERVING ■

Transfer cauliflower to heated dish and pour sauce over. If liked, sprinkle with chopped green onion and finely chopped ham or presoaked, chopped dried shrimp.

- 1 large cauliflower
- 2 egg whites
- ½ cup ground breast of chicken
- ¼ cup good stock (see page 56)
- 1½ tablespoons cornstarch blended with ¼ cup water
- Salt and pepper to taste
- ¼ teaspoon MSG (optional)
- ¼ cup milk

BEAN CURD AND EGGS

A simple bean curd stir-fry (*left*).
A selection of Chinese eggs (*above*); see page 27.

豆腐和蛋

BEAN CURD

One of the most widely eaten foods in China, bean curd may seem bland to the average Westerner, whose palate may not readily appreciate the subtle yet, to attuned taste buds, nutty flavor to be experienced when eating this unusual food. Bean curd is made from a thick, soy bean milk, derived from soy bean purée which has been boiled with water and then filtered for the milk. The milk is then induced to set through overnight cooling and the addition of a small amount of plaster of Paris. Once set the bean curd can be cut into various shapes and sizes, but it is usually sold in 3 × 3-inch cakes, about 1-inch thick.

Bean curd is reputed to be highly nutritious and easily digestible, and is rapidly gaining in popularity among health-conscious Westerners. A very attractive yet useful vegetarian food – one that can be cooked into innumerable dishes with all kinds of vegetables – bean curd can also be mixed and married successfully with almost any meat, fish, seafood and poultry. So, not only does this seemingly non-descript food possess great culinary versatility, but nutritionally it is one of the pillars of the Chinese diet.

---

5 tablespoons dried shrimp
2 tablespoons dry sherry or rice wine
1½ tablespoons drained, canned Sichuan hot Ja Chai pickles
1½ tablespoons drained, canned snow pickles
2 garlic cloves
2½ tablespoons vegetable oil
1½ tablespoons sesame oil
2 tablespoons dark soy sauce
3 tablespoons lemon juice or vinegar
2 teaspoons sugar
¼ teaspoon MSG (optional)
3 cakes bean curd

COLD TOSSED BEAN CURD

Because bean curd has already been cooked (boiled) during its preparation, it usually requires very little cooking and heating when incorporated into a dish; or it may not need any cooking at all, as shown in the following recipe.

■ PREPARATION ■

Soak dried shrimp in hot water to cover for 15 minutes. Add sherry or wine and soak for further 15 minutes. Drain shrimp and finely chop. Finely chop both types of pickle. Crush garlic. Place shrimp, pickle and garlic in bowl with the oils, soy sauce, lemon juice, sugar and monosodium glutamate, if using; mix well.

■ SERVING ■

Cut bean curd into cubes and place on a serving dish. Spoon sauce mixture over bean curd and toss lightly. Serve with plain boiled rice.

★

Preparation time: about 10 minutes, plus soaking

Serves: 5–6

Quick to prepare

Useful starter for vegetarian or meat meal

BEAN CURD WITH CRAB MEAT AND PEAS

★★
Cooking time: about 6 minutes
Serves: 4–6
Cooking method: stir-fry, p.42
Quick to prepare
Illustrated on p.103

■ PREPARATION ■

Cut bean curd into ¼-inch slices, then quarter each slice. Shred green onions. Flake crab meat.

■ COOKING ■

Heat oil in wok or skillet. When hot, stir-fry ginger for 10–15 seconds. Stir in crab meat and peas and stir-fry for 45 seconds. Add bean curd pieces, green onions, salt and pepper to taste, soy sauce and sherry; toss for 1½ minutes. Sprinkle with blended cornstarch, then turn and toss for further 45 seconds.

2 cakes bean curd

2 green onions

5–6 oz crab meat

2½ tablespoons vegetable oil

1 teaspoon finely chopped fresh ginger root

1 tablespoon peas

Salt and pepper to taste

2 teaspoons light soy sauce

1 tablespoon dry sherry

3 teaspoons cornstarch blended with 3 tablespoons good stock (see page 56)

STIR-FRIED BEAN CURD WITH SHRIMP

★★
Cooking time: 4–5 minutes
Serves: 4–6
Cooking method: stir-fry, p.42
Quick to prepare
Suitable for family meal

■ PREPARATION ■

Soak dried shrimp in hot water to cover for about 5 minutes, then drain. Cut bean curd into cubes. Cut green onions into ½-inch sections.

■ COOKING ■

Heat oil in wok or skillet. When hot, stir-fry ginger and dried shrimp over medium heat for about 30 seconds. Add white parts of green onions, fresh or frozen shrimp, salt, pepper and stock. Bring to boil and add bean curd, soy sauce, oyster sauce and green parts of green onions. Turn and stir contents around gently. Simmer for 2 minutes.

2 teaspoons dried shrimp

3 cakes bean curd

3 green onions

3 teaspoons vegetable oil

3 slices fresh ginger root

⅓ cup fresh or frozen shrimp

½ teaspoon salt

Pepper to taste

¼ cup good stock (see page 56)

1½ tablespoons light soy sauce

1 tablespoon oyster sauce

Sichuan Ma Po Tofu (*above left*), sprinkle with chopped green onion and serve with chili dip; recipe page 106.
Stir-fried Chinese Omelet with Tomatoes (*below left*), a simple, light yet colorful dish; recipe page 109.
Bean Curd with Crab Meat and Peas (*right*), a quick to prepare dish; recipe page 101.

2 cakes bean curd

²/₃ cup button mushrooms

2 oz chicken breast

2 oz chicken livers

2 oz lamb's kidney

½ cup drained, canned sliced bamboo shoots

2 garlic cloves

2 green onions

1 tablespoon cornstarch

3 tablespoons water

Vegetable oil for deep-frying, about 1½ cups

¾ teaspoon salt

Pepper to taste

¼ cup vegetable oil

1 tablespoon shortening

½ teaspoon finely chopped fresh ginger root

⅓ cup shrimp

2 tablespoons white wine

1½ tablespoons light soy sauce

3 tablespoons good stock (see page 56)

¼ teaspoon MSG (optional)

½ teaspoon sesame oil

BEAN CURD WITH EIGHT PRECIOUS INGREDIENTS

The appeal of this dish lies in the savoriness of the sauce coating all the ingredients and in the different textures of the foods.

■ PREPARATION ■

Cut bean curd into cubes. Quarter mushrooms. Cut chicken breast meat and livers into bite-sized pieces if necessary. Score kidney in criss-cross pattern on surface and then cut into bite-sized pieces. Trim bamboo shoots into small wedges. Finely chop garlic and green onions. Blend cornstarch with 3 tablespoons water. Heat oil in wok or deep-fryer. When hot, gently fry bean curd for about 1 minute. Drain thoroughly, pour away oil for other uses. Sprinkle chicken breast meat, chicken livers and kidney with salt and pepper and 1 tablespoon oil.

■ COOKING ■

Heat 3 tablespoons oil in wok or skillet until hot, then add shortening. Add ginger, garlic and half the green onions and stir together briefly over a high heat. Add chicken meat, shrimp, chicken livers and kidney and stir-fry over medium heat for about 1½ minutes. Stir in vegetables and toss together for further 1½ minutes. Mix in bean curd, then pour in wine, soy sauce and stock. Bring to boil then simmer gently for 3–4 minutes. Finally sprinkle on monosodium glutamate, if using, blended cornstarch and sesame oil. Turn them over a few times and serve.

■ SERVING ■

Serve in a very large plate or bowl. This dish is served in China both as an accompaniment for rice and as a snack for nibbling when sipping wine. Part of its attraction lies in the fact that there are so many different ingredients to choose from.

★ ★ ★

Cooking time: about 10 minutes

Serves: 6–8

Cooking method: stir-fry, p.42

Needs time to prepare

Serve as part of a multi-dish meal

Scoring kidney p.39

Cooking time:
about 15 minutes

Serves: 4–6

Cooking methods:
stir-fry p.42, deep-
fry p.45 and
simmer

Good family dish

★ ★ ★

BRAISED BEAN CURD FAMILY-STYLE

Family-style simply means bean curd which has been braised with whatever bits and pieces are available in the family kitchen; in a typical Chinese kitchen, this includes cooked pork (usually Soy Braised Pork), ginger, bamboo shoots, green onions, soy sauce and oyster sauce.

■ PREPARATION ■

Cut bean curd into 10–12 pieces per cake. Heat oil in wok or deep-fryer. When hot, fry bean curd for about 2 minutes. Drain, saving oil for other cooking. Cut green onions into 1-inch sections. Cut pork into bite-sized pieces if necessary. Trim bamboo shoots into 1½-inch wedges. Blend cornstarch with 3 tablespoons water.

■ COOKING ■

Heat 3–4 tablespoons oil in wok or skillet. When hot, stir-fry ginger and half of green onions for about 1 minute. Add bamboo shoots, pork and bean curd pieces. Turn them over high heat for about 1½ minutes. Stir in stock, soy sauce, hoisin sauce, oyster sauce, sugar and monosodium glutamate, if using. Bring to boil and stir gently. Reduce heat and simmer gently for further 10 minutes. Finally, add blended cornstarch and wine and stir until thickened. Sprinkle remaining green onions over dish and serve.

3 cakes bean curd
Vegetable oil for deep-frying, about 1½ cups
3 green onions
1 lb soy braised pork (see page 196)
⅔ cup drained, sliced canned bamboo shoots
1 tablespoon cornstarch
3 tablespoons water
3 slices fresh ginger root
⅔ cup good stock (see page 56)
3 tablespoons soy sauce
1 tablespoon hoisin sauce
1 tablespoon oyster sauce
1 tablespoon sugar
¼ teaspoon MSG (optional)
3 tablespoons rice wine

3 cakes bean curd
2 tablespoons salted black beans
3 green onions
2 slices fresh ginger root
2 small chilies, dried or fresh
3 slices drained, canned Sichuan hot Ja Chai pickle
1½ tablespoons cornstarch
¼ cup water
¼ cup vegetable oil
8 oz ground pork
½ teaspoon salt
¼ cup good stock (see page 56)
2 tablespoons white wine
2 tablespoons light soy sauce
¼ teaspoon pepper
2 teaspoons chili sauce
2 teaspoons sesame oil

SICHUAN MA PO TOFU

(HOT BEAN CURD WITH GROUND PORK)

This dish, which has always been popular in Japan, is now gaining in popularity in the West.

■ PREPARATION ■

Cut bean curd into cubes. Place in pan of boiling water and simmer for 3 minutes, then drain. Soak black beans in hot water for 5 minutes, then drain and crush. Remove seeds from chilies. Coarsely chop green onions. Finely chop ginger, chilies, and pickle. Blend cornstarch with ¼ cup water.

■ COOKING ■

Heat vegetable oil in wok or skillet. When hot, stir-fry ginger, chili, pickle and black beans for about 1 minute. Add pork, green onions and salt and continue to stir-fry for another 4 minutes. Pour in stock, wine and soy sauce and simmer for further 2 minutes. Add bean curd to pan and toss gently to coat. Bring to boil and sprinkle on pepper, chili sauce and blended cornstarch. Stir gently for another 30 seconds. Finally, sprinkle on sesame oil and serve immediately.

★★★
Cooking time: 8–10 minutes

Serves: 5–6

Cooking method: stir-fry, p.42

Fairly quick to prepare

Serve this spicy dish with plenty of rice for hungry appetites

Illustrated on p.102

2 cakes bean curd
8 oz button mushrooms
6 medium dried Chinese mushrooms
1 tablespoon dried shrimp
3 tablespoons water
1 tablespoon cornstarch
3 tablespoons vegetable oil
1 tablespoon shortening or lard
½ tablespoon bean curd 'cheese' (optional)
3 tablespoons light soy sauce
2 tablespoons white wine
7 tablespoons good stock (see page 56)
¼ teaspoon pepper
1½ teaspoons sesame oil

BRAISED BEAN CURD WITH MUSHROOMS

■ PREPARATION ■

Cut bean curd into cubes. Halve fresh mushrooms. Soak dried mushrooms and dried shrimp separately in hot water to cover for 25 minutes. Drain, retaining liquid in which shrimp was soaked. Discard tough mushroom stalks then cut caps into quarters. Blanch bean curd in boiling water for 2 minutes. Drain thoroughly. Blend cornstarch with 3 tablespoons water.

■ COOKING ■

Heat vegetable oil and shortening in wok or skillet. When hot, stir-fry dried mushrooms for about 30 seconds. Add shrimp and stir-fry for 30 seconds before adding bean curd 'cheese', bean curd, soy sauce and wine. Blend together and put in fresh mushrooms, shrimp soaking water and stock. Bring to boil, stir gently and simmer for

★★
Cooking time: about 6 minutes

Serves: 4–6

Cooking methods: stir-fry p.42 and simmer

Quick to prepare

A light dish that goes well with any combination

2 minutes. Sprinkle on blended cornstarch and turn over once more to combine. Finally, sprinkle on pepper and sesame oil. By this time bean curd will have absorbed much of the mushroom flavor.

★★★★

Cooking time: 20 minutes

Serves: 6–8

Cooking method: steam, p.49

Requires time and care in preparation

Serve as part of a multi–dish party dinner

STEAMED STUFFED BEAN CURD

Bean curd is often steamed in China. Stuffed bean curd is a little more difficult to prepare than diced bean curd dishes, as the cakes must be cut with more care. It is often served at party meals.

■ PREPARATION ■

Cut each cake of bean curd into 4 pieces. Scoop out deep hollow in center of each piece, about half–way through. Soak dried shrimp in hot water for 5 minutes, then drain and finely chop. Crush garlic. Mix pork, garlic, shrimp, salt, pepper, ½ tablespoon oil and egg white together in a bowl. Spoon mixture into bean curd and place a whole shrimp firmly on top.

■ COOKING ■

Arrange 12 pieces of stuffed bean curd on heatproof dish, place in steamer and steam for 20 minutes. Meanwhile, heat oil for sauce in small pan. When hot, add the ginger, green onions, stock, oyster sauce and soy sauce. Bring to boil and stir well. When bean curd is ready, add sesame oil to sauce and pour evenly over bean curd.

3 cakes bean curd

1 tablespoon dried shrimp

1 garlic clove

4 oz ground pork

¼ teaspoon salt

Pepper to taste

½ tablespoon vegetable oil

1 egg white

12 medium shrimp, fresh or frozen

Sauce:

1½ tablespoons vegetable oil

1½ teaspoons finely chopped fresh ginger root

2 teaspoons coarsely chopped green onions

3 tablespoons good stock (see page 56)

1 tablespoon oyster sauce

½ tablespoon light soy sauce

1 teaspoon sesame oil

EGGS

There is poultry in abundance in China, so it follows that eggs should be one of the most popular foods eaten there. Eggs in China are usually eaten either boiled, scrambled, stir-fried or steamed in the form of savory custards. They are often hard cooked and seasoned; for example, as soy eggs, marbled tea eggs, salted eggs or preserved and pickled 'hundred-year-old' eggs.

These latter are buried in a mixture of mud and lime, and the heat generated by the small amount of water added to the lime cooks the eggs. They are usually stored in stone jars with pine-ash and salt added – ingredients which seem to pickle the eggs. During their two months of maturation the eggs become encrusted in dried mud and lime and are covered with straw to separate them. When these layers have been removed and the eggs shelled, the whites of the eggs will be green in color and the yolks a dark yellowish-green. These eggs have a very pungent and cheesey flavor. They are often eaten at breakfast with congee (rice gruel) or cut into slices and used as an hors d'oeuvres.

The majority of eggs consumed at mealtimes in China are usually stir-fried or scrambled. Chinese scrambled eggs bear little similarity to Western scrambled eggs, being only lightly stirred. There are innumerable ingredients that can be mixed and cooked with beaten eggs, enabling a large variety of stir-fried egg dishes. The most popular ingredients used for this purpose are ham, bacon, tomatoes, mushrooms, shrimp, peas, green onions, shredded meats and chicken. Invariably, a large pinch of finely chopped green onions and a little soy sauce or sherry are sprinkled over the top shortly before the dish is served. To any hungry Chinese, such a dish eaten with plain boiled rice is as appetizing as any other in the entire Chinese culinary repertoire.

CHINESE STIR-FRIED 'OMELETS'

Chinese 'omelets' are not strictly omelets in the Western sense. In China, the eggs are stirred during frying rather than being allowed to set before they are folded over. In Chinese cooking, the stirring should be done just as half of the eggs have set. The final product should be 85-90 per cent set. Since almost any kind of food suitably chopped or shredded can be combined and cooked in this manner with the eggs, there is almost an unlimited number of variations of these stir-fried omelets. The following are just a few examples. The two indispensable requisites for the success of such a dish are finely chopped green onion and a spoonful or two of good quality soy sauce, which are sprinkled over the omelets just before serving.

BASIC PLAIN STIR-FRIED OMELET

★★

Cooking time:
2½ minutes

Serves 4-6

Cooking method:
stir-fry, p.42

Quick and easy to prepare

Serve as part of an informal family meal.

■ PREPARATION ■

Break eggs into bowl with salt and pepper and beat lightly with fork.

■ COOKING ■

Heat oil in wok or skillet. When hot, pour in eggs. When edges of egg begin to set, continue to cook over medium heat for further 15 seconds. Stir and turn mixture over several times until it is almost all set and then arrange on heated dish. Sprinkle omelet evenly with chopped green onion and soy sauce.

4-5 eggs
½ teaspoon salt
Pepper to taste
5-6 tablespoons vegetable oil
1½ tablespoons finely chopped green onions
1½ tablespoons good quality dark soy sauce

STIR-FRIED CHINESE OMELET WITH TOMATOES

★★

Cooking time:
about 4 minutes

Serves: 4-6

Cooking method:
stir-fry, p.42

Makes a light snack

Illustrated on p.102

■ PREPARATION ■

Break eggs into bowl with salt and pepper and beat lightly with fork. Peel and finely slice onion. Cut each tomato into 8 segments.

■ COOKING ■

Heat vegetable oil in wok or skillet. When hot, gently stir-fry onion for about 30 seconds, then add tomatoes. Spread evenly over bottom of pan. Pour over beaten egg and allow to flow over base of pan. When edges of egg have begun to set, gently turn and stir several times, allowing uncooked liquid to come in contact with surface of pan. Sprinkle on sesame oil and arrange omelet on a heated dish. Sprinkle over chopped green onion, with extra green onion shreds if liked, and soy sauce and serve.

4-5 eggs
½ teaspoon salt
Pepper to taste
1 medium onion
3 medium tomatoes
4-5 tablespoons vegetable oil
1 teaspoon sesame oil
1½ tablespoons finely chopped green onion
1½ tablespoons good quality dark soy sauce

4–5 eggs

½ teaspoon salt

Pepper to taste

1 medium onion

3 slices bacon

4–5 tablespoons vegetable oil

1½ tablespoons finely chopped green onion

1½ tablespoons good quality dark soy sauce

STIR-FRIED CHINESE OMELET
WITH ONION AND BACON

■ PREPARATION ■

Break eggs into bowl with salt and pepper and beat lightly with fork. Peel and finely slice onion. De-rind and finely chop bacon.

■ COOKING ■

Heat oil in wok or skillet. When hot, stir-fry onion and bacon for about 1½ minutes. Spread evenly over bottom of pan. Pour over beaten egg and allow to flow over base of pan. When edges of egg have begun to set, gently turn and stir several times, allowing any uncooked liquid to come in contact with surface of pan. Arrange on heated dish, sprinkle over green onion and soy sauce and serve.

★★

Cooking time: about 5 minutes

Serves: 4–6

Cooking method: stir-fry, p.42

Quick to prepare

Serve as a snack or part of a multi-dish meal.

---

8 oz jumbo shrimp, fresh or frozen, shelled

1 teaspoon salt

Pepper to taste

5 tablespoons vegetable oil

2 teaspoons cornstarch

2 garlic cloves

3 green onions

4 eggs

1 tablespoon dry sherry

STIR-FRIED SHRIMP 'SOUFFLE'

■ PREPARATION ■

Sprinkle shrimp with salt, pepper, ½ tablespoon of oil and dust with cornstarch. Crush garlic. Cut green onions into 1-inch sections. Beat eggs in small bowl.

■ COOKING ■

Heat remaining oil in wok or skillet. When hot, stir-fry garlic and shrimp for 1½ minutes. Pour in beaten egg and let egg flow over surface of the pan. Reduce heat to low, sprinkle on green onions and cook for 1½ minutes. When eggs are almost set, toss with metal spoon. Sprinkle on sherry and place on heated serving plate.

★★

Cooking time: about 5–7 minutes

Serves: 4–6

Cooking method: stir-fry, p.42

Easy to prepare

A light dish to serve as part of a multi-dish meal.

★ ★ ★

Cooking time:
about 10 minutes

Serves: 4–6

Cooking method:
stir-fry, p.42

An attractive stacked pancake dish to serve as a light meal or part of a multi-dish meal

HUANG-PU BOATMEN'S EGG OMELET

This is a favorite dish invented by the boatmen of Huang-Pu, which is a stretch of the Pearl River just below Canton. The contrast in colors between the dark soy sauce and the different colored pancakes makes the dish visually attractive as well as appealing in flavor.

▩ PREPARATION ▩

Break eggs into bowl with salt and pepper and beat lightly with fork.

▩ COOKING ▩

Heat 3 tablespoons of oil in wok or skillet. When hot, stir-fry onion for few seconds. Add crab meat and spread evenly over bottom of pan. Pour in one-third of eggs and cook until almost set. With aid of fish slice, transfer to heated dish. Reheat wok or pan with about 2 tablespoons oil and, when hot, add shrimp. Spread over bottom of pan and then pour on another third of eggs. Cook until almost set, then stack on top of first 'pancake'. Reheat wok or pan with about 2 tablespoons oil and, when hot, add peas and green onions. Stir-fry for few seconds, then spread evenly over bottom of pan. Pour in remaining egg and cook until almost set, then stack on top of other 2 pancakes.

▩ SERVING ▩

Cut the 'triple pancake' into 8 segments. Sprinkle with soy sauce.

7 eggs
1 teaspoon salt
Pepper to taste
8 tablespoons vegetable oil
1 tablespoon finely chopped onion
¼ cup cooked crab meat
¼ cup fresh shrimp, shelled
3 tablespoons peas
2 tablespoons finely chopped green onions
1½ tablespoons soy sauce

2 eggs

1¼ cups good stock (see page 56) or water

salt and pepper to taste

1 tablespoon soy sauce

1 tablespoon chopped green onion

Optional extras:

2-3 tablespoons shredded crab meat or shrimp

pinch of MSG (optional)

1-2 tablespoons chopped ham

1-2 tablespoons petits pois

BASIC STEAMED EGG AND FANCY STEAMED EGGS

★★

Cooking time: about 15 minutes

Serves: 4–6

Cooking method: steam, p.49

Easy to prepare

Excellent with rice

Illustrated opposite

Chinese steamed egg would be called egg custard in Western cuisine, except that in the West they are usually sweet; in China they are invariably savory.

The most basic Chinese steamed egg dish consists of no more than 2 eggs mixed with 1¼ cups stock or water in a dish with seasoning added and cooked in a steamer for about 15 minutes, or until the custard has set. It is then topped with a spoonful of soy sauce and a scattering of chopped green onions.

A more elaborate version consists of using the best grade stock, perhaps with a little shredded crab meat or shrimp added, and a pinch of monosodium glutamate stirred into the stock to help enhance the flavors, if liked. After steaming, the top of the custard should be set and firm enough so that more shrimp or crab meat can be arranged on top, together with some chopped ham and petits pois. The dish is then returned to the steamer for a further 3-4 minutes. After the second steaming, a large pinch of chopped green onion is sprinkled over the top. When cooking this dish, never use too many eggs, as this will cause the custard to become too firm and hard after steaming. The dish is meant to be very light, for this is the appeal of the dish.

6 eggs

½ teaspoon salt

Pepper to taste

4–5 tablespoons vegetable oil

★★

Cooking time:
about 2½ minutes
per pouch (plus
time for making
filling)

Serves: 4–6

Cooking method:
shallow-fry

EGG POUCHES (OR SMALL OMELETS)

These pouches can be filled with any kind of filling. The most common ones are ground pork, beef, ham, shrimp and fish, which have been stir-fried with shredded green onions, seasonings, salt and pepper and a small amount of finely chopped ginger. The pouches themselves are made as follows:

■ PREPARATION ■

Break eggs into bowl with salt and pepper and beat lightly with fork.

■ COOKING ■

Heat small wok or skillet and add 2 tablespoons oil. Ensure oil coats entire base of pan. When hot, add 1 tablespoon of egg mixture and tilt pan so it also coats most of base. Cook quickly over high heat until underneath is cooked but top surface is still moist. At this point, spoon on to center of omelet about 1½ teaspoons chosen filling. Fold omelet over to form half circle, press edges together and then cook for further 30 seconds. Remove and keep warm on plate on top of double boiler.

■ SERVING ■

These egg 'pouches' can be served on a bed of shredded lettuce with a dash of soy sauce and tomato sauce spooned over.

3 salt eggs

3 'hundred year old' eggs

2 fresh eggs

1 teaspoon salt

Pepper to taste

½ tablespoon cornstarch

⅔ cup good stock (see page 56)

½ teaspoon MSG (optional)

1½ tablespoons chopped green onion

★

Cooking time:
15–18 minutes

Serves: 4–6

Cooking method:
steam, p.49

Easy to prepare

STEAMED EGGS IN THREE COLORS

■ PREPARATION ■

Shell salt eggs and 'hundred year old' eggs. Cut them into 6 segments each. Arrange in pattern in bottom of flat ovenproof dish. Beat together in bowl fresh eggs, salt, pepper, cornstarch, stock, and monosodium glutamate, if using. Pour mixture into ovenproof dish, nearly covering eggs already in dish.

■ COOKING ■

Place dish in steamer and steam vigorously for 15–18 minutes or until set. Sprinkle with green onion and serve with rice.

★★
Cooking time:
about 5 minutes

Serves: 4–6

Cooking method:
stir-fry, p.42

Easy to prepare

STIR-FRIED EGGS WITH OYSTERS

This is a somewhat unusual dish by Western standards, but it is quite common along the coastal provinces of China.

■ PREPARATION ■

Break eggs into bowl with half of salt and beat lightly with fork. Mix ginger and remaining salt with oysters and marinate for 15 minutes, then drain. Coarsely chop green onions.

■ COOKING ■

Heat oil and shortening or lard in wok or skillet. When hot, stir-fry ginger, oysters and green onions for 1 minute. Pour in eggs and, when they are almost set, stir a few times and sprinkle on wine or sherry. Cook for further 30 seconds and serve.

5–6 eggs
1/2 teaspoon salt
2 teaspoons chopped fresh ginger root
4–5 fresh shucked oysters or 4–5 oz canned oysters, drained
2 green onions
3 tablespoons vegetable oil
2 tablespoons shortening or lard
1 tablespoon rice wine or dry sherry

★★
Cooking time:
about 3 minutes

Serves: 4–6

Cooking method:
shallow-fry

Quick to prepare

■ YELLOW FLOWING ■ EGG – LUI HUANG DAN

Like Mu Shu Rou (see page 250), this is a popular dish in Peking and the north of China.

■ PREPARATION ■

Mix together in bowl egg yolks, eggs, salt, shortening, cornstarch, stock and monosodium glutamate, if using.

■ COOKING ■

Heat oil in wok or skillet. When hot, pour in egg mixture. Stir quickly over high heat for about 2 1/2 minutes or until mixture is steaming and beginning to set.

■ SERVING ■

Pour mixture into heated dish and sprinkle top with ham. Ladle spoonfuls of egg mixture into rice bowls and mix with boiled rice.

3 egg yolks
2 eggs
1 1/2 teaspoons salt
2 1/2 tablespoons melted shortening or lard
2 tablespoons cornstarch
1 1/2 cups good stock (see page 56)
1/2 teaspoon MSG (optional)
3 tablespoons vegetable oil
3 tablespoons finely chopped ham

FISH AND SEAFOOD

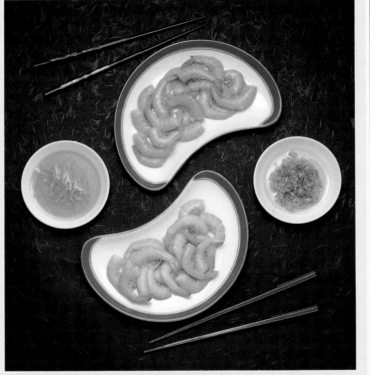

Cantonese Poached Shrimp with Two Dips (*above*);
recipe page 137.

魚類和海鮮

FISH

It seems strange but nevertheless is true that the Chinese enjoy fresh fish more than do the residents of an island such as Britain. Although a continental country, China has countless rivers, streams, canals, lakes and ponds, not to mention tens of thousands of miles of coastline. China has fish in abundance, not only from these natural sources but from her cultivation of fish farming which has been widely practised in China for centuries. And, until the recent advent of refrigeration in China, fish was eaten fresh and kept alive in water.

Whenever I become nostalgic about meals I have had in China, invariably it is fish dishes which come to mind, for Chinese culinary practice has been particularly successful with fish. The reason for this success lies in the Chinese chef's ability to preserve the freshness of the fish by careful heat control.

The Chinese art of marrying the spicy and seasoned with the sweet and fresh in all dishes is particularly effective with fish; if using quantities of ginger, garlic and onions, and seasoned oil into which the flavor of these strong-tasting vegetables have been impregnated. The fish is then briefly cooked in the ingredients with the result that the sweet freshness of the fish and seafood is enhanced. When strong-tasting ingredients are not cooked with the fish or seafood, they are invariably used as dip sauces or 'mixes' (aromatic mixed condiments) to accompany the dish.

I have chosen some typical Chinese fish dishes (ranging from basic dishes to classical and regional) to illustrate the characteristics of the methods and ingredients used.

---

1 lb sole or flounder fillets
1½ teaspoons salt
Pepper to taste
1½ teaspoons sesame oil
3 green onions
3 garlic cloves
5 eggs
6 tablespoons vegetable oil
Sauce:
6 tablespoons good stock (see page 56)
1½ tablespoons light soy sauce
1½ tablespoons dry sherry

PEKING SLICED FISH OMELET

▦ PREPARATION ▦

Cut each fillet into 3 equal-sized pieces. Sprinkle with salt, pepper and sesame oil. Cut green onions into 1½-inch shreds. Crush garlic. Beat eggs lightly in bowl. Mix sauce ingredients together in separate bowl.

▦ COOKING ▦

Heat vegetable oil in wok or skillet. When hot, gently fry fish slices for about 45 seconds. Pour over the beaten eggs; these should completely immerse fish. Cook for 2½ minutes and, when quite set, turn fish over. Fry over medium heat for another 2½ minutes. Add green onions and garlic. Pour over half sauce mixture which will begin to boil immediately. Cover and simmer very gently for about 3 minutes. Remove egg-covered fish slices and arrange on heated serving dish. Heat remaining sauce in wok or skillet and pour over fish.

★★★

Cooking time: 12 minutes
Serves: 4–6
Cooking method: shallow-fry
Care required in cooking
Goes well with rice to complement meat and vegetable dishes

FISH FU-YUNG

■ PREPARATION ■

Coarsely chop fish. Finely chop ginger. Mix fish, ginger, salt, pepper, monosodium glutamate, if using, and egg whites in bowl and beat for 20 seconds with fork. Coarsely chop green onions and ham.

■ COOKING ■

Heat oil in wok or deep-fryer. When hot, add chopped fish and egg-white mixture, stirring all the time with pair of chopsticks. Cook over medium heat for 1½ minutes. Pour contents through strainer to remove oil and transfer mixture to heated plate. Reheat wok with 2 tablespoons oil. When hot, stir-fry ham and peas over medium heat for 1 minute. Add soy sauce, stock, vinegar and green onions and stir-fry for a further 30 seconds.

■ SERVING ■

Pour ham, peas and green onion mixture over the fish fu-yung.

★★★

Cooking time: about 12 minutes

Serves: 6–7

Cooking methods: deep-fry p.45 and stir-fry p.42

Quite easy to prepare

Good with most combinations, particularly red-cooked meat dishes and vegetables

12 oz white fish

2 slices fresh ginger root

1½ teaspoons salt

Pepper to taste

Pinch of MSG (optional)

6 egg whites

2 green onions

2 oz ham

Vegetable oil for deep-frying

3 tablespoons peas

1 tablespoon light soy sauce

3 tablespoons good stock (see page 56)

2 tablespoons vinegar

POACHED FISH BALLS WITH SHRIMP AND MUSHROOMS

■ PREPARATION ■

Grind fish finely. Add 1½ teaspoons of salt, pepper, cornstarch and egg white and beat thoroughly until smooth. Form the fish paste into balls half the size of a medium egg. Cut mushrooms into quarters. Cut green onions into 1-inch sections. Coarsely chop garlic and ginger.

■ COOKING ■

Poach fish balls in pan of boiling water for 3½ minutes, then drain. Heat vegetable oil in wok or skillet. When hot, add garlic, ginger, green onions, mushrooms and shrimp, sprinkle with remaining salt and stir-fry quickly for 1½ minutes. Add sherry, stock and soy sauce. Turn ingredients over a few times, then add fish balls. Turn and toss together for 1 minute. Reduce heat to low and continue to cook for further 1½ minutes. Sprinkle with sesame oil.

★★★★

Cooking time: about 12–15 minutes

Serves: 4–6

Cooking methods: poach and stir-fry, p.42

Quite easy to prepare

Serve with meat and vegetable dishes

1 lb white fish

2½ teaspoons salt

Pepper to taste

2½ tablespoons cornstarch

1 egg white

5–6 medium button mushrooms

2 green onions

2 garlic cloves

3 tablespoons vegetable oil

2 slices fresh root ginger

3–4 oz shelled shrimp

1½ tablespoons dry sherry

2 tablespoons good stock (see page 56)

3 tablespoons light soy sauce

1 teaspoon sesame oil

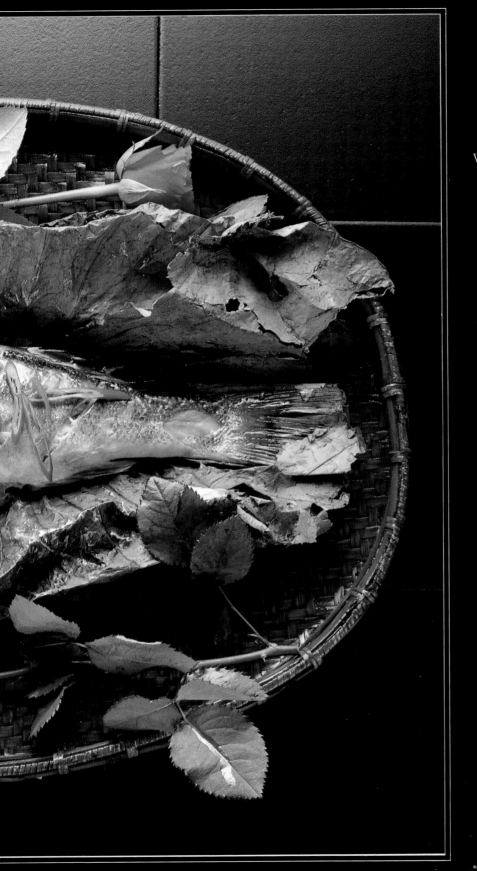

Steamed Whole Fish
Wrapped in Lotus Leaves,
an unusual presentation;
recipe page 122.

1 sea bass, about 2 lb

2 tablespoons dark soy sauce

3 garlic cloves

3 slices fresh ginger root

2 green onions

2 dried chilies

Vegetable oil for deep-frying

1½ teaspoons salt

Pepper to taste

4 oz ground pork

Sauce:

2 tablespoons light soy sauce

2 tablespoons red wine

1¼ cups good stock (see page 56)

1½ tablespoons cornstarch blended with 4 tablespoons water

2 teaspoons sesame oil

DEEP-FRIED AND BRAISED SEA BASS

■ PREPARATION ■

Clean fish and dry well. Rub inside and out with dark soy sauce. Coarsely chop garlic, ginger, green onions and chilies.

■ COOKING ■

Heat oil in wok or deep-fryer. When hot, fry fish for 5 minutes. Drain. Reserve oil. Heat 3 tablespoons of reserved oil in a wok or skillet. When hot, stir-fry green onions, garlic, ginger, chilies, salt, pepper and ground pork for 4 minutes. Add light soy sauce, wine and stock and bring to boil. Place fish on top of mixture in wok or skillet, cover and simmer gently for about 6 minutes. Lift out fish and place on heated serving plate. Add blended cornstarch and sesame oil to wok. Stir until sauce comes back to boil and thickens. Pour over fish.

★★★★

Cooking time: about 15–18 minutes

Serves: 4–6

Cooking methods: deep-fry p.45 and braise

Goes well with lightly cooked meat and vegetable dishes

---

1 whole fish, about 2 lb

1½ tablespoons dark soy sauce

2 lotus leaves

3 tablespoons vegetable oil

Garnish and sauce:

3–4 oz canned snow pickles

3 slices fresh ginger root

3 green onions

2 small fresh red chilies

2 tablespoons light soy sauce

2 tablespoons dry sherry

6 tablespoons good stock (see page 56)

2 teaspoons sugar

STEAMED WHOLE FISH WRAPPED IN LOTUS LEAVES

■ PREPARATION ■

Clean fish and dry well. Rub inside and out with dark soy sauce. Shred pickles, ginger, green onions, and fresh chilies, discarding seeds. Soak lotus leaves in warm water for 10 minutes to soften. Drain.

■ COOKING ■

Heat oil in wok or skillet. When hot, stir-fry pickles, green onions, ginger and chilies over medium heat for 1 minute. Add soy sauce, sherry, stock and sugar, bring to boil and stir for 30 seconds. Place fish on lotus leaves. Pour half contents of wok over length of fish. Turn fish over and pour over remainder. Wrap fish completely in lotus leaves. Secure by tying with string. Place in a steamer and steam for 25 minutes.

★★★★

Cooking time: about 30 minutes

Serves: 4–6

Cooking methods: stir-fry p.42 and steam p.49

An interesting addition to a multi-course meal

Illustrated on p.120–121

SAUTEED FISH STEAKS WITH GARNISH

■ PREPARATION ■

Clean and dry fish steaks. Rub inside and out with salt, pepper and 1 tablespoon of oil. Soak dried mushrooms in hot water to cover for 25 minutes. Drain. Discard tough stalks. Cut mushroom caps into matchstick-size shreds. Cut green onions into 1-inch sections.

■ COOKING ■

Heat remaining oil in wok or skillet. When hot, add ginger slices and spread out evenly to flavor oil. Lay fish steaks in hot flavored oil and shallow fry or sauté for 2 minutes on each side. Pour away any excess oil and remove from heat. Heat fat in separate pan. When hot, stir-fry chopped onion, ginger and mushrooms for 1 minute. Add ground pork and stir over high heat for 3 minutes. Mix in soy sauce, stock, sherry and green onions. Bring to boil and continue to stir-fry for 1 minute. Meanwhile, reheat first pan and return fish steaks to it. Heat through; and pour sauce and garnish over fish. Transfer contents to heated serving plate.

1½–2 lb fish, cut into 4–6 steaks
2 teaspoons salt
Pepper to taste
6 tablespoons vegetable oil
5 slices fresh ginger root
Garnish and sauce:
4 medium dried Chinese mushrooms
2 green onions
3 tablespoons shortening or lard
2 tablespoons coarsely chopped onion
1½ tablespoons chopped fresh ginger root
4 oz ground pork
3 tablespoons soy sauce
¼ cup good stock (see page 56)
2 tablespoons dry sherry

SOY-BRAISED SLICED FISH

■ PREPARATION ■

Cut fish into 2½ × 1½ × 1-inch pieces. Toss in salt, pepper and 2 teaspoons of oil. Dust in cornstarch. Cut green onions into 1-inch sections, separating the green from the white parts. Combine soy sauce, stock, sherry and sugar into a sauce.

■ COOKING ■

Heat oil in wok or skillet. When hot, stir-fry ginger and white parts of green onions for about 15 seconds, to flavor the oil. Add fish pieces, one by one, spacing them in pan. Fry for 1½ minutes on either side. Drain off excess oil. Pour sauce over fish pieces. Sprinkle with green parts of the green onions and bring to boil. Baste fish with sauce, turning fish after 1½ minutes. Simmer for another 2 minutes and then transfer to heated plate. Pour sauce and green onions over fish.

1½ lb fish steak, eg cod, haddock, halibut, snapper, etc.
1½ teaspoons salt
Pepper to taste
6½ tablespoons vegetable oil
1½ tablespoons cornstarch
3 green onions
4 slices fresh ginger root
¼ cup soy sauce
3 tablespoons good stock (see page 56)
1½ tablespoons dry sherry
2 teaspoons sugar

■

Steamed Fish with Garnish
(*above*), serve the garnished
fish with lemon slices;
recipe page 126.
Braised Whole Fish in Hot
Vinegar Sauce (*right*), a
colorful dish for a multi-
course meal; recipe page
127.

1 lb fish fillets, eg cod,
   haddock, sole, turbot

1½ teaspoons salt

1 egg

½ cup cornstarch

3 slices fresh ginger root

3 stalks celery

3 green onions

1½ cups bean sprouts

Vegetable oil for deep-
   frying

2 tablespoons light soy sauce

1½ tablespoons wine vinegar

1 tablespoon chili sauce

1 teaspoon sesame oil

YANGTZE 'FISH SALAD'

Ideal dish for those vegetarians who eat fish. In the way it is prepared, this dish can justifiably be called a salad. An excellent dish for a light meal. The contrast between the crunchiness of the vegetables and the crispy fish makes for an interesting variation in texture.

■ PREPARATION ■

Cut fish into thin slices, then cut slices into matchstick-sized strips. Rub in salt, coat with beaten egg and dust with cornstarch. Cut ginger into thin shreds. Cut celery into thick matchstick-size strips. Blanch celery in pan of boiling water for 1½ minutes, then drain. Cut green onions into 2-inch sections. Wash bean sprouts and drain thoroughly.

■ COOKING ■

Heat oil in wok or deep-fryer. When hot, fry fish in 2 batches for about 2 minutes. Drain.

■ SERVING ■

Place celery and bean sprouts in base of deep-sided dish. Arrange strips of fish, like French fries, in one layer on top. Sprinkle with ginger, green onions, soy sauce, vinegar, chili sauce and sesame oil. Toss salad before eating.

★★★

**Cooking time:
about 5 minutes**

Serves: 5-8

**Cooking method:
deep-fry, p.45**

**Excellent starter
for a multi-dish
meal**

---

1 whole fish, about 1½-2 lb

2 teaspoons salt

Pepper to taste

1½ tablespoons finely
   chopped fresh ginger
   root

Garnish and sauce:

2-3 green onions

3 slices fresh ginger root

3 large fresh or Chinese
   dried mushrooms
   (optional)

1 tablespoon dry sherry

2½ tablespoons soy sauce

¼ cup vegetable oil

STEAMED FISH WITH GARNISH

As often as not, the Chinese steam their fish, since steam is widely used in the Chinese kitchen. When fish is steamed, there is a tendency to undercook it; hence, a characteristic process to complete the cooking of the fish is to pour a few tablespoons of very hot oil over the length of the fish and its garnish. The oil and the fish are impregnated with the flavor of the garnish, usually green onions and ginger. Alternatively, after the fish has been steamed or poached, lay it on the serving dish. Fry the garnish and sauce, usually consisting of a little chopped or shredded green onion, ginger, mushrooms, pork, with a sprinkling of dried shrimp and soy sauce, for a minute or two. When very hot, pour over the length of the fish or pieces of fish.

■ PREPARATION ■

Clean fish and dry well. Rub inside and out with salt,

★★★

**Cooking time:
about 15 minutes,
plus seasoning
time**

Serves: 4-5

**Cooking method:
steam, p.49**

**Fairly simple to
prepare**

**Serve with meat
and vegetable
dishes**

Illustrated on p.124

pepper and finely chopped ginger. Leave to season for 30 minutes. Shred green onions and ginger. Slice mushroom caps; if using dried, soak first in hot water for 25 minutes.

■ COOKING ■

Place fish on a heatproof dish and put into steamer. Steam vigorously for 10 minutes. Remove dish from steamer and pour away any excess water which has collected. Pour sherry and soy sauce along length of fish and garnish with green onions, mushrooms and ginger. Heat oil in a small pan and, when smoking hot, pour in a thin stream down length of fish over green onions, mushrooms and ginger. The fish is brought to the table on the dish in which it was cooked.

■ BRAISED WHOLE FISH IN HOT VINEGAR SAUCE ■

★ ★ ★

Cooking time: about 10 minutes, plus seasoning time

Serves: 4–6

Cooking methods: shallow-fry and braise

Fairly simple to prepare

Serve with meat and vegetable dishes

Illustrated on p.125

■ PREPARATION ■

Finely chop 2 slices of ginger. Clean fish and dry well. Rub inside and out with salt, pepper, chopped ginger and 1 tablespoon oil. Leave to season for 30 minutes. Remove seeds from chilies. Shred 3 slices of ginger, bamboo shoots, red pepper, carrot, seeded chilies and green onions.

■ COOKING ■

Heat remaining oil in wok or skillet. When hot, fry fish for 2½ minutes on each side. Remove and drain. Add shredded ginger, bamboo shoots, red pepper, carrot, chilies and green onions to remaining oil and stir-fry over medium heat for 1 minute. Add shortening, soy sauce, stock and half vinegar and cook for another minute. Lay fish back in wok or pan and cook gently for 2 minutes on both sides, basting. Transfer fish to serving dish. Stir remaining vinegar into wok, then add blended cornstarch, stirring over high heat until sauce thickens.

■ SERVING ■

Pour sauce from wok over length of fish. Garnish with shredded vegetables.

---

2 slices fresh ginger root

1 whole fish, 1½–2lb

1 teaspoon salt

Pepper to taste

¼ cup vegetable oil

Sauce:

3 slices fresh ginger root

3 tablespoons drained, canned sliced bamboo shoots

½ red pepper

1 small carrot

2 small dried chilies

1 small green chili

2 green onions

2 tablespoons shortening or lard

2 tablespoons light soy sauce

3 tablespoons good stock (see page 56)

6 tablespoons vinegar

½ tablespoon cornstarch blended with 2 tablespoons water

Cantonese Ginger and
Onion Crab (*left*), makes a
spectacular starter; recipe
page 140.
Peking 'Pomegranate'
Snow Flake Shrimp Balls
(*above*), an attractive party
dish; recipe page 135.

1 whole fish, about 1½-2 lb

2 teaspoons salt

Pepper to taste

4 slices fresh ginger root

Garnish and sauce:

3 slices fresh ginger root

3 green onions

2 slices bacon

3 tablespoons vegetable oil

1 tablespoon shortening or lard

1 tablespoon vinegar

3 tablespoons soy sauce

2 tablespoons dry sherry

2 tablespoons good stock (see page 56)

1½ teaspoons chili sauce

POACHED FISH WITH GARNISH

■ PREPARATION ■

Clean fish and dry well. Rub inside and out with salt and pepper. Leave to season for 30 minutes. Heat 4 ginger slices in water in pan until boiling. For the garnish, shred ginger, green onions and bacon.

■ COOKING ■

Immerse fish in ginger water, making sure fish is completely covered. Simmer gently for 8 minutes. Remove, drain and place on heated serving dish. Meanwhile, heat oil and fat in small pan. When hot, fry bacon over high heat for 1½ minutes. Add ginger and green onions and continue to stir-fry for another 30 seconds. Pour in vinegar, soy sauce, sherry, stock and chili sauce. Mixture will boil almost immediately. Stir once more and then pour boiling sauce and garnish over fish. Spread garnish out evenly to serve.

★★★

Cooking time: about 12 minutes, plus seasoning time

Serves: 4-5

Cooking methods: simmer and stir-fry, p.42

Fairly simple to prepare

Complements meat and vegetable dishes

1 whole fish, 1½-2 lb

3 slices fresh ginger root

1½ teaspoons salt

Pepper to taste

3-4 tablespoons cornstarch

Vegetable oil for deep-frying

Sauce:

2 tablespoons wood ears

6 medium dried Chinese mushrooms

2 green onions

2 tablespoons shortening or lard

2 tablespoons drained, canned sliced bamboo shoots

3 tablespoons soy sauce

1 tablespoon sugar

¼ cup good stock (see page 56)

2 tablespoons wine vinegar

2 tablespoons dry sherry

'SQUIRREL' FISH

This dish derives its name from the fact that, when cooked and served, the fish's tail curves up like a squirrel; also, when the hot sauce is poured over the hot freshly cooked fish, it 'chatters'!

■ PREPARATION ■

Clean fish and slit open from head to tail on underside so that it lays flat. Cut 7-8 deep slashes on one side of fish and only 2 on the other. Finely chop ginger. Rub fish inside and out with salt, pepper and ginger, then coat in cornstarch. Soak wood ears and mushrooms separately in hot water to cover for 25 minutes. Drain and discard tough stalks. Cut mushroom caps into shreds. Finely slice wood ears. Cut green onions into 2-inch sections.

■ COOKING ■

Heat oil in wok or deep-fryer. When hot, gently fry fish over medium heat for 4 minutes, then reduce heat to low. Meanwhile, melt fat in a smaller wok or saucepan. When hot, stir-fry wood ears, mushrooms, green onions and bamboo shoots over medium heat for 1½ minutes. Add soy sauce, sugar, stock, vinegar and sherry. Stir ingredients over low heat for about 2 minutes. Raise heat under wok containing fish and fry for another 2 minutes. The tail should have curled by now due to the uneven amount

★★★★

Cooking time: about 8 minutes

Serves: 4-6

Cooking methods: deep-fry p.45 and stir-fry p.42

Serve as part of a multi-course meal

of cuts on the fish. Lift out fish, drain and place on heated dish.

■ SERVING ■

During last minute of the fish cooking, raise heat under the smaller wok or saucepan and boil sauce rapidly. Pour sauce over hot fish as soon as it has come out of the oil – the fish will sizzle and 'chatter'. The noise should draw the attention of the diners, reminding them that it is a dish to be eaten quickly while the fish is freshly cooked and crisp.

★ ★ ★

Cooking time: about 12 minutes

Serves: 4–6

Cooking method: shallow-fry

Care required in cooking

Goes well with red-cooked meat dishes and vegetables

SOFT-FRIED PEKING SLICED FISH IN WINE

The white of the fish contrasts well with the black of the wood ears. Being only quickly cooked, the taste of the wine and spirit in the sauce is very pronounced.

■ PREPARATION ■

Cut fish into 1½ × 1-inch slices. Rub evenly with salt, dust with cornstarch and coat with egg white. Soak wood ears in hot water to cover for 10 minutes. Drain. Shred ginger.

■ COOKING ■

Heat oil in wok or skillet. When hot, lay out fish slices evenly on bottom of wok and turn after 30 seconds. Cook for a further 1 minute, then remove wok from heat. Carefully remove fish and arrange on heated serving dish. Pour away oil except about 2 tablespoons and reheat wok. When hot, cook ginger for 30 seconds to flavor oil, then remove from wok. Add wood ears and fry for 30 seconds, then push to side of wok. Mix together stock, white wine, vodka, sugar and blended cornstarch in bowl. Add to wok and and stir until thickened. Return fish slices to wok and reheat.

■ SERVING ■

Transfer fish and wood ears to heated serving dish, then pour over sauce.

1 lb fish fillets, eg sole or flounder
1½ teaspoons salt
2 tablespoons cornstarch
1 egg white
2 oz wood ears
1¼ cups vegetable oil
Sauce:
2 slices fresh ginger root
5 tablespoons good chicken stock (see page 56)
¼ cup white wine
2 teaspoons vodka or wine-lee if available
1½ teaspoons sugar
2½ teaspoons cornstarch blended with 1½ tablespoons water

Quick-fried Crystal Shrimp (*above left*), a simple yet delicious dish; recipe page 143. Steamed Scallops with Black Bean Sauce (*below left*), a popular starter served in their shells with parsley and radish garnish; recipe page 138. Braised Mussels with Bean Curd and Mushrooms (*right*), served with rice to mop up the juices; recipe page 142.

SEAFOOD AND CRUSTACEANS

Fresh-water crustaceans abound in many areas of China, and, indeed, a sizeable proportion of all Chinese crustaceans are found in fresh water. I have many happy, childhood memories of fishing for crabs and shrimp or digging them up from muddy river banks and along the sides of canals, ponds and lakes. These crustaceans are found in profusion during certain seasons and a celebration of their coming is made.

The east coast of China is another rich source of both crustaceans and other seafood, stretching as it does from the frozen wastes of Manchuria to the tropical waters of Vietnam. Many dishes have been created from the enormous harvest yielded annually by these waters and fresh-water sites. Here are some of the better known, many of which can be cooked as readily in the West as in the East.

1 lb shrimp, fresh or frozen, shelled
¼–⅓ cup pork fat
4 water chestnuts
1 teaspoon salt
1 tablespoon dry sherry
2 green onions
5 slices fresh ginger root
2 egg whites
8 teaspoons cornstarch
Vegetable oil for deep-frying
1½ tablespoons salt and pepper dip (see page 93)

DEEP-FRIED CRISPY SHRIMP BALLS

■ PREPARATION ■

Mince or finely chop shrimp, pork fat and water chestnuts. Place in bowl and add salt and sherry. Mix together thoroughly. Cut green onions into shreds. Finely chop ginger. Place green onions and ginger in small saucepan with ⅔ cup water and bring to boil. Simmer until liquid has reduced by half, about 2 tablespoons. Leave to cool, then add to shrimp mixture, straining out green onion and ginger. Beat egg whites until stiff and fold into shrimp mixture with the cornstarch. Fold together until mixture is smooth. Form into 24 even-sized balls.

■ COOKING ■

Heat oil in wok or deep-fryer. When hot, add shrimp balls one at a time and fry in about 2 batches over medium heat for about 3 minutes until golden brown. Remove with a slotted spoon and drain on paper towels.

■ SERVING ■

Transfer shrimp balls to heated serving dish. Serve with a small bowl of salt and pepper dip. Another dip which could be used is the Peking duck sauce (see page 178).

★ ★ ★ ★

Cooking time: about 6–8 minutes

Serves: 5–7

Cooking method: deep-fry, p.45

Requires some time to prepare

Ideal starter for a party meal

★ ★ ★ ★

**Cooking time:
about 10 minutes**

Serves: 5-7

**Cooking method:
deep-fry, p.45**

**Requires some
time to prepare**

**Excellent starter
for a dinner party**

Illustrated on p.129

VARIATION

*PEKING 'POMEGRANATE' SNOW FLAKE
SHRIMP BALLS*

*This is a popular version of Deep-Fried Crispy Shrimp Balls,
often served during parties in Peking.*

This is very similar to the previous recipe but only half of
the egg white is beaten stiffly and the other half is beaten
only lightly. The stiff egg white is added first, then the
lightly beaten egg white, making the mixture much
wetter. After forming into balls, they are rolled evenly
and firmly in croûtons.

To make croûtons, cut 4–5 slices of white bread into
small cubes, then dry in a preheated to moderate oven
180°C, 350°F for about 3 minutes.

The coated shrimp balls are then deep-fried as in the
previous recipe and served in the same way. They are,
however, crisper as the croûton coating crisps up well
during frying.

★ ★ ★ ★

**Cooking time:
about 6 minutes**

Serves: 5-6

**Cooking method:
deep-fry, p.45**

**A little fiddly to
make**

**An excellent
starter**

DEEP-FRIED
CRAB CLAWS

This dish makes a popular starter.

▥ PREPARATION ▥

Defrost claws and chop in half lengthwise. Finely chop
ginger. Beat eggs. Add salt and ginger to shrimp and
finely chop, mixing well. Divide shrimp mixture into 10
portions, and press each portion on to meat of crab claws.
Sprinkle shrimp mixture with cornstarch, dip each meat
side of claw into beaten egg, and coat with bread crumbs.
Place shrimp-filled claws on a plate and chill for 1 hour.

▥ COOKING ▥

Heat oil in wok or deep-fryer. When hot, fry claws in
about 2 batches for 3 minutes. Drain.

▥ SERVING ▥

Serve hot on a heated dish, garnished with wedges of
lemon and sprigs of parsley.

10 large frozen crab claws
2 slices fresh ginger root
3 eggs
1 teaspoon salt
1⅓ cups shelled shrimp
3 tablespoons cornstarch
2 cups dry bread crumbs
Vegetable oil for deep-frying

★★
Cooking time:
about 5 minutes

Serves: 4–5

Cooking method:
poach

Easy to prepare

Serve as a starter

Illustrated on p.117

CANTONESE POACHED SHRIMP WITH TWO DIPS

1¼ lb fresh shrimp, unshelled

1½ tablespoons salt

Dip 1:

2 green onions

3 slices fresh ginger root

2 green chilies

3 tablespoons vegetable oil

3 tablespoons light soy sauce

1 tablespoon wine vinegar

½ tablespoon sesame oil

Dip 2:

1 tablespoon shredded fresh ginger root

3 tablespoons vinegar

■ PREPARATION ■

Wash shrimp thoroughly under running water. Finely chop green onions, ginger and chilies, discarding seeds. Place them in small heatproof bowl.

■ COOKING ■

Bring 5 cups water to boil in saucepan; add salt. Simmer shrimp for 2 minutes, then leave to stand in water, off heat, for a further minute. Drain.

■ SERVING ■

Place shrimp in medium bowl; set aside. Heat vegetable oil in pan. When smoking hot, pour over ginger, green onions and chilies. Let stand for 30 seconds, then add soy sauce, vinegar and sesame oil; stir well. For other dip, place shredded ginger in small bowl and spoon over vinegar. Serve sauce as dip for shrimp. To eat, peel shrimp up to its tail and then, holding tail, dip into sauces.

★★★
Cooking time:
about 3 minutes
per batch

Serves: 4–6

Cooking method:
deep-fry, p.45

Serve as a dinner
party starter or
part of a multi-
dish meal

Illustrated
opposite

DEEP-FRIED CRISPY JUMBO SHRIMP

1 slice fresh ginger root

2 eggs

¾ cup all-purpose flour

2 tablespoons self-rising flour

1½ teaspoons salt

¼ cup water

1½ lb jumbo shrimp, fresh or frozen, unshelled

Vegetable oil for deep-frying

■ PREPARATION ■

Finely chop ginger. Beat eggs for 15 seconds, then fold in both types of flour, salt, ginger and ¼ cup water. Beat for 1 minute until light batter. Shell shrimp, leaving tail shells on. Clean, scraping away any dark or gritty bits.

■ COOKING ■

Heat oil in wok or deep-fryer. When hot, hold each shrimp by tail and dip fish into batter. Lower into oil, frying 6 shrimp at a time for 3 minutes. Remove with perforated spoon and drain. When first batch has been fried, keep hot and crispy in oven while frying remaining shrimp.

■ SERVING ■

Serve with lemon slices and salt and pepper dip (see page 93)

12 fresh scallops, with shells

Sauce:

1½ tablespoons salted black beans

¼ cup vegetable oil

1 tablespoon finely chopped fresh ginger root

½ tablespoon finely chopped red chili

½ tablespoon crushed garlic

1 teaspoon pounded Sichuan peppercorns

1 tablespoon finely chopped green onions

2 tablespoons soy sauce

1 tablespoon dry sherry

2 tablespoons good stock (see page 56)

1 teaspoon sesame oil

STEAMED SCALLOPS WITH BLACK BEAN SAUCE

■ PREPARATION ■

Scrub scallops under cold running water, then discard flat shell. Soak black beans in hot water for 5 minutes, then drain and crush.

■ COOKING ■

Put the scallops on large heatproof dish, place in steamer and steam for 1-2 minutes. Meanwhile, heat vegetable oil in a small wok or saucepan. When hot, stir-fry ginger, chili, garlic, peppercorns, green onion and black beans for 30 seconds. Add soy sauce, sherry and stock and continue to stir-fry for another 15 seconds. Sprinkle on sesame oil.

■ SERVING ■

Transfer one scallop to each shell and sprinkle about 2 teaspoons of sauce over each one. The diners should be able to remove the scallops from their shells with a pair of chopsticks or a fork, then drink the remaining sauce from the shells.

★★★

Cooking time: 1-2 minutes

Serves: 6-8

Cooking methods: steam p.49 and stir-fry p.42

Easy if you have a large steamer

Excellent starter

Illustrated on p.132

1 lb jumbo shrimp

½ cup vegetable oil

2 green onions

2 garlic cloves

2 dried chilies

1½ teaspoons Sichuan peppercorns

1½ teaspoons salt

SALT AND PEPPER SHRIMP

The impact of the heat on the salt and pepper coating on the shrimp makes this a very aromatic dish. A very suitable dish as an hors d'oeuvre for nibbling with wine.

■ PREPARATION ■

Wash and shell shrimp. Sprinkle on 1½ teaspoons of oil. Cut green onions into 1-inch sections. Thinly slice garlic. Shred chilies. Lightly pound peppercorns and mix with salt.

■ COOKING ■

Heat remaining oil in wok or skillet. When hot, stir-fry shrimp over high heat for 1 minute. Remove shrimp and pour away oil to use for other purposes, except for 1 tablespoon. Reheat oil in wok or skillet. When hot, quickly stir-fry chili, garlic and green onion. Spread out green onion and chilli and add shrimp. Sprinkle on salt and pepper mixture and stir-fry for another 45 seconds.

★★★

Cooking time: about 6 minutes

Serves: 6-7

Cooking method: stir-fry, p.42

Quite easy to prepare

A good starter dish

★ ★ ★ ★

Cooking time:
about 10 minutes

Serves: 2-3

Cooking method:
steam, p.49

Easy, except for
killing and
preparing lobster

Serve with grated
ginger and vinegar
dip

STEAMED LOBSTER

■ PREPARATION ■

Kill lobster (see recipe for Cantonese Ginger and Onion Crab, page 140). Cut in half lengthwise, discarding stomach sac and dark intestinal vein, then cut into 2-inch sections. Place in heatproof dish. Finely chop green onions and ginger. Mix with sherry. Sprinkle this mixture on to lobster.

■ COOKING ■

Place lobster in steamer and steam for about 10 minutes.

■ SERVING ■

To prepare dip sauce, finely chop green onions, ginger and chili. Place in a small heatproof bowl. Heat oil in pan until smoking hot. Pour into bowl. Stir a few times, then add soy sauce, vinegar and sesame oil, mixing well. Serve with freshly steamed lobster.

1 live lobster, about 1-1½lb

2 green onions

2 slices fresh ginger root

1 tablespoon dry sherry

2½ tablespoons vegetable oil

Dip sauce:

2 green onions

2 slices fresh ginger root

2 dried red chilies

3 tablespoons soy sauce

1 tablespoon vinegar

½ teaspoon sesame oil

★ ★

Cooking time:
about 5 minutes

Serves: 4-6

Cooking method:
stir-fry, p.42

Quick and easy to
prepare

Goes well with
meat and
vegetable dishes

SHRIMP FU-YUNG

The pink of the shrimp, the whiteness of the egg white and the green of the green onions make an attractive color combination.

■ PREPARATION ■

Finely chop green onions. Finely shred ginger. Place shrimp in bowl with ginger and cornstarch. Beat egg whites in bowl with salt and half chopped green onions for 15 seconds with fork.

■ COOKING ■

Heat 2 tablespoons oil in wok or skillet. When hot, stir-fry shrimp with sherry over medium heat for 1½ minutes. Remove shrimp from wok and place in bowl with egg whites. Mix together well. Heat remaining oil in wok or skillet. When hot, pour in egg white and shrimp mixture. Stir quickly for 1 minute, then add shortening. Sprinkle on remaining green onions. Turn and scramble for further minute. When mixture has just set, transfer to heated serving dish.

2 green onions

2 slices fresh ginger root

¾ cup shrimp, fresh or frozen, shelled

2 teaspoons cornstarch

5 egg whites

1 teaspoon salt

5 tablespoons vegetable oil

1 tablespoon dry sherry

1 tablespoon shortening or lard

20-25 medium-sized oysters

1 teaspoon salt

Pepper to taste

2 teaspoons finely chopped fresh ginger root

Vegetable oil for deep-frying

1½ tablespoons finely chopped green onion

Batter:

1 egg

5 tablespoons all-purpose flour

1 tablespoon cornstarch

5 tablespoons water

½ teaspoon baking powder

DEEP-FRIED OYSTERS

■ PREPARATION ■

Shell and drain oysters. Sprinkle with salt, pepper and ginger. Combine ingredients for the batter until smooth.

■ COOKING ■

Heat the oil in wok or deep-fryer. When very hot, dip oysters individually into batter, then fry in batches for about 2½-3 minutes until golden brown. Drain.

■ SERVING ■

Transfer crispy-fried oysters to heated serving dish and sprinkle with green onion.

★★★

Cooking time: 2½-3 minutes per batch

Serves: 4-6

Cooking method: deep-fry, p.45

Serve as a starter with grated ginger and vinegar or salt and pepper dips

---

3 lb crab or 2 lb live lobster

5 slices fresh ginger root

4 green onions

1 medium sized pepper

Vegetable oil for deep-frying

½ teaspoon salt

⅔ cup good stock (see page 56)

2 tablespoons light soy sauce

3 tablespoons dry sherry

1 teaspoon sesame oil

CANTONESE GINGER AND ONION CRAB OR LOBSTER

Crab or lobster cooked this way is an outstanding dish by any standards. The Chinese chop up their lobsters while still alive! If you prefer to kill the lobster first, tie the pincers up firmly and cover the tail with a cloth. Holding the tail firmly, plunge the pointed end of a sharp knife into the place where the head and body meet, to cut the nerve cord. This kills the lobster instantly.

■ PREPARATION ■

Scrub crab thoroughly under running water. Chop crab into 4 pieces, discarding grey dead men's fingers. Alternatively, scrub lobster under cold running water and chop into bite-sized pieces, discarding the hard stomach sac behind the head and the black intestinal vein. Crack claws with the back of a chopper. Cut ginger and green onions into matchstick-size shreds. Thinly slice red pepper.

■ COOKING ■

Heat the oil in wok or deep-fryer. When very hot, add crab or lobster pieces one by one to the oil. Fry over high heat for 2½ minutes. Remove and drain. Pour away oil to use for other purposes, reserving about 2 tablespoons. Reheat oil in wok or skillet. When hot, stir-fry ginger, green onion, red pepper and salt over medium heat for 1 minute. Pour in stock, soy sauce and sherry. Bring to boil and return crab or lobster to pan. Toss a few times, then

★★★★

Cooking time: 15 minutes

Serves: 5-6

Cooking methods: deep-fry p.45 and stir-fry p.42

Best eaten by itself, perhaps as a starter to a multi-dish meal

Illustrated on p.128

cover and cook for 3–4 minutes until sauce is reduced by about half. Sprinkle on sesame oil; toss and transfer to heated serving dish.

★ ★ ★ ★

Cooking time: 12-15 minutes

Serves: 5-6

Cooking methods: stir-fry p.42 and deep-fry p.45

Needs a little time to prepare

Excellent as part of a multi-dish meal

■ QUICK-FRIED SHRIMP IN SAUCE ON CRISPY RICE ■

In China, the scrapings of rice from the bottom of the rice cooking pan are often dried and fried to form a crispy sizzling bed for a saucey mixture of food.

■ PREPARATION ■

Rub shrimp with salt. Dust with cornstarch and coat with egg white. Cut green onions into ½-inch shreds. Cut bamboo shoots into pieces.

■ COOKING ■

Heat 8 tablespoons vegetable oil in wok or skillet. When hot, stir-fry shrimp for about 1½ minutes. Remove and drain. Pour away oil to use for other purposes, leaving only about 1 tablespoon. Reheat pan. When hot, stir-fry peas, mushrooms, green onions and bamboo shoots over medium heat for 30 seconds. Add stock, sugar, monosodium glutamate, if using, soy sauce, sherry, tomato paste and blended cornstarch. Bring to boil, stirring gently, until sauce thickens, then return shrimp to wok or skillet. Continue to simmer very gently over low heat for a further minute. Meanwhile, heat oil in wok or deep-fryer. When smoking hot, place rice scrapings into a wire basket and fry for about 2 minutes. The rice will puff up immediately. Drain and place in heated deep-sided serving dish.

■ SERVING ■

Place dish of crispy rice scrapings in the center of the table and pour over the shrimp sauce. Serve immediately while the rice is still crisp.

1 cup shrimp, fresh or frozen, shelled

½ teaspoon salt

1 tablespoon cornstarch

1 egg white

2 green onions

3 oz drained, canned bamboo shoots

Vegetable oil for deep-frying

¾ cup peas

⅓ cup drained, canned straw mushrooms

2 cups good stock (see page 56)

3 teaspoons sugar

Pinch of MSG (optional)

1½ tablespoons light soy sauce

1½ tablespoons dry sherry

1½ tablespoons tomato paste

1 teaspoon cornstarch blended with 2 tablespoons water

¾–1 cup rice scrapings (see above)

3 pints mussels

4 slices fresh ginger root

6 medium-sized dried
Chinese mushrooms

2 cakes bean curd

3 garlic cloves

3 green onions

2 cups good stock (see page
56)

4–5 tablespoons dry sherry or
white wine

½ teaspoon salt

Pepper to taste

1 chicken bouillon cube

1 tablespoon cornstarch
blended with
2 tablespoons water

1 teaspoon sesame oil

■ BRAISED MUSSELS WITH BEAN CURD AND MUSHROOMS ■

■ PREPARATION ■

Scrub mussels thoroughly. Poach in large saucepan of simmering water with ginger for 1½ minutes, then drain. Discard any unopened ones. Transfer mussels to large pan or flameproof casserole. Soak dried mushrooms in hot water to cover for 25 minutes. Drain and discard tough stalks. Cut mushroom caps into quarters. Cut bean curd into cubes or rectangles. Finely chop garlic and shred green onions.

■ COOKING ■

Place pan of mussels over medium-high heat. Pour in stock and sherry or wine, then add bean curd, mushrooms, garlic, half green onions, salt and pepper. Bring to boil and sprinkle in crumbled bouillon cube. Stir, then simmer gently for 10 minutes. Stir in blended cornstarch. Sprinkle with remaining green onions and sesame oil.

★★★

Cooking time:
15 minutes

Serves: 5–6

Cooking methods
poach and simmer

Fairly easy to
prepare

A useful starter to
eat by itself

Illustrated on p.13

1 lb fresh squid

1 teaspoon salt

1 medium-sized red pepper

1 medium-sized green
pepper

3 tablespoons vegetable oil

3 slices fresh ginger root

Sauce:

1½ tablespoons shortening
or lard

2 teaspoons finely chopped
garlic

1½ tablespoons yellow bean
paste

2 teaspoons sugar

1 tablespoon soy sauce

1 tablespoon tomato paste

1 teaspoon red chili oil

2 teaspoons chili sauce

1 tablespoon dry sherry or
white wine

2 teaspoon cornstarch
blended with
1½ tablespoons water

HUNAN CHILI SQUID

■ PREPARATION ■

Clean squid under running cold water. Cut into 1 × ½-inch pieces. Sprinkle and rub with salt. Cut peppers into similar-sized pieces.

■ COOKING ■

Heat oil in wok or skillet. When hot, stir-fry ginger over medium heat for 30 seconds. Add squid and stir-fry for 1½ minutes. Remove and drain. Add shortening to wok. When hot, add garlic, yellow bean paste, sugar, soy sauce, tomato paste, red chili oil and chili sauce and stir together over medium heat for 30 seconds. Add sherry and blended cornstarch. Stir and mix for 15 seconds. Return squid to pan, stirring and coating with sauce. Stir in peppers, turn and stir in sauce for 1 minute.

★★★

Cooking time:
about 8 minutes

Serves: 4–6

Cooking method:
stir-fry, p.42

Quite easy to
prepare

Goes well with
most lightly
flavored dishes

★ ★ ★

Cooking time:
about 6 minutes

Serves: 4-5

Cooking methods:
shallow-fry and
stir-fry, p.42

Quick to do

A nice light dish
that combines well
with other dishes

Illustrated on p.132

Shell shrimp, p.40

QUICK-FRIED CRYSTAL SHRIMP

■ PREPARATION ■

Shell shrimp. Wash them in salted water, then rinse under cold running water. Drain well. Place in bowl. Add salt, cornstarch, egg white, sugar, pepper and ½ teaspoon vegetable oil. Mix well. Finely chop green onions and ginger.

■ COOKING ■

Heat oil in wok or deep skillet. When hot, add shrimp, stir around and fry over medium heat for 1¾ minutes. Remove and drain. Pour away oil to use for other purposes leaving only 1-1½ tablespoons. Reheat wok or pan. When hot, stir-fry ginger, green onions and peas over high heat for 15 seconds. Add stock and wine or sherry. As the sauce boils, return shrimp and adjust seasoning. Fry for 1 minute.

6-8 jumbo shrimp, fresh or frozen, unshelled

1 teaspoon salt

1½ tablespoons cornstarch

1 egg white

½ teaspoon sugar

Pepper to taste

⅔ cup vegetable oil

2 green onions

2 slices fresh ginger root

3-4 tablespoons green peas (optional)

2½ tablespoons good stock (see page 56)

1½ tablespoons dry sherry or white wine

★ ★ ★

Cooking time:
about 6-8 minutes

Serves: 5-6

Cooking methods:
shallow-fry and
stir-fry, p.42

Quick to make

Will accompany
most other
Chinese dishes

Shell shrimp, p.40

QUICK-FRIED CHILI SHRIMP

■ PREPARATION ■

Shell shrimp. Wash in salted water, then rinse under cold running water. Drain well. Finely chop chilies, discarding seeds. Coarsely chop ginger and green onions. Place shrimp in bowl. Add 1 teaspoon of salt, cornstarch, egg white and wine or sherry and mix well.

■ COOKING ■

Heat oil in wok or deep skillet. When hot, add shrimp, stir around and fry for 2 minutes. Remove and drain. Pour away oil to use for other purposes leaving only 2 tablespoons. Reheat wok or pan. When hot, stir-fry chilies and ginger over medium heat for 30 seconds. Add sugar, yellow bean paste, tomato paste, stock, remaining salt, vinegar and green onions. Toss and stir for 15 seconds. Return shrimp to pan. Stir and turn for 30 seconds. Pour in blended cornstarch. Sprinkle over sesame oil. Stir and turn once more.

8-12 jumbo shrimp, fresh or frozen, unshelled

1 small fresh green chili

2 small dried red chilies

2 slices fresh ginger root

2 green onions

1½ teaspoons salt

1½ tablespoons cornstarch

1 egg white

1 tablespoon dry sherry or white wine

⅔ cup vegetable oil

1½ teaspoons sugar

1 tablespoon yellow bean paste

1 tablespoon tomato paste

2½ tablespoons good stock (see page 56)

1 tablespoon wine vinegar

2 teaspoons cornstarch blended with 2 tablespoons water

1 teaspoon sesame oil

2lb crab (about 2 crabs)

5-6 green onions

5-6 slices fresh ginger root

3 tablespoons dry sherry

1½ teaspoons salt

5 tablespoons vegetable oil

2 eggs

Sauce:

1 red chili

3 garlic cloves

2 tablespoons salted black beans

2 tablespoons good stock (see page 56)

2 tablespoons vinegar

1 tablespoon sugar

2 teaspoons cornstarch blended with 2 tablespoons water

1½ teaspoons sesame oil

QUICK-FRIED CRAB IN HOT BLACK BEAN SAUCE

■ PREPARATION ■

Scrub crabs under cold running water. Break each crab into 6 pieces, discarding grey dead men's fingers. Crack claws and legs with the back of a chopper. Cut green onions in ½-inch shreds. Finely chop ginger and chili, discarding seeds. Crush garlic. Soak black beans in hot water for 5 minutes, then drain and crush. Place crab pieces in bowl with half of green onions and the ginger, sherry and salt. Mix together and leave to marinate for 15 minutes.

■ COOKING ■

Heat the vegetable oil in wok or skillet. When hot, stir-fry crab pieces over high heat for 2½ minutes. Remove and drain. Pour away oil to use for other purposes leaving about 1 tablespoon. Reheat the wok or skillet. When hot, stir-fry remaining green onion, garlic, chili and black beans over medium heat for 30 seconds. Add stock, vinegar and sugar. Continue to stir-fry quickly, then return crab pieces to wok or skillet. Turn and stir for 1 minute, then add beaten egg and cook for 30 seconds, stirring. Add blended cornstarch and sesame oil. Turn and stir until thickened.

★★★

Cooking time: about 10 minutes

Serves: 5-6

Cooking method: stir-fry, p.42

A dish that is good by itself, perhaps as an hors d'oeuvre

2 green onions

2 eggs

3 tablespoons vegetable oil

4-5 large fresh scallops, shelled

1 teaspoon salt

½ teaspoon sugar

1½ tablespoons dry sherry

Pepper to taste

1½ tablespoons shortening or lard

1½ tablespoons finely chopped ham

STIR-FRIED SCALLOPS WITH EGG

■ PREPARATION ■

Coarsely chop green onions, dividing white and green parts. Lightly beat eggs.

■ COOKING ■

Heat the oil in wok or skillet. When hot, stir-fry scallops and white parts of green onions over medium heat for 1 minute. Add salt, sugar, sherry and pepper. Continue to stir-fry for 1 minute. Remove from pan. Add shortening to wok or skillet. When hot, pour in beaten eggs. Stir them a couple of times and, before they have set, return scallops to pan. Turn and stir with egg for 30 seconds. Sprinkle with green parts of green onion. Stir once more, then transfer to heated serving dish. Sprinkle with chopped ham.

★★

Cooking time: 6-8 minutes

Serves: 4-6

Cooking method: stir-fry, p.42

Quick and easy to prepare

Goes well with most Chinese dishes. Serve with good quality soy sauce or grated ginger and vinegar dip sauce

STIR-FRIED SHRIMP IN GARLIC AND TOMATO SAUCE

12 oz shrimp, fresh or frozen, shelled
1 teaspoon salt
³⁄₄ tablespoon cornstarch
1 egg white
2 garlic cloves
2 green onions
2 small firm tomatoes
6 tablespoons vegetable oil
Sauce:
2 tablespoons tomato sauce or paste
¼ teaspoon salt
1 tablespoon sugar
Pinch of MSG (optional)
6 tablespoons good stock (see page 56)·
1½ tablespoons cornstarch blended with 3 tablespoons water
1 teaspoon sesame oil

★★

Cooking time:
10 minutes

Serves: 5–6

Cooking method:
stir-fry, p.42

Quick and easy to prepare

Versatile dish for any part of a Chinese meal

■ PREPARATION ■

Toss shrimp in salt, dust with cornstarch and coat with egg white. Crush garlic. Cut green onions into shreds. Skin tomatoes and cut into eighths.

■ COOKING ■

Heat oil in wok or skillet. When hot, stir-fry shrimp over high heat for 1½ minutes. Remove from wok or skillet. Pour away excess oil and reheat wok. When hot, stir-fry garlic, tomatoes and half of green onions over high heat for 30 seconds. Add tomato paste, salt, sugar, monosodium glutamate, if using, and stock and continue stir-frying for further 30 seconds. Stir blended cornstarch until the sauce thickens. Sprinkle on sesame oil and remaining green onions. Return shrimp to wok, stir once more and serve.

FUKIEN CLAM SOUP

3 lb fresh clams
2 tablespoons salt
1½ tablespoons dried shrimp
2 slices fresh ginger root
3 green onions
2 garlic cloves
2 teaspoons salt
Pepper to taste
1½ chicken bouillon cubes
4 cups good stock (see page 56)
1½ tablespoons light soy sauce
1 teaspoon vinegar
½ tablespoon sesame oil

★★★

Cooking time:
20 minutes

Serves: 4–5

Cooking method:
poach

A good starter

■ PREPARATION ■

Wash and clean clams well with stiff brush under running water. Bring 5 cups water to boil in saucepan and add salt. Simmer clams for 2 minutes, then leave to stand in water off heat, for a further minute. Drain. Discard any unopened clams. Soak dried shrimp in hot water to cover for 5 minutes, then drain. Finely shred ginger and green onions. Crush garlic.

■ COOKING ■

Place poached clams in saucepan. Add dried shrimp, ginger, garlic, salt, pepper and crumbled bouillon cubes. Pour in stock and bring to boil. Reduce heat and simmer for 10 minutes. Add green onions, soy sauce and vinegar and continue to simmer for another 5 minutes.

■ SERVING ■

Place clams and soup in heated, large serving bowl and sprinkle on sesame oil. Serve in individual bowls and eat like 'Moules Marinière', or dish can be eaten from a large central bowl in the normal Chinese way.

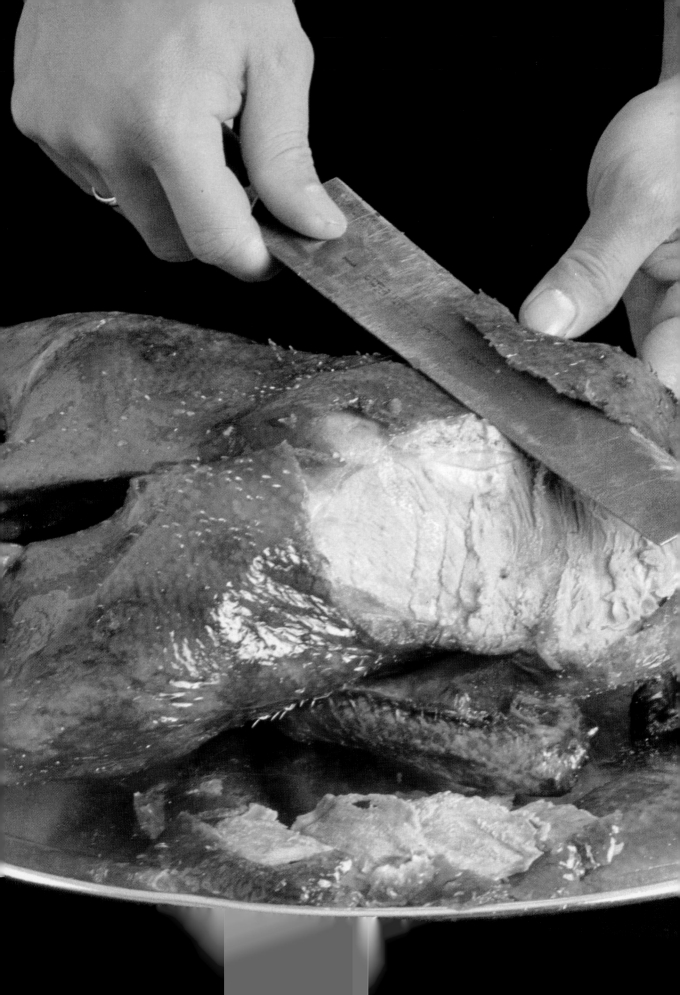

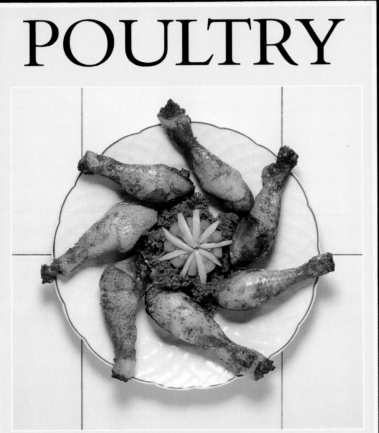

POULTRY

Carving Peking Duck (*left*); recipe page 178.
Crispy 'Five Spice' Chicken Legs (*above*); recipe page 166.

CHICKEN

Chicken is regarded as a greater delicacy than pork on the Chinese menu and is nearly as widely used, mainly because of its convenient unit size. It is a relatively simple matter for a Chinese family to kill a chicken in order to provide an extra large dish for visiting guests or relatives. This is especially true of peasant families, who make up over 90 percent of the Chinese population.

Visitors to China often find the free-range chickens produced there tough but full of flavor. This natural flavor is heightened by the unique Chinese treatment of chicken as a dish. Indeed, the Chinese knack of incorporating a wide range of ingredients in their dishes is an example that many Western cooks would do well to follow. The flavor blending and flavor development techniques used can compensate for the reduction in flavor of the mass-produced chicken commonly found in the West.

Chinese chicken, like pork, has a neutral savoriness which enables it to combine easily with other foods and ingredients, a characteristic which has allowed almost unlimited potential for the development of new dishes. The cooking and flavoring techniques used for many of these dishes are similar, as you will see.

RED-COOKED CHICKEN

- 3-4 lb chicken
- 1¼ cups good stock (see page 56)
- 1 chicken bouillon cube
- 4 slices fresh ginger root
- ¼ teaspoon salt
- 1½ tablespoons sugar
- Pepper to taste
- 5-6 tablespoons soy sauce
- 2 pieces star anise

★★

Cooking time: 1 hour 20 minutes

Serves: 6-8

Cooking method: casserole

Easy and straightforward

A main meal to accompany most vegetable and savory dishes

'Red-cooked' means that the chicken is cooked with soy sauce instead of in stock and water with seasonings added. Red-cooked chicken is about the most common chicken dish in China.

PREPARATION

Bring large pan of water to boil, add chicken and simmer for about 8 minutes. Remove and drain thoroughly. Place bird in flameproof casserole, add stock, crumbled bouillon cube, ginger, salt, sugar, pepper, soy sauce and star anise. Bring to boil.

COOKING

Cover and place casserole in preheated oven at 200°C, 400°F and cook for 30 minutes. Turn bird over, reduce oven temperature to 180°C, 350°F and cook for further 25 minutes, turn bird over again and continue to cook for final 25 minutes.

WHITE-CUT CHICKEN

★★

Cooking time:
15 minutes, plus
cooling time

Serves: 4

Cooking method:
simmer

Easy to prepare

▩ PREPARATION ▩

Wash chicken thoroughly. Cut the green onions into 2-inch sections.

▩ COOKING ▩

Bring about 7½ cups water to boil in saucepan. Add ginger, salt, green onions and sherry. Place chicken in water, bring to boil and simmer for about 15 minutes. Remove from heat and allow the bird to cool in water. To make dip sauce, heat oil in small saucepan. Add garlic, then soy sauce and mustard. Stir together well. Take out chicken and drain. Cut into large bite-sized pieces. Arrange chicken on large platter and serve with dip sauce.

2½lb young chicken
3 green onions
4–5 slices fresh ginger root
3 teaspoons salt
3 tablespoons dry sherry
Dip sauce:
2 tablespoons peanut oil
2 garlic cloves, crushed
¼ cup soy sauce
1 tablespoon prepared English mustard

STIR-FRIED CHICKEN

WITH GARLIC AND CUCUMBER

★★★

Cooking time:
about 5–6 minutes

Serves: 5–6

Cooking method:
stir-fry, p.42

Fairly quick and
easy to make

A light dish. Serve
as a starter or with
vegetables and
red-cooked dishes

Illustrated on p.154

▩ PREPARATION ▩

Cut chicken into ½-inch cubes. Cut cucumber into similar-sized cubes. Sprinkle and rub chicken evenly with 1 teaspoon salt, pepper and half cornstarch, then wet with egg white. Crush garlic. Chop shortening. Blend remaining cornstarch with 2 tablespoons stock. Cut green onions into 1½-inch sections.

▩ COOKING ▩

Heat vegetable oil in wok or skillet. When hot, stir in ginger slices for 15 seconds to flavor oil. Remove and discard ginger. Add chicken cubes to pan and stir-fry over medium to high heat for 45 seconds. Remove and drain. Add shortening and garlic to wok or pan and stir over medium heat for 15 seconds. Add cucumber cubes and sprinkle with ½ teaspoon salt, pepper and monosodium glutamate, if using. Stir-fry for 1 minute. Add sherry, soy sauce and green onion. Return chicken to pan and stir-fry for 1 minute. Add blended cornstarch and sesame oil and stir-fry for 10 seconds.

5–8 oz boneless chicken breast
1 medium cucumber
1 teaspoon salt
Pepper to taste
4 teaspoons cornstarch
½ egg white
2 garlic cloves
1 tablespoon cold shortening or lard
2 tablespoons good stock (see page 56)
2 green onions
3 tablespoons vegetable oil
2 slices fresh ginger root
½ teaspoon salt
¼ teaspoon MSG (optional)
1½ tablespoons dry sherry
1 tablespoon light soy sauce
½ teaspoon sesame oil

▩ SERVING ▩

Serve this lightly colored dish as a starter to a multi-course Chinese meal.

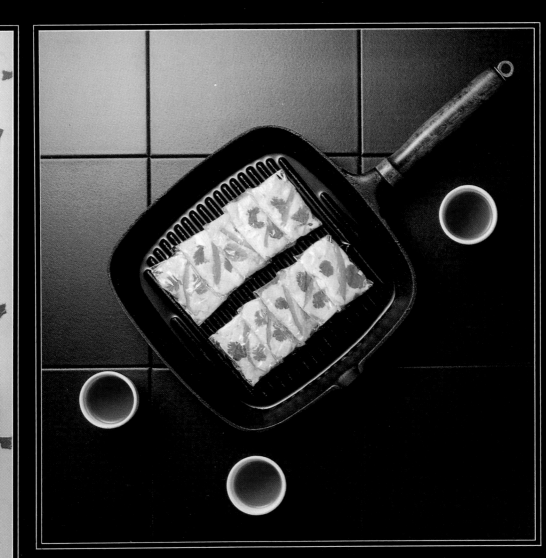

Stir-fried Chicken and
Celery on Rice (*left*),
spoonfuls of chicken and
rice can be wrapped in
lettuce leaves for serving;
recipe page 152.
Paper-wrapped Deep-fried
Chicken (*above*), these
pretty parcels can be
garnished any way you
like; recipe page 152.

2-3 medium dried Chinese mushrooms
1 half chicken breast
1 stalk celery
2 oz canned bamboo shoots
2 slices fresh ginger root
2 green onions
Salt and pepper to taste
3 tablespoons vegetable oil
2 tablespoons good stock (see page 56)
2 tablespoons dry sherry
1 tablespoon light soy sauce
½lb boiled rice or 4-5 oz crispy rice (see page 68 or 141)

STIR-FRIED CHICKEN AND CELERY ON RICE

■ PREPARATION ■

Soak dried mushrooms in hot water to cover for 25 minutes. Drain and discard tough stalks. Cut mushroom caps into small cubes. Dice chicken into small cubes. Dice celery and bamboo shoots into similar sized cubes. Finely chop ginger. Chop green onions.

■ COOKING ■

Heat oil in wok or skillet. When hot, stir-fry ginger, green onion, mushrooms, celery and bamboo shoot over high heat for 1 minute. Add chicken and stir-fry for 1 minute. Sprinkle with salt and pepper to taste. Add stock, sherry and soy sauce, turn and toss for further minute.

■ SERVING ■

Serve on boiled or crispy rice. If liked, wrap spoonfuls of chicken and rice in lettuce leaves to eat with fingers.

★★

Cooking time: about 5 minutes

Serves: 4

Cooking method: stir-fry, p.42

Quick to prepare

Illustrated on p.150

1lb boned chicken breasts
5 dried Chinese mushrooms
2 slices ham
2 green onions
2 bunches parsley
15 sheets waxed paper – not plastic wrap
2 tablespoons sesame oil
Vegetable oil for deep-frying
Marinade:
3 tablespoons light soy sauce
½ teaspoon salt
1½ tablespoons dry sherry
½ teaspoon sugar
¼ teaspoon pepper
2 teaspoons sesame oil
2 teaspoons cornstarch

PAPER-WRAPPED DEEP-FRIED CHICKEN

Serve these savory parcels as part of an hors d'oeuvres selection. The parcels can be garnished in many different ways.

■ PREPARATION ■

Cut chicken into 2 × ½-inch strips. Place in bowl and add all ingredients for marinade. Mix well and leave to marinate for 20 minutes. Soak dried mushrooms in hot water to cover for 25 minutes. Drain and discard tough stalks. Cut mushroom caps into about 6 pieces each. Cut ham into 2-inch strips. Cut green onions into 2-inch sections. Cut and divide parsley into about 15 portions. Brush 1 sheet of waxed paper with sesame oil and place spray of parsley in middle. Divide and place small quantity of mushroom and ham on either side, lay some sliced chicken on top and green onion on top of that. Fold waxed paper to completely enclose filling.

■ COOKING ■

Heat oil in wok or deep-fryer. When hot, fry envelopes for about 2 minutes. Remove. Reheat oil and fry again for 2 minutes. Drain. Serve envelopes arranged on large heated plate.

★★★★

Cooking time: about 5 minutes

Serves: 5-6

Cooking method: deep-fry, p.45

Takes time to prepare

An attractive hot starter

Illustrated on p.151

SIMULATED BEGGARS' CHICKEN

I recommend this Simulated Beggars' Chicken in preference to the original recipe which requires encasing the whole chicken in a layer of mud. Since suitable mud is difficult to find in the West, this recipe is much easier.

■ PREPARATION ■

Bring large pan of water to boil. Add chicken and simmer for about 5 minutes. Remove, drain and dry very thoroughly. Finely chop ginger. Mix together salt, hoisin sauce, oyster sauce, sherry, soy sauce, sugar and ginger. Rub about three-quarters of this mixture both inside and outside the chicken. Leave chicken to season for 30 minutes.

For the stuffing, soak dried mushrooms in hot water to cover for 25 minutes. Drain and discard tough stalks. Finely slice mushroom caps. Cut pork, bamboo shoots and pickles into similar-sized shreds. Place pork into remaining marinade and leave to marinate. Heat oil in small skillet. When hot, stir-fry mushrooms and pork for about 2 minutes. Add pickle and bamboo shoots and stir-fry for 1 minute. Stuff these ingredients into the chicken cavity. Soak lotus leaves in water for 10 minutes until soft. Wrap chicken in suet, then the lotus leaves. Mix together flour and water to form thick dough and wrap the chicken in the dough. Finally, cover the chicken completely in foil.

■ COOKING ■

Place foil parcel in preheated oven at 200°C, 400°F and cook for 45 minutes. Reduce oven temperature to 190°C, 375°F and cook for further 45 minutes. Reduce heat again to 180°C, 350°F and cook for additional 45 minutes.

■ SERVING ■

Remove foil and crack the tough casing with a hammer. Lift out the lotus-wrapped chicken and serve on a heated platter straight from the leaves.

3½-4 lb chicken

2 slices fresh ginger root

2 teaspoons salt

1 tablespoon hoisin sauce

1½ tablespoons oyster sauce

3½ tablespoons dry sherry

2½ tablespoons soy sauce

2 teaspoons sugar

Stuffing:

6 medium dried Chinese mushrooms

1 lb lean pork

10 oz drained, canned sliced bamboo shoots

4 oz drained, canned Sichuan hot Ja Chai pickles

2 tablespoons vegetable oil

Wrapping:

2 large lotus leaves

1 large sheet of suet

4 cups all-purpose flour

2 cups water

Chicken Fu-Yung (*above left*), a light chicken dish with egg garnished with chopped dried shrimp; recipe page 167. Stir-fried Chicken with Garlic and Cucumber (*below left*), a quick stir-fried dish; recipe page 149. Shanghai Quick-braised Chicken on the Bone (*above*), garnished with green onion tassels and served with extra soy sauce; recipe page 164.

1 tablespoon salt

2 teaspoons crushed Sichuan peppercorns

1½ teaspoons ground ginger

1½ teaspoons sugar

3–3½ lb chicken

Cooking stock:

5 cups good stock (see page 56)

2 teaspoons salt

2 teaspoons crushed Sichuan peppercorns

½ teaspoon five spice powder

6 green onions

6 slices fresh ginger root

Fuel for smoking:

4–5 tablespoons damp tea leaves

2 teaspoons five spice powder or in pieces

2 tablespoons brown sugar

½ cup sawdust, pine, oak, etc.

Garnish:

2 tablespoons sesame oil

2½ tablespoons chopped coriander (cilantro) leaves

3½–4 lb chicken

Vegetable oil for deep-frying

2 tablespoons soy sauce

1 tablespoon oyster sauce

3 medium onions

4 slices fresh ginger root

3 garlic cloves

1⅓ cups button mushrooms

8 oz pork shoulder or fresh pork sides

2 teaspoons salt

1¼ cups good stock (see page 56)

1 chicken bouillon cube

1 cup dry white wine

2 cups dry sherry

■ SIMPLE SICHUAN SMOKED CHICKEN

■ PREPARATION AND COOKING ■

Mix together salt, peppercorns, ground ginger and sugar. Wash chicken and dry thoroughly. Rub chicken inside and out with this mixture and leave to marinate overnight. Bring large pan of water to boil, add chicken, making sure it is covered with water, and simmer for about 5 minutes. Mix stock ingredients together. Pour away water and replace with cooking stock. Bring to boil and simmer gently for 25 minutes. Drain.

■ SMOKING ■

Use an old pot, pan or wok large enough to suspend chicken in. Mix fuel together and place in bottom of pan. Arrange wire rack about 2–3 inches above fuel. Place pan over high heat and, when smoke rises, place chicken on rack. Cover with large lid or another pan. Smoke chicken for 10 minutes, then turn it over, cover and smoke again for 10 minutes.

■ SERVING ■

Rub the chicken evenly with sesame oil, then chop it into about 24 bite-sized pieces. Reassemble the chicken on a large heated platter and sprinkle on the coriander leaves.

ROYAL CONCUBINE CHICKEN

This dish is said to date from Yan Kwie-Fei, a royal concubine who was drunk more often than not; it might also be called 'Chinese Coq au Vin'.

■ PREPARATION ■

Wash chicken and dry thoroughly. Heat oil in wok or deep-fryer. When hot, gently fry chicken for about 7 minutes. Drain. Plunge chicken momentarily into pan of boiling water to remove any fat. Dry, then rub bird inside and out with soy and oyster sauces. Place chicken in casserole and leave to season. Peel and thinly slice onions. Crush ginger and garlic. Cut mushrooms in half. Cut pork into 1½ × 3-inch slices.

★★★★★

Cooking time: 30 minutes, plus 20 minutes smoking time

Serves: 8–10 (at a party)

Cooking methods: simmer and smoke

Takes time and a lot of preparation

An unusual dish to serve as a change from stir-fried

★★★★★

Cooking time: about 1½ hours

Serves: 6–8

Cooking methods: deep-fry p.45, stir-fry p.42 and casserole

A rich dish to serve with vegetables and stir-fried dishes

■ COOKING ■

Heat 3 tablespoons oil in wok or skillet. When hot. stir-fry pork over high heat for about 2 minutes. Add ginger, onion, garlic and salt and continue to stir-fry for 2 minutes. Pour in stock and add crumbled bouillon cube and white wine. Bring to boil and pour over chicken in casserole. Cover casserole and place in preheated oven at 200°C, 400°F for 30 minutes. Reduce oven temperature to 190°C, 375°F and turn bird over. Continue to cook for another 30 minutes. Turn bird over again, add sherry and mushrooms and cook for an additional 30 minutes.

■ SERVING ■

Serve this dish straight from the casserole at the table. Spoon liquid into individual bowls to serve as a soup.

PEKING DICED CHICKEN STIR-FRIED IN CAPITAL SAUCE

★ ★

Cooking time: about 5 minutes

Serves: 5-6

Cooking method: stir-fry, p.42

Quick and easy

Serve alone or accompany with other stir-fried dishes

Capital Sauce is used and served more frequently in Peking than anywhere else in China. It consists of a mixture of yellow bean paste, soy sauce, sugar, ginger or ginger water, sesame oil, a small amount of sherry and cornstarch all blended together over high heat.

■ PREPARATION ■

Cut chicken into cubes, then toss them in salt and cornstarch and wet with egg white. To make ginger water, boil 3 slices of fresh ginger in 6 tablespoons water until reduced by half.

■ COOKING ■

Heat vegetable oil in wok or skillet. When hot, add chicken and separate cubes. Stir-fry over high heat for about 30 seconds, then remove and keep warm. Pour away excess oil. Reheat wok or pan and add yellow bean paste and ginger water. Add sherry, sugar and soy sauce, then stir in blended cornstarch over high heat. Add chicken and stir in thickened sauce. Add sesame oil and stir together.

■ SERVING ■

Serve hot on its own to nibble while sipping wine; or eat as a dish with rice as part of a meal.

1 lb boneless chicken breast

¾ teaspoon salt

1 tablespoon cornstarch

1 egg white

6 tablespoons vegetable oil

Sauce:

1¾ tablespoons yellow bean paste

1½ tablespoons ginger water (see Preparation)

1 tablespoon dry sherry

2 teaspoons sugar

2 teaspoons soy sauce

2 teaspoons cornstarch blended with 1½ tablespoons water

1 teaspoon sesame oil

3–3½ lb chicken

Sea salt

★★★
Cooking time:
1 hour 25 minutes

Serves: 4–6

Cooking method:
bake

Illustrated
opposite

SALT-BURIED BAKED CHICKEN

This is a favorite Cantonese dish, producing a chicken with crispy dry skin. As long as the salt and the chicken are both dry, the chicken will not be over-salty when cooked.

■ PREPARATION ■

Wash chicken and dry very carefully. Hang up overnight in well-ventilated place to ensure chicken is perfectly dry. Heat salt in saucepan to ensure it too is dry.

■ COOKING ■

Spoon layer of salt in bottom of flameproof casserole. Put chicken in casserole and cover with salt. Place heavy lid on casserole and cook over low heat for about 15 minutes. Place in preheated oven at 190°C, 375°F and cook for 30 minutes. Reduce temperature to 180°C, 350°F and continue to cook for another 40 minutes without lifting the lid.

■ SERVING ■

Remove the chicken from the salt and chop it into small bite-sized pieces. Arrange on a heated platter. If liked, a mixture of 3 chopped green onions fried in 3 tablespoons vegetable oil can be poured over the chicken.

½ medium chicken

1 medium onion

3 teaspoons salt

3 slices fresh ginger root

1 medium cucumber

Sauce:

1½ tablespoons chili sauce or red chili oil

1 tablespoon chopped garlic

1 tablespoon chopped fresh ginger root

1 tablespoon peanut butter

1 tablespoon chopped green onion

2 teaspoons sesame oil

1½ tablespoons vegetable oil

¼ cup good stock (see page 56)

½ teaspoon salt

¼ teaspoon MSG (optional)

★★
Cooking time:
45 minutes, plus
cooling time

Serves: 4–6

Cooking method:
simmer

Easy to prepare

Usually served as a starter

HOT-TOSSED SHREDDED CHICKEN IN RED CHILI OIL

This dish is usually eaten cold or as a starter. It can be a useful dish to serve while waiting for stir-fried dishes to appear.

■ PREPARATION AND COOKING ■

Bring about 5 cups water to boil in pan. Add chicken and simmer for about 10 minutes. Peel and slice onion. Pour away quarter of water and add salt, ginger and onion. Cook for another 35 minutes. Cut cucumber into shreds, leaving skin on. Remove chicken and cool. Shred meat into pieces of similar size to cucumber shreds.

■ SERVING ■

Place all sauce ingredients in bowl and mix well. Arrange cucumber on plate and pile chicken on top. Pour over sauce.

3½–4 lb chicken

1½ teaspoons salt

6 tablespoons vegetable oil

6 slices fresh ginger root

1½ cups good stock (see page 56)

2 tablespoons light soy sauce

2 tablespoons dark soy sauce

2 tablespoons yellow bean paste

1½ teaspoons sugar

¼ cup dry sherry or rice wine

5 tablespoons honey

QUICK BRAISED CHICKEN WITH HONEY

★★
Cooking time: about 20 minutes

Serves: 6–8

Cooking method: stir-fry p.42 and quick-braise

Easy to prepare

A main item in a multi-dish meal

The sweetness of the honey contrasts well with the savory soy chicken.

■ PREPARATION ■

Chop chicken through bone into about 30 bite-sized pieces. Sprinkle and rub with salt.

■ COOKING ■

Heat oil in wok or flameproof casserole. When hot, add ginger and stir over high heat for 30 seconds. Add chicken, stir and turn in gingered oil over high heat for 5 minutes. Drain away excess oil. Pour stock, soy sauces, yellow bean paste, sugar and sherry or wine evenly over chicken. When contents begin to boil, turn and stir chicken in sauce for 2 minutes over high heat. Cover wok or casserole and continue to boil for further 10 minutes. Remove lid and turn chicken so that all pieces are coated in sauce. Continue to boil rapidly until sauce is reduced to less than 10 per cent of its original volume, stirring now and then. The consistency will be very sticky and rich. Stir chicken pieces to coat in thickened sauce. Pour honey evenly over chicken. Turn contents once more, then serve.

1 lb boneless chicken breast

Salt and pepper to taste

2 eggs

2 green onions

2 garlic cloves

4–5 tablespoons vegetable oil

5 tablespoons good stock (see page 56)

2 teaspoons wine vinegar

1½ tablespoons dry sherry

¼ teaspoon MSG (optional)

PEKING SLICED EGG-BATTERED CHICKEN
IN GARLIC AND ONION SAUCE

★★
Cooking time: about 8 minutes

Serves: 4–6

Cooking method: shallow-fry

Easy to prepare

Serve as part of a multi-dish meal

■ PREPARATION ■

Cut chicken meat into approximately 2 × 4¼-inch thick slices. Sprinkle and rub with salt and pepper. Beat eggs in bowl, add chicken slices and coat thoroughly. Finely chop green onions and garlic.

■ COOKING ■

Heat oil in wok or skillet over medium heat. Add battered chicken slices, one by one, and spread them out evenly over surface of wok or pan. Shake pan and reduce heat to low. Cook chicken pieces for 1½ minutes. Once egg has set, turn chicken slices over to cook for 30 seconds.

Sprinkle chicken with garlic and onion. Mix stock in bowl with 1½ teaspoons salt, vinegar and sherry. Pour half this mixture evenly over chicken pieces. Simmer gently for 1¾ minutes.

■ SERVING ■

Remove chicken slices with perforated spoon and place them on chopping board. Cut into ¼-inch wide strips. Arrange them on heated serving dish. Add ¼ teaspoon salt, monosodium glutamate, if using, and remaining stock to pan. Bring to boil and pour it evenly over chicken pieces.

DRUNKEN CHICKEN

★ ★ ★

Cooking time: 15 minutes, plus cooling and soaking time

Serves: 8–10 (as a starter)

Cooking method: simmer

Quite easy to prepare, but time needed for soaking

A good starter

3–3½ lb chicken
2 medium onions
6 slices fresh ginger root
1½ teaspoon salt
5 cups water
2½ cups rice wine or dry sherry

This is a dish which is often used as part of a multi-dish hors d'oeuvres. Although it takes time to make, the process is comparatively straightforward. If liked, the remaining wine or sherry may be reused in cooking.

■ PREPARATION ■

Wash, dry and cut chicken in half. Peel and thinly slice onions. Cut ginger into shreds. Place onion and ginger in saucepan, add salt and pour in 5 cups water. Bring to boil and simmer for 10 minutes.

■ COOKING ■

Add chicken halves to pan, making sure they are totally immersed. Bring slowly to boil and simmer gently for 15 minutes. Turn off heat and allow chicken to cool in water for 1 hour.

■ SOAKING ■

Remove chicken pieces from pan and drain. Transfer to bowl. Pour wine or sherry over chicken. Turn halves over a few times, making sure they are completely covered. Place bowl in refrigerator overnight (or longer), again turning chicken over a couple of times during this time.

■ SERVING ■

When required, lift the chicken pieces out of the wine or sherry and place them on a chopping board. Chop each half of the chicken through the bones into 10–12 pieces. Arrange them attractively on a serving dish or as an item on a much larger platter.

家禽類

3½-4½ lb chicken

1 medium Chinese white cabbage

6 slices fresh ginger root

5 cups good stock (see page 56) or water

2½ teaspoons salt

2 chicken bouillon cubes

Pepper to taste

½ teaspoon MSG (optional)

WHITE-COOKED OR CLEAR-SIMMERED CHICKEN

WITH CHINESE WHITE CABBAGE

★★

Cooking time: about 2 hours

Serves: 6-8

Cooking method: simmer

Easy to prepare

Unlike red-cooked chicken, the aim of which is to produce a very rich meaty dish with a highly savory gravy or sauce suitable for serving with rice, the aim of white-cooked chicken is to produce a dish where the richness of the chicken combines with the sweet freshness of the cabbage. As a whole chicken is cooked, there is likely to be more than 4 cups of liquid, therefore the Chinese call this recipe a semi-soup dish.

■ PREPARATION ■

Bring large pan of water to boil, add chicken and boil for about 7 minutes. Remove and drain thoroughly. Cut cabbage into about 5 even sections and wash carefully.

■ COOKING ■

Arrange slices of ginger in bottom of large flameproof casserole and place chicken on top. Add stock or water and salt and bring to boil. Simmer gently for 30 minutes and then turn bird over. Add crumbled bouillon cubes, pepper and monosodium glutamate, if using, and simmer for another 30 minutes, then turn bird over once more. After 1½ hours, remove bird from casserole and place cabbage in bottom of casserole. Put chicken back on top to submerge all the cabbage. Simmer again for another 30 minutes.

■ SERVING ■

Serve the dish straight from the casserole at the table with the help of a small ladle. The chicken will be tender enough to serve with the chopsticks and can be dipped into good quality soy sauce.

Note: The above recipe can be made into a more elaborate party meal by adding ⅓ cup smoked diced ham and 6-8 medium Chinese dried mushrooms (soaked for 25 minutes, stalks removed). These should be added at the beginning of the cooking. At a party, serve the dish as a soup or semi-soup, divide the chicken and cabbage and ladle into the individual bowls adding a tablespoon of Chinese rice wine.

CHICKEN WITH CHILIES AND RED PEPPER

★ ★ ★

Cooking time: about 5-7 minutes

Serves: 5-6

Cooking method: stir-fry, p.42

Quick to prepare

A spicy dish, best served with vegetables and lighter tasting dishes

■ PREPARATION ■

Skin chicken and cut into cubes. Add salt, cornstarch, wine and egg white. Mix together thoroughly. Finely chop together ginger, garlic and fresh and dried chilies, discarding seeds. Shred green onions. Cut red pepper into cubes.

■ COOKING ■

Heat oil in wok or skillet. When hot, stir-fry chicken cubes over high heat for about 45 seconds. Drain and pour away oil to use for other purposes. Reheat wok or pan. Stir-fry chilies, ginger and garlic over high heat for a few seconds until fragrance begins to rise. Add green onions and red pepper and stir-fry for 30 seconds. Return chicken to wok or pan and add stock, sugar, soy sauce and vinegar. Turn all ingredients together for 15 seconds.

1 lb boneless chicken breasts

1 teaspoon salt

1½ tablespoons cornstarch

1½ tablespoons rice wine

1 egg white

2 slices fresh ginger root

1 garlic clove

1 fresh medium chili

1 dried small chili

2 green onions

1 red pepper

⅔ cup vegetable oil

2 tablespoons good stock (see page 56)

1 tablespoon sugar

1 tablespoon light soy sauce

1¼ tablespoons wine vinegar

STEAMED CHICKEN IN AROMATIC GROUND RICE

★ ★ ★

Cooking time: 1 hour

Serves: 6-8

Cooking method: steam, p.49

Excellent as variety to stir-fried dishes

Ground rice, which has coarser grains than rice flour, can be made aromatic either by roasting or frying in a dry skillet until slightly browned. It is then used much as breadcrumbs are used in Western cooking, for coating meats and fish.

■ PREPARATION ■

Chop ginger. Chop chicken into 20 bite-sized pieces. Sprinkle with salt, pepper and ginger and leave to season for 10 minutes. Dip in egg white and coat with ground rice.

■ COOKING ■

Place coated pieces of chicken on to heatproof dish, place in steamer and steam for 1 hour. Drain off liquid which has collected in the dish into a small pan. Add chicken fat and bring to boil. Add rest of sauce ingredients and stir together for about 15 seconds. Arrange chicken pieces on heated plate and pour over sauce.

2 slices fresh ginger root

3½-4lb chicken

2 teaspoons salt

Pepper to taste

1 egg white

6 tablespoons roasted ground rice

Sauce:

1 tablespoon chicken fat

2 tablespoons light soy sauce

½ teaspoon salt

3 tablespoons good stock (see page 56)

1 tablespoon malt vinegar

1½ tablespoons dry sherry

1 tablespoon chopped green onions

2 garlic cloves, crushed

12 oz chicken breast

3 medium zucchini

1 teaspoon salt

2½ teaspoons cornstarch

1 egg white

6½ tablespoons vegetable oil

3 slices fresh ginger root

2 tablespoons good stock
(see page 56)

1 tablespoon dry sherry

1 tablespoon soy sauce

1 tablespoon chili sauce

Pepper to taste

¼ teaspoon MSG (optional)

1½ teaspoons cornstarch
blended with
2 tablespoons water

STIR-FRIED SLICED CHICKEN WITH ZUCCHINI

★★★

Cooking time:
about 8 minutes

Serves: 6–7

Cooking method:
stir-fry, p.42

Quick to prepare

Goes well with
most dishes

■ PREPARATION ■

Cut chicken into flat sheets. Cut zucchini into ¼-inch slices. Place chicken into bowl and mix with salt, cornstarch and egg white.

■ COOKING ■

Heat 5 tablespoons oil in wok or skillet. When hot, add ginger and heat until oil begins to smoke. Remove ginger and discard. Add chicken slices and stir-fry for about 1½ minutes. Remove with perforated spoon and place in bowl. Add remaining 1½ tablespoons oil and heat. When hot, stir-fry zucchini for about 1½ minutes. Add stock, sherry, soy sauce, chili sauce, pepper and monosodium glutamate, if using. Remove zucchini and arrange on plate in circle. Return chicken pieces to pan and stir over high heat for 1 minute to reheat. Add blended cornstarch, stirring until sauce thickens. Spoon into the middle of zucchini circle.

3–4 lb chicken

1 tablespoon cornstarch

¼ cup vegetable oil

5 slices fresh ginger root

2 tablespoons sugar

3 tablespoons light soy sauce

3 tablespoons dark soy sauce

1 tablespoon hoisin sauce

1 tablespoon oyster sauce

½ teaspoon MSG (optional)

¼ cup rice wine

2 cups good stock (see page 56)

Garnish:

Green onion tassels

■ SHANGHAI QUICK-BRAISED CHICKEN ON THE BONE ■

★★★

Cooking time:
about 25 minutes

Serves: 6–8

Cooking methods:
stir-fry p.42 and
boiling

Quite easy to
prepare

A main item for a
multi-course meal

Illustrated on p.155

This dish can only be successfully made if cooked over very high heat.

■ PREPARATION ■

Chop chicken through bone into about 30 bite-sized pieces. Bring large pan of water to boil, add chicken and simmer for about 5 minutes. Remove and drain thoroughly. Blend cornstarch with 3 tablespoons water.

■ COOKING ■

Heat oil in wok or pan. When hot, stir in ginger for about 1½ minutes. Add chicken pieces and stir-fry for about 3 minutes. Put in sugar, soy sauces, hoisin sauce, oyster sauce, monosodium glutamate, if using, wine and stock. Bring to boil and continue to stir over highest heat until sauce begins to thicken and reduce. Add blended cornstarch and stir until sauce is thick and coats chicken pieces.

★ ★ ★ ★ ★

Cooking time:
1 hour 35 minutes

Serves: 6–8

Cooking methods:
steam p.49 and
stir-fry p.42

Takes time and
care in preparation

An attractive item
for a multi-dish
dinner party

Illustrated on p.172

MELON CHICKEN

Melon chicken is simply chicken cooked and served in a melon. It is a very popular way of serving chicken at a Chinese dinner party.

■ PREPARATION ■

Soak dried mushrooms and dried shrimp separately in hot water to cover for 25 minutes. Slice off top of melon and reserve for a lid. Scrape out most of the flesh and reserve about a quarter for cooking with the chicken. Drain and discard tough mushroom stalks. Cut mushroom caps in quarters. Dice ham and bamboo shoots.

■ COOKING ■

Place chicken in steamer and steam for about 1 hour. Leave to cool. When cool enough to handle, remove meat from bones and cut into cubes. Heat oil in wok or large skillet. When hot, stir-fry ginger, dried shrimp and dried mushrooms over high heat for about 2 minutes. Add ham, half chicken, bamboo shoots, reserved melon, fresh mushrooms, salt and pepper. Stir-fry for further 3 minutes. Pack all stir-fried ingredients into melon. Add any excess to remaining chicken. Mix crumbled bouillon cube with stock and sherry and pour on to melon until it fills to the brim. Replace melon lid and fasten it with a few cocktail sticks. Place on heatproof plate and steam for 30 minutes.

■ SERVING ■

Bring the whole melon to the table to serve. This is a pretty dish and the different savory flavors in the chicken-ham-mushroom stuffing and the sweetness of the melon give it a unique appeal. At a banquet in Canton, I have had a similar dish where frogs' legs were used instead of chicken. Accompany the dish with the remaining chicken and stir-fried ingredients.

3 large dried Chinese mushrooms
1/3 cup dried shrimp
1 large melon, approximately 8-inch diameter
1/2 cup diced ham
3/4 cup diced bamboo shoots
2 1/2 –3 lb chicken
2 tablespoons vegetable oil
2 slices fresh ginger root
1 cup button mushrooms
1 teaspoon salt
Pepper to taste
1 chicken bouillon cube
1 1/2 cups good stock (see page 56)
2 tablespoons dry sherry

家
禽
類

3 tablespoons rice

3 pieces lotus leaf

3½–4 lb chicken

2 tablespoons dark soy sauce

Vegetable oil for deep-frying

2 medium onions

2 green onions

2 tablespoons drained, canned chopped winter pickles

2 tablespoons drained, canned chopped snow pickles

1 tablespoon drained, canned, chopped Sichuan hot Ja Chai pickles

2 teaspoons salt

2 tablespoons dry sherry

LONG-STEAMED LOTUS LEAF–WRAPPED CHICKEN

★★★★★

Cooking time: 2½ hours

Serves: 6–8

Cooking method simmer, deep-fry p.45 and steam p.

Takes time to prepare

A main item for a multi-dish meal

■ PREPARATION ■

Soak rice in cold water to cover for 20 minutes. Drain. Soak lotus leaves in warm water for 15 minutes. Drain. Bring large pan of water to boil, add chicken and simmer for 5 minutes. Drain thoroughly. Brush chicken with soy sauce. Heat oil in wok or deep-fryer. When hot, fry chicken until brown all over. Drain. Chop onions and mix with pickles, salt, rice and sherry. Stuff this mixture into chicken cavity. Wrap chicken in lotus leaves to form neat parcel.

■ COOKING ■

Place wrapped chicken in steamer and steam for about 2½ hours.

■ SERVING ■

Bring chicken to the table still wrapped in the lotus leaves. Open the parcel and serve the chicken with the stuffing.

8 chicken drumsticks

2½ teaspoons salt

Pepper to taste

1 teaspoon ground ginger

Vegetable oil for deep-frying

Cooking sauce:

1½ cups good stock (see page 56)

1½ tablespoons hoisin sauce

1½ tablespoons yellow bean paste

¾ teaspoon pepper

1½ tablespoons mixed five spice pieces

CRISPY 'FIVE SPICE' CHICKEN LEGS

★★★

Cooking time: about 25 minutes, plus seasoning and cooling time

Serves: 4–6

Cooking methods simmer and deep-fry, p.45

Useful dish for a party buffet

Illustrated on p.14

■ PREPARATION ■

Rub chicken drumsticks with mixture of salt, pepper and ground ginger. Leave to season for 30 minutes. Bring pan of water to boil, add drumsticks and cook for 3 minutes. Drain and cool.

■ COOKING ■

Place cooking sauce ingredients in wok or pan and bring to boil. Add drumsticks and simmer for about 15 minutes. Leave drumsticks to cool in sauce for 15 minutes, then remove and drain thoroughly. Heat oil in wok or deep-fryer. When hot, gently fry chicken for about 5 minutes until golden brown.

■ SERVING ■

If liked, remove knuckle from drumstick and put cutlet frill on exposed bone. Arrange on heated plate and serve with Peking Duck Sauce (see page 178).

★ ★ ★

Cooking time:
6–7 minutes

Serves: 6–8

Cooking methods:
deep-fry p.45 and
stir-fry p.42

Quite easy to
prepare

A good contrast to
darker colored
dishes

Illustrated on p.154

CHICKEN FU-YUNG

PREPARATION

Cut chicken meat into 1½ × 2½-inch thin slices. Place them in a bowl. Add 1½ tablespoons cornstarch and coat chicken pieces evenly. Beat egg whites lightly in another bowl. Blend 2½ teaspoons cornstarch with 2 tablespoons water.

COOKING

Heat oil in wok or deep-fryer. When hot, gently fry chicken pieces over low to medium heat for 1½ minutes. Pour in egg white slowly and evenly over contents of pan. When egg white rises, turn it around once with the chicken pieces. Transfer with a perforated spoon to a bowl. Pour away oil to use for other purposes. Return wok or pan to heat. Add stock, salt, peas and monosodium glutamate, if using. Bring to boil and stir in blended cornstarch until thickened. Return chicken and egg-white pieces to pan. Bring back to boil and serve. If liked, sprinkle with presoaked, chopped dried shrimp.

| 12 oz chicken breasts |
| 1½ tablespoons cornstarch |
| 8 egg whites |
| 2½ teaspoons cornstarch |
| Vegetable oil for deep-frying |
| ⅔ cup good stock (see page 56) |
| 1 teaspoon salt |
| 3 tablespoons peas |
| ¼ teaspoon MSG (optional) |

★ ★ ★

Cooking time:
about 30 minutes

Serves: 6–8

Cooking methods:
simmer and stir-
fry, p.42

Usually served as a
starter

STRANGE FLAVOR CHICKEN

I am not certain why the people in Sichuan have come to call this dish 'Strange Flavor' since its hot nutty flavor is quite common-place in the Province. However, the presence of both sugar and vinegar in the sauce does make the final taste somewhat unusual.

PREPARATION AND COOKING

Place salt and ginger in a saucepan with 3¾ cups water. Bring to boil, add chicken and simmer gently for 25 minutes. Drain. Remove bone from drumstick with a sharp knife, making as small a cut as possible. Thinly slice onions and arrange them in serving dish.
Place sesame seeds and peppercorns in wok or small skillet. Stir them over low heat for 2½ minutes, until seeds have browned. Reserve half of this mixture and add remainder to a bowl. Mix in remaining sauce ingredients.

SERVING

Cut meat from the boned drumsticks slantwise into thin circular slices. Sprinkle them with reserved roasted sesame seeds. Arrange chicken over bed of onion on serving dish. Pour over sauce evenly.

| 1 tablespoon salt |
| 3 slices fresh ginger root |
| 8 chicken drumsticks |
| 1 large or 2 medium onions |
| Sauce: |
| ¼ cup sesame seeds |
| 1 teaspoon pounded Sichuan peppercorns |
| 2 tablespoons sesame paste or peanut butter |
| 1 tablespoon sugar |
| 1 tablespoon chili sauce |
| 3 tablespoons vinegar |
| 1½ tablespoons dry sherry |
| 3 tablespoons dark soy sauce |

DUCK

In China, ducks are reared with much greater care and produced in larger concentrations than chickens. Around Nanking, which is situated just south of the Yangtze river, over 40 million ducks are produced annually for a dish called Nanking Pressed Duck, and vast quantities of duck are raised for probably one of the most famous Chinese dishes, Peking Duck.

Duck is not commonly found on the average Chinese dining table and for every duck dish served there are probably as many as ten chicken dishes. In my father's household, which was considered well-to-do, I don't recollect eating duck more than three or four times a year. Chicken was consumed at least once a week.

What has made Peking Duck famous is not the quality of the bird, but the way it is cooked. A typical restaurant specializing in this dish in Peking will cook several thousand duck each day. The bird is roasted in a room-size oven, the heat source for which is a large bed of glowing, red embers. Dozens of ducks are hung on sticks and suspended from just below the ceiling of the oven. The cooking of each bird can be conveniently checked at any time and the stick removed from the heat. The sticks can also be moved around to hotter or cooler parts of the oven; whatever is required. For a chef to make a success of this dish, he needs a thorough knowledge of the heat distribution of his particular oven and of the particular fuel he is using.

4–5 lb duck

3–4 oz lotus seeds

8 medium dried Chinese mushrooms

4–5 oz drained, sliced canned bamboo shoots

4 slices fresh ginger root

2 teaspoons salt

1 chicken bouillon cube

4–5 oz smoked ham (in one piece)

4–5 tablespoons dry sherry

2 tablespoons finely chopped green onions

BASIC WHITE-SIMMERED DUCK

In China, when poultry is not cooked with soy sauce, it is called white-cooked or white-simmered. A variety of ingredients can be added to the poultry to vary the flavor as well as adding substance to the dish. So duck cooked this way is enjoyed as much as the popular red-cooked duck in soy sauce. Although apparently less rich, it is just as flavorsome, and the soup is excellent served during the course of a long meal.

■ PREPARATION ■

Place duck and lotus seeds in large pan of water. Bring to boil and simmer for 7–8 minutes. Drain and transfer to flameproof casserole or pan. Soak dried mushrooms in hot water to cover for 25 minutes. Drain and discard tough stalks. Trim bamboo shoots if necessary.

■ COOKING ■

Add mushrooms, ginger and bamboo shoots to casserole. Pour in 6 cups water and bring to boil. Reduce heat to very low and simmer for 2 hours, turning bird every 30 minutes. Add salt, crumbled bouillon cube, ham and sherry and continue to simmer for another 30 minutes.

★★

Cooking time: 2½ hours

Serves: 6–8

Cooking method: long simmer

Easy to make

A main item for a multi-dish meal

■ SERVING ■

Remove ham, place on chopping board and cut into 1½ × 2½-inch thin slices and use them to garnish the bird in the casserole. Sprinkle duck with the green onion and serve directly from casserole at the table.

BASIC RED-COOKED DUCK

★★

Cooking time: about 2 hours

Serves: 6–8

Cooking method: long simmer

A good centerpiece for a family meal, surrounded by smaller vegetable and savory dishes

4–5lb duck

3 green onions

4 slices fresh ginger root

Sauce:

½ teaspoon salt

6 tablespoons soy sauce

2 tablespoons yellow bean paste

2½ teaspoons sugar

¼ cup dry sherry

■ PREPARATION ■

Wipe duck inside and out with damp cloth. Place breast side up in flameproof casserole and cover with water. Bring to boil for 10 minutes, then pour out about quarter of water. Cut green onions into 1½-inch sections.

■ COOKING ■

Add ginger, green onions, salt, soy sauce, yellow bean paste to casserole. Bring to boil, cover and simmer for about 1 hour, turning duck over a couple of times during cooking. Add sugar and sherry and continue to cook, covered, for another 45 minutes.

■ SERVING ■

Serve duck whole, or chopped through bone into bite-sized pieces. The remaining sauce can be reduced over high heat and thickened with small amount of cornstarch mixed with little water, if liked. Two teaspoons sesame oil can also be added. Pour sauce over whole duck or pieces of duck arranged on large heated plate.

VARIATION
RED-COOKED DUCK
WITH CHESTNUTS AND CHINESE MUSHROOMS

★★

Cooking time: 2¾ hours

Serves: 6–8

Cooking method: long simmer

Serve as Basic Red-cooked Duck

Two traditional ingredients used for stuffing poultry are often added to Red-Cooked Duck; namely chestnuts and dried Chinese mushrooms.

Soak about 8–10 medium dried Chinese mushrooms in hot water to cover for 25 minutes. Drain and discard tough stalks. Cut mushroom caps in half. Place about 12oz chestnuts in pan of boiling water and simmer for about 15 minutes. Peel. Both these ingredients can withstand lengthy cooking, so add to casserole at beginning of cooking. They add to the flavor of the dish and complement the duck. Serve with rice and steamed buns (see page 240), the staple food of the North.

2 tablespoons soy sauce

1½ tablespoons yellow bean
    paste

1½ tablespoons oyster sauce

4–4½ lb duck

2–3 large sheets lotus leaf

Stuffing:

1 cup glutinous rice

2 medium onions

6 medium dried Chinese
    mushrooms

2 tablespoons dried shrimp

3 slices fresh ginger root

2 garlic cloves

¼ cup vegetable oil

3–4 tablespoons diced ham

7–8 fresh chestnuts

4 tablespoons drained, diced,
    canned bamboo shoots

1 teaspoon salt

2 tablespoons good stock
    (see page 56)

1½ tablespoons hoisin sauce

LOTUS LEAF-WRAPPED LONG-STEAMED DUCK

■ PREPARATION ■

Mix together soy sauce, yellow bean paste, and oyster sauce. Use to rub inside and outside of duck. Leave to marinate for 30 minutes. Soak lotus leaves in warm water for about 3 minutes, then drain. Soak glutinous rice in cold water to cover for 30 minutes, then drain. Peel and finely dice onions. Soak dried mushrooms and dried shrimp separately in hot water to cover for 25 minutes. Drain and discard tough mushroom stalks. Cut caps into quarters. Coarsely chop shrimp and ginger. Crush garlic.

■ COOKING ■

Heat oil in wok or skillet. When hot, stir-fry onions, ginger, garlic, shrimp and mushrooms over medium heat for 3–4 minutes. Add ham, chestnuts and bamboo shoots and stir-fry for another 2 minutes. Finally, add rice, salt, stock and hoisin sauce and stir-fry for another 2 minutes. Leave to cool. Stuff all stir-fried ingredients into cavity of duck and sew up to secure. Wrap bird in lotus leaves, then wrap in large sheet of foil. Place foil parcel in steamer and steam for about 3 hours.

■ SERVING ■

Unwrap the duck at the table – the meat will be tender enough to be taken apart with a pair of chopsticks. Spoon out the stuffing and serve with the duck.

★ ★ ★ ★ ★

Cooking time:
about 3 hours

Serves: 6–8

Cooking methods:
stir-fry p.42 and
long steam

A principal dish
for a multi-dish
dinner party

stir-fry p.42

4–5 lb duck

1½ tablespoons soy sauce

1½ tablespoons vegetable oil

2 medium onions

3 pieces star anise

2 pieces dried tangerine peel

4 slices fresh ginger root

Sauce:

1½ tablespoons cornstarch
    blended with
    3 tablespoons water

1 teaspoon salt

1½ tablespoons soy sauce

1½ tablespoons oyster sauce

Lettuce leaves

WHITE-SIMMERED DOUBLE-COOKED TANGERINE DUCK

■ PREPARATION ■

Dry duck both inside and out and rub evenly with 1½ tablespoons soy sauce and oil. Peel and thinly slice onions. Place in cavity of duck with star anise. Soak tangerine peel in warm water for about 15 minutes, then break into small pieces.

■ COOKING ■

Put duck on wire rack over roasting dish. Place in preheated oven at 200°C, 400°F and roast for 30 minutes,

★ ★ ★ ★

Cooking time:
about 2 hours

Serves: 6–8

Cooking methods:
roast and simmer

A main item for a
multi-dish meal

turning over once. Heat 5 cups water in large casserole or pan and, when boiling, add duck, together with tangerine peel and ginger. Bring to boil and simmer gently for 1½ hours. Turn duck over every 30 minutes. Remove duck from casserole and leave to cool. Cut into large bite-sized pieces. Strain liquid from pan and reduce to half volume over high heat. Stir in blended cornstarch, salt, soy sauce and oyster sauce. When liquid has thickened, pour it into 2 small bowls.

■ SERVING ■

Arrange the duck pieces on top of lettuce leaves. Use the 2 bowls of liquid as dipping sauce for the duck.

★ ★ ★ ★

Cooking time: about 50 minutes

Serves: 6–8

Cooking methods: simmer and deep-fry, p.45

Interesting to eat between stir-fried dishes

KOU SHOA DEEP-FRIED BONELESS DUCK

4–5 lb duck

6 cups cooking sauce (see page 174)

Vegetable oil for deep-frying

Batter:

1 egg

5 tablespoons cornstarch

2 tablespoons self-rising flour

■ PREPARATION ■

Parboil duck in pan of boiling water for about 5 minutes, then drain. Mix ingredients for batter in bowl until smooth.

■ COOKING ■

Heat cooking sauce in heavy pan. Add duck and simmer gently for 45 minutes. Remove duck and drain thoroughly. Allow duck to cool for 30 minutes, then remove meat from bones, leaving meat in large pieces if possible. Turn meat in batter mixture until evenly coated. Heat oil in wok or deep-fryer. When hot, fry coated duck for about 5 minutes. Drain.

■ SERVING ■

Place the large duck pieces on a chopping board and cut each into 3–4 pieces. Place small bowl of Duck Sauce (see page 178) in center of a heated dish and surround with the fried duck pieces. Each piece of duck should be dipped in the sauce before eating.

Melon Chicken (*left*), an
attractive party dish; recipe
page 165.
Aromatic and Crispy
Duck (*above*), an
entertaining dish served
and eaten as Peking Duck;
recipe page 174.

4–5 lb duck

Vegetable oil for deep-frying

Cooking sauce:

6 cups good stock (see page 56)

6 tablespoons sugar

6 slices fresh ginger root

2/3 cup soy sauce

4 teaspoons yellow bean paste

6 tablespoons dry sherry

6 pieces star anise

1/2 teaspoon five spice powder

1/4 teaspoon pepper

Garnish:

Radish rose

AROMATIC AND CRISPY DUCK

This dish is served and eaten in the same way as Peking Duck – wrapped in a pancake along with shredded green onions and cucumber and duck sauce. In a restaurant, this dish can be much more conveniently served than Peking Duck because a quantity of ducks can be precooked in the marinade or cooking sauce and put aside. When required, they are simply deep-fried for 10–11 minutes and served; because of the final deep-frying, the duck meat will invariably be crisper and without the care and precise timing required when preparing and cooking traditional Peking Duck.

PREPARATION

Mix ingredients for cooking sauce together in large saucepan. Clean duck thoroughly and cut in half down backbone. Place into liquid and submerge.

COOKING

Simmer duck gently for 2 hours. Remove from cooking liquid and leave to cool. When required to serve, heat oil, place duck gently in oil and fry for 10–11 minutes. Drain well.

SERVING

Place duck on large heated platter. Serve by taking meat off the carcass at the table and wrapping it in pancakes. For the preparation of pancakes and duck sauce, see Peking Duck on page 178.

★★★★★

Cooking time: 2 hours 10 minutes

Serves: 6–8

Cooking method: simmer and deep-fry, p.45

Needs preparation beforehand

A main dish for a multi-dish dinner party

Illustrated on p.173

---

about 1 cup skinned, boneless duck meat, breast and leg

3 young leeks

3 slices fresh ginger root

2 garlic cloves

1/4 cup vegetable oil

1 1/2 teaspoons salt

1 tablespoons shortening or lard

2 teaspoons soy sauce

2 teaspoons sugar

2 tablespoons good stock (see page 56)

2 tablespoons prepared English mustard

QUICK-FRIED DUCK IN SOY AND MUSTARD SAUCE

PREPARATION

Cut duck meat into 2 × 1-inch strips. Wash and cut leeks slantwise into 1-inch sections. Shred ginger. Crush garlic.

COOKING

Heat 3 tablespoons oil in wok or skillet. When hot, fry ginger and salt over high heat for 10 seconds. Add duck meat and stir-fry for 1 minute. Remove meat with perforated spoon and put to one side. Add remaining oil and reheat. Stir-fry garlic and leeks for 1 1/2 minutes, then remove with perforated spoon and reserve. Add shorten-

★★

Cooking time: about 8 minutes

Serves: 4–6

Cooking method: stir-fry, p.42

Easy to make

A very tasty dish which complements most others

ing to wok or pan. When melted, add soy sauce, sugar and stock. Stir together until creamy bubbling mixture, then return duck meat to pan. Stir into sauce, then add leek mixture and toss quickly with duck.

■ SERVING ■

Remove contents from the wok to a heated dish. Spread the mustard over evenly and serve.

★ ★ ★ ★ ★

Cooking time: about 1½ hours, plus hanging time

Serves: 6–8

Cooking method: roast

Preparation requires attention

Excellent with any combination of dishes

CANTONESE ROAST DUCK

Cantonese roast duck is the duck most often seen hanging in the windows of Cantonese restaurants abroad. The duck is filled with a sauce and basted with a different mixture several times during roasting.

■ PREPARATION ■

Wash and dry duck. Rub duck inside and out with salt. Hang it up to dry for 2½–3 hours. Shred ginger. Chop garlic. Coarsely chop green onions. Mix ginger, garlic and green onions together with remaining filling ingredients.

Tie neck of duck securely so that there is no leakage. Place duck in large bowl, back side up, and pour in filling mixture. Sew skin up securely. Mix basting ingredients together.

■ COOKING ■

Place duck on a wire rack over roasting pan filled with 1½ inches of water. (In a restaurant, the bird is normally hung up to roast, tail end up.) Brush duck with basting mixture and roast in preheated oven at 200°C, 400°F for 30 minutes. Brush again with basting mixture, reduce oven temperature to 190°C, 375°F and roast for 30 minutes. Brush duck once more, reduce oven temperature to 180°C, 350°F and roast for further 20 minutes.

■ SERVING ■

Drain liquid from duck into large bowl. Place duck on chopping board and chop through bones into 3 × 2-inch pieces. Reassemble duck on heated serving dish. Boil liquid from inside duck in small pan until reduced by quarter. Pour this sauce over duck. Serve hot or cold.

Ingredients
1 duck, about 3½ lb
3 teaspoons salt

Filling:

3 slices fresh ginger root
3 garlic cloves
2 green onions
3 tablespoons soy sauce
¾ tablespoon sugar
½ tablespoon pounded Sichuan peppercorns
⅔ cup good stock (see page 56)
1 tablespoon yellow bean paste
2 pieces star anise
1 tablespoon broken dried tangerine peel

Baste:

⅔ cup boiling water
2 tablespoons vinegar
2 tablespoons soy sauce
2 tablespoons honey

Peking Duck, the famous
dish for special occasions
that is such fun to eat.
Slices of Peking Duck are
wrapped in Chinese
pancakes with cucumber,
green onions and sauce;
recipe page 178.

3–4 lb duck

1 medium cucumber

1 bunch green onions

Duck sauce:

2–3 tablespoons vegetable oil

7–8 tablespoons yellow bean
    paste

3–4 tablespoons sugar

1 teaspoon sesame oil

Chinese pancakes

Garnish:

Radish rose

PEKING DUCK

Peking duck is now a world famous dish, partly due to the way it is eaten and also the delicious flavors – a combination of crispy duck, fresh vegetables and tasty sauce all wrapped individually in Chinese pancakes.

■ PREPARATION ■

Wash and dry duck thoroughly. Hang it up to dry in a well-ventilated place overnight to dry skin (at least 4–5 hours or if in a great hurry use a hair drier). Cut cucumber into matchstick-sized shreds. Cut green onions into similar-sized shreds.

■ COOKING ■

Place duck on wire rack over roasting dish. Place in preheated oven at 200°C, 400°F for 1 hour 10 minutes. It is important to make sure the oven is correctly preheated for a good result. Do not open the oven door during roasting; the duck requires no basting.

Meanwhile, to make Duck Sauce, heat oil in small saucepan. When hot, add yellow bean paste and stir over low heat for 2–3 minutes. Add sugar and 3 tablespoons water and stir for another 2–3 minutes. Finally, add sesame oil and stir for further 30 seconds.

■ SERVING ■

Slice off all crispy skin with sharp knife into 2-inch pieces and arrange on heated plate. Carve meat into similar-sized pieces and arrange on separate heated plate. Brush each pancake with 1–1½ teaspoons duck sauce, and add a little shredded cucumber and green onion. Place a little duck skin and meat overlapping on each pancake. Roll up, turning up one end of pancake to stop filling falling out. Eat using the fingers.

★★★★

Cooking time:
1 hour 10 minutes,
plus drying time

Serves: 6–8

Cooking method:
roast

**Care is needed
with preparation
and timing**

**Excellent
centerpiece for a
dinner party**

**Illustrated on
pp.176–177**

---

4 cups all-purpose flour

1½ teaspoons sugar

1 teaspoon oil

CHINESE
PANCAKES

■ PREPARATION ■

Sift flour into bowl and stir in sugar, oil and 1 cup warm water. Stir and mix with pair of chopsticks or wooden spoon until smooth. Knead dough on lightly floured surface for about 5 minutes using a little more flour, if necessary, to make smooth, non-sticky dough, then form into 2 even 'sausages'. Cut each sausage into 8–10

★★★

Cooking time:
about 3 minutes
per 2 pancakes

Makes: 16–20

Cooking method:
dry-fry

**These versatile
pancakes can hold
all kinds of fillings**

pieces and roll each piece into a ball. Flatten each ball into a round. Brush top of each round with oil and place another round on top to form a sandwich. Roll pancakes together with small rolling pin into flat pancake about 6 inches in diameter. Repeat process until all dough is rolled out.

■ COOKING ■

Heat dry skillet over medium heat. When hot, place 'pancake sandwich' in pan and shake pan around. After 1½ minutes, turn pancake over with fish slice and cook other side in same way. The pancake should bubble and puff slightly. The pancake is ready when brown spots begin to show on the underside. Now, very gently peel pancake sandwich apart into 2 pancakes. Fold each pancake in half and stack under damp cloth. You can heat them in a steamer for a few minutes to soften before serving, if necessary.

DUCK CARCASS SOUP

★ ★

Cooking time: about 30 minutes

Serves: 6–8

Cooking method: boil

Easy to prepare

A good dish to end a meal

1 duck carcass

6–7 cups water

2 lb Chinese white cabbage

Salt and pepper to taste

Duck Carcass Soup is the customary soup to serve after a Peking Duck dinner. In the winter in Peking, where the temperature seldom rises above freezing, a large hot bowl of soup is ideal food.

This soup is cooked and prepared in a short time. Simply boil the duck carcass in water for 15 minutes. Cut white cabbage into 3-inch sections and add to the soup. Continue to cook for another 15 minutes. The only seasoning required is salt and pepper added to taste. If liked, 1 tablespoon dried shrimp, 2 tablespoons wine vinegar and a crumbled chicken bouillon cube can be included. During the cooking, keep the soup boiling. The resulting soup will be very white. If not white enough, add a couple of tablespoons of milk. This soup is relatively light and is much appreciated after a rich meal. When the bowl of soup is drunk at the end of a lengthy meal, it should bring beads of perspiration to the forehead of every diner, an indication of the comfort and satisfaction derived from life and eating.

MEAT

Peking Mongolian Hot Pot (*left*); recipe page 211.
Sichuan Yu-hsiang Shredded Pork; recipe page 190.

肉
類

PORK

Pork is used for cooking more frequently than any other type of meat in China, partly because it is so versatile. It can be short-cooked, quick stir-fried, or long steam-braised to produce highly delectable dishes. Pork can be cooked for its fresh sweet savoriness, its rich succulent tenderness or its crisp, crackling qualities; and its neutral flavor means that it can impart taste to other foods as well as receive and absorb them from numerous other ingredients.

The Chinese are thus unconcerned by the fattiness of pork, the effects of which are more than offset by their high intake of cereals and low consumption of dairy products. The problem of cholesterol – Western man's dietary preoccupation – has not arisen there.

The Chinese consider lean meat to be too dry for prolonged cooking, and prefer cuts like pork shoulder (called 'five flower pork' by the Chinese, meaning that the meat consists of five layers of skin, lean, fat, lean, fat) which are used for long-steaming or stewing. This type of cooking produces the best gravies, which are wonderful to consume with rice and plain-cooked vegetables. The following pork dishes are probably the most commonly cooked in China and, therefore, probably the most widely eaten dishes in the world.

1¾ lb pork shoulder or fresh pork sides
1½ tablespoons dark soy sauce
Vegetable oil for deep-frying
3 tablespoons light soy sauce
3 slices fresh ginger root
1¼ cups good stock (see page 56)
3 tablespoons dry sherry
1½ tablespoons sugar
3 pieces star anise

■ LONG-BRAISED TUNG PO SOY PORK ■

Su Tung Po, one of China's foremost poets, is reputed to have invented this dish, hence it bears his name.

■ PREPARATION ■
Cut pork through skin into 4 equal pieces. Plunge them in boiling water for about 5 minutes, then drain. Rub pork, especially skin, with dark soy sauce. Heat oil in wok or deep-fryer. When hot, fry the pork pieces over a medium heat for about 3 minutes. Drain.

■ COOKING ■
Place 4 pieces of pork, skin-side down, in flat-bottomed casserole and add light soy sauce, ginger, stock, sherry, sugar and star anise. Bring to boil, turn pork pieces over several times. Place open casserole into steamer, with pork skin-side down, for about 2 hours until tender.

■ SERVING ■
Serve the pork, skin-side up, in a heated deep dish, if liked, arranging 3 pieces in the bottom and the fourth piece on top across the others. Pour over the remaining sauce. The pork should be tender enough to break with a pair of chopsticks.

★ ★ ★

Cooking time: good 2 hours
Serves: 5–6
Cooking methods: deep-fry p.45 and braise
Quite easy to prepare but takes time to cook
Excellent served with rice and accompanied by lighter dishes and vegetables

CRISPY FIVE SPICE PORK

★★★

Cooking time:
about 10 minutes

Serves: 5–6

Cooking methods:
deep-fry p.45 and
stir-fry p.42

**An excellent
starter**

1 lb lean pork	
1 teaspoon salt	
½ teaspoon five spice powder	
1½ tablespoons cornstarch	
2 slices fresh ginger root	
2 garlic cloves	
Vegetable oil for deep-frying	
1½ tablespoons soy sauce	
2 teaspoons granulated sugar	
2 teaspoons sea salt	
1½ teaspoons pounded Sichuan peppercorns	

Wrapping:

10–12 well-shaped lettuce leaves	
6 tablespoons Peking Duck Sauce (see page 178)	

■ PREPARATION ■

Cut pork into thick strips. Sprinkle and rub with salt, five spice powder and cornstarch. Leave to season for 30 minutes. Finely chop ginger and garlic.

■ COOKING ■

Heat oil in wok or deep-fryer. When hot, fry half pork strips over medium heat for 3½ minutes. Drain and place in a bowl. Fry remaining pork strips for 3½ minutes, then drain and add to bowl. Add soy sauce and sugar to pork, mixing well. Pour away oil to use for other purposes, leaving 2 tablespoons. Reheat wok or pan. When hot, stir in ginger, garlic, sea salt and pepper over medium heat for 25 seconds. Pour once-fried and seasoned pork into pan. Turn and stir around quickly so that pork is evenly coated by spicy ingredients. Turn, toss and stir for 1 minute.

■ SERVING ■

Transfer to a heated serving dish. To serve, take a lettuce leaf, add a portion of pork, spoon on some duck sauce, then fold and wrap lettuce up enclosing pork. Eat with fingers.

CRISPY SKIN ROAST PORK

★★

Cooking time:
1½ hours, plus
seasoning time

Serves: 5–6

Cooking method:
roast

**Takes a little time,
but easy to prepare**

**Excellent with
rice, accompanied
by other savory
dishes**

2½ lb pork shoulder or fresh pork sides	
1½ teaspoons ground ginger	
3½ teaspoons salt	
1 tablespoon honey	
1½ tablespoons light soy sauce	

■ PREPARATION ■

Score pork skin in 1-inch diamond pattern and rub in ginger and salt. Leave to season for 2 hours. Bring large pan of water to boil, add pork and simmer for about 5 minutes. Remove, drain and wipe very dry.

■ COOKING ■

Put pork on rack with skin side down. Place in preheated oven at 200°C, 400°F and roast for about 45 minutes. Turn pork and paint on mixture of honey and soy sauce. Reduce oven temperature to 180°C, 350°F and roast again for about 45 minutes. By this time skin should be very crisp and brown.

■ SERVING ■

Chop pork into bite-sized pieces. The crispy skin and tenderness of pork fat makes an interesting combination. Soy sauce may be used as dip for pork.

Pearl-studded Pork Balls
(*above*), a steamed dish of
pork balls coated with rice;
recipe page 194.
Steamed Ground Pork
with Chinese Sausages
(*right*), an easy family dish
to serve with rice; recpie
page 187.

1½ lb meaty pork spareribs

2 tablespoons salted black beans

1 medium onion

2 garlic cloves

2 tablespoons vegetable oil

½ teaspoon salt

2 tablespoons good stock (see page 56)

2 teaspoons sugar

1½ tablespoons light soy sauce

1½ tablespoons dry sherry

1½ tablèspoons cornstarch

1½ tablespoons seeded chopped red chilies

CANTONESE STEAMED SPARERIBS WITH BLACK BEANS

Chinese-style spareribs differ from those usually served in the West mainly in that they are cut shorter, into 1-1½-inch sections, so they can be eaten whole and the bone spat out! Westerners need much practice to perfect this technique, if they wish to acquire the skill at all. It also means that the cooking time is considerably shorter.

■ PREPARATION ■

Chop spareribs into 1-1½ inch pieces. Place in large pan of water, bring to boil and simmer for 2 minutes. Drain well and place spareribs into bowl. Soak black beans in cold water to cover for 5 minutes. Drain and crush lightly. Peel and finely chop onion. Crush garlic. Heat oil in wok or skillet. When hot, stir-fry onion for about 30 seconds. Add black beans, salt, stock, sugar, soy sauce and sherry and stir-fry for about 15 seconds. Pour mixture into bowl with spareribs and toss together. Mix in cornstarch.

■ COOKING ■

Transfer spareribs to heatproof dish and sprinkle on chili and garlic. Place in steamer and cook for 25–30 minutes.

■ SERVING ■

Spareribs are often served as a dim sum item in tea houses, where they are eaten as nibbles to accompany drinks. Included as part of a multi-course meal, this dish makes a delicious hot starter.

★ ★ ★

Cooking time: about 30 minutes

Serves: 5–6

Cooking method: steam, p.49

Ideal snack or starter

Meat balls:

8 medium dried Chinese mushrooms

4 oz pork fat

4 oz pork skin

5 water chestnuts

2 green onions

1½ lb ground lean pork

2 tablespoons cornstarch

1 egg

1½ teaspoons salt

1½ tablespoons dark soy sauce

1 teaspoon yellow bean paste

LION'S HEAD MEAT BALLS IN CLEAR BROTH

'Lion's head' meat balls differ from ordinary meat balls in that they are much larger, cooked for much longer and are very succulent when prepared well.

■ PREPARATION ■

Soak dried mushrooms in hot water to cover for 25 minutes. Drain. Discard tough stalks and finely chop half mushroom caps. Mince pork fat and skin or grind briefly in a food processor. Chop the water chestnuts and green onions. Mix all ingredients for meat balls together in a

★ ★ ★ ★

Cooking time: about 1½ hours

Serves: 6–8

Cooking methods: deep-fry p.45 and simmer

Rather time-consuming

Serve with rice. Goes well with most dishes

Illustrated on p.192

large bowl, except whole mushroom caps. Form mixture into 3-5 large meat balls. Heat oil in wok or deep-fryer. When hot, add meat balls, one by one, and fry each one gently for 6-7 minutes until brown all over. Drain on absorbent kitchen paper. Cut Chinese cabbage into large sections.

■ COOKING ■

Heat stock and whole mushroom caps in flameproof casserole or Chinese clay pot. When boiling, add meat balls. Cover and simmer gently for 1 hour. Add Chinese cabbage sections, cover and continue to simmer for about 20 minutes.

■ SERVING ■

Place meat balls on large heated serving dish and serve soup separately. They are too large to eat whole and need to be eaten broken into quarters or pieces, then accompanied by rice.

5 tablespoons finely chopped shrimp, fresh or frozen
Vegetable oil for deep-frying
1 Chinese white cabbage
3¾ cups good stock (see page 56)

★★

Cooking time: 30 minutes

Serves: 6-8

Cooking method: steam, p.49

Easy to prepare

Good family fare

Illustrated on p.185

STEAMED GROUND PORK WITH CHINESE SAUSAGES

■ PREPARATION ■

Cut sausages slantwise into 1½-inch sections. Mix pork with salt, pepper, soy sauce, cornstarch and egg. Blend thoroughly until smooth. Cut cauliflower into 2-inch florets. Space cauliflower evenly on bottom of deep heatproof dish. Cover with thick layer of ground pork. Stud top of pork evenly with pieces of sausage.

■ COOKING ■

Place dish in steamer and steam for 30 minutes.

2 Chinese wind-dried sausages
1 lb ground pork
1 teaspoon salt
Pepper to taste
1½ tablespoons light soy sauce
1½ tablespoons cornstarch
1 egg
1 cauliflower

Deep–fried Crispy Fingers of Pork (*above*);
recipe page 191.
Opposite
Capital Spareribs (*above left*); recipe page 196.
Sichuan Double Cooked Pork (*above right*);
recipe page 264.
Sichuan Hot Crispy-Fried Shredded Beef (*center
left*); recipe page 203.
Sliced Beef in Black Bean and Chili Sauce (*center
right*); recipe page 201.
Quick-fried Shredded Beef with Ginger and
Onions (*below left*); recipe page 201.
Soy-braised Pork – Long Cooked Version
(*below right*), dried squid and Sichuan pickles can
be used to flavor this dish; recipe page 196.

8 oz boneless pork loin

2 green onions

2 slices fresh ginger root

2 fresh chilies

1 garlic clove, crushed

3–4 dried Chinese mushrooms

1/4 cup drained, canned bamboo shoots

2 egg whites

2 teaspoons cornstarch

Vegetable oil for deep-frying

1/2 teaspoon salt

1 tablespoon yellow bean paste

1 tablespoon good stock (see page 56)

1 tablespoon dry sherry or rice wine

1 1/2 tablespoons soy sauce

1 1/2 tablespoons vinegar

1/2 teaspoon white pepper

2 teaspoons cornstarch blended with 2 tablespoons cold stock

1 teaspoon sesame oil

2 teaspoons red chili oil or chili sauce

1 teaspoon crushed Sichuan peppercorns

SICHUAN YU-HSIANG SHREDDED PORK

■ PREPARATION ■

Shred pork finely. Shred green onions, ginger, chilies, discarding seeds, and garlic. Soak dried mushrooms in boiling water to cover for 25 minutes. Drain and discard tough stalks. Shred mushroom caps. Shred bamboo shoots. Put pork in bowl with egg whites, cornstarch and 1 tablespoon oil. Toss together very well.

■ COOKING ■

Heat oil in wok or deep-fryer. When medium hot, fry pork for about 1 1/2 minutes. Add bamboo shoots and mushrooms and stir for about 1 1/2 minutes. Drain and pour away oil to use for other purposes. Reheat wok or pan with about 1 tablespoon oil. When hot, stir-fry ginger, garlic, green onions, salt and chilies for 1 minute. Add bean paste, stock, sherry or wine, soy sauce, vinegar and white pepper. Stir and bring to boil. Add shredded pork and vegetables to wok. Thicken sauce with blended cornstarch. At the last minute, trickle over sesame oil and toss together.

■ SERVING ■

Transfer to a heated plate and sprinkle on the red chili oil and crushed peppercorns.

★★★

Cooking time: about 10 minutes

Serves: 4–6

Cooking methods: deep-fry p.45 and stir-fry p.42

A spicy dish. Serve with rice and vegetables and other savory dishes

Illustrated on p.181

3–4 lotus leaves

1 1/2 lb pork shoulder or fresh pork sides

2 tablespoons light soy sauce

Vegetable oil for deep-frying

2 slices fresh ginger root

2 green onions

1 1/2 tablespoons oyster sauce

1/2 teaspoon salt

1 1/2 teaspoons sugar

1/4 teaspoon MSG (optional)

2 garlic cloves

3 tablespoons ground rice

1 1/2 teaspoons sesame oil

STEAMED GROUND RICE-PORK IN LOTUS LEAVES

Although not considered haute cuisine, this is a prized dish in domestic cooking, beloved of all the connoisseurs of pork, which must be 98 per cent of the Chinese population.

■ PREPARATION ■

Immerse lotus leaves in warm water for 3–4 minutes to soften. Bring large pan of water to boil, add pork and simmer for 10 minutes. Remove and drain. Rub pork with soy sauce. Heat oil in wok or deep-fryer. When hot, fry pork for about 3 minutes. Drain. Cut pork into 1/2-inch slices. Finely chop ginger and green onions. Mix together oyster sauce, salt, sugar, ginger, monosodium

★★★★

Cooking time: about 3 hours

Serves: 6–7

Cooking methods: deep-fry p.45 and steam p.49

Good family fare

Illustrated on p.209

glutamate, if using, garlic and green onions. Add ground rice and sesame oil. Mix in pork slices and make sure they are evenly coated. Pile slices neatly into stack, then wrap in softened lotus leaves. Tie securely with string.

■ COOKING ■

Place parcel in heatproof dish, put in steamer and steam for 3 hours.

■ SERVING ■

When ready, drain away excess water and serve straight from the lotus leaves. The pork will be tender and the ground rice will have soaked up any fattiness.

Note: The pork mixture can be wrapped in individual lotus leaf parcels.

★ ★ ★

Cooking time: about 4–5 minutes per batch

Serves: 5–6

Cooking method: deep-fry, p.45

Quite easy to prepare

Good starter for a party meal

Illustrated on p.189

DEEP-FRIED CRISPY FINGERS OF PORK

■ PREPARATION ■

Cut pork into finger-sized strips. Mix salt, pepper, ginger, wine or sherry and sesame oil together. Add pork and mix thoroughly. Leave to marinate for 10 minutes. To make batter, mix egg, flour and cornstarch together. To make dip sauce, heat oil in wok or pan. When hot, add onion, garlic, chili and ginger and stir for a few seconds. Add rest of dip sauce ingredients. Bring to boil, then pour into small heatproof bowl.

■ COOKING ■

Heat oil in wok or deep-fryer. When very hot, dip pork fingers in batter and put gently into oil. Fry for about 3 minutes. Drain. Allow oil to reheat, then fry pork again for 30 seconds. Drain.

■ SERVING ■

Arrange pork fingers on heated plate and serve with dip sauce. Sweet and sour sauce (see page 197) can also be used with these pork fingers, or a simple dip sauce of shredded fresh ginger root in vinegar.

1½ lb lean pork

1 teaspoon salt

¼ teaspoon pepper

½ teaspoon ground ginger

1 tablespoon rice wine or dry sherry

1 teaspoon sesame oil

Vegetable oil for deep-frying

Batter:

1 egg

5 tablespoons all-purpose flour

1½ tablespoons cornstarch

Dip sauce:

1½ tablespoons vegetable oil

1½ tablespoons chopped green onions

2 teaspoons crushed garlic

2 teaspoons chopped fresh chili

1½ tablespoons chopped fresh ginger root

5 tablespoons good stock (see page 56)

2 tablespoons vinegar

2 tablespoons light soy sauce

1 teaspoon salt

1 teaspoon sugar

Garnish:

Radish rose

Halved lemon slices

191

Quick-fried Shredded
Pork in Capital Sauce
(*above*), spoonfuls of pork
and rice can be wrapped in
lettuce leaves to eat with
the fingers; recipe page
193.
Lion's Head Meat Balls in
Clear Broth (*right*), serve
with rice to mop up the
juices; recipe page 186.

BARBECUE SPARERIBS

Barbecue Spareribs evolved in the West comparatively recently. Here Chinese ingredients and cooking methods are used to produce spareribs to suit the Western palate.

■ PREPARATION ■

Separate spareribs. Parboil them in pan of boiling water for 5 minutes. Drain, sprinkle and rub them with salt and pepper. Heat oil in flameproof casserole. When hot, stir in ginger for 1½ minutes, then add ribs. Turn and stir ribs for 4–5 minutes. Drain away all excess oil. Cut green onions into ¼-inch sections.

■ COOKING ■

Add sauce ingredients to casserole, partly submerging ribs. Bring to boil, stir and turn ribs in sauce over high heat for 5 minutes. Reduce heat to low, cover and cook for 40 minutes, turning ribs after 20 minutes. If there is a fair quantity of the sauce left in casserole, raise heat to high and turn ribs in thickening sauce until sauce is well reduced. Sprinkle ribs with green onions and serve.

★★★

Cooking time: 50 minutes

Serves: 5-6

Cooking methods: stir-fry p.42 and stew p.46

Quite easy to prepare

Can be served alone or as a starter

To reduce sauce, p.46

3-3½ lb pork spareribs

1½ teaspoons salt

Pepper to taste

6 tablespoons vegetable oil

3-4 slices fresh ginger root

3 green onions

Sauce:

2½ cups good stock (see page 56)

1 chicken bouillon cube

3 tablespoons soy sauce

1 tablespoon yellow bean sauce

3 pieces star anise

6 tablespoons dry sherry

2 tablespoons sugar

QUICK-FRIED SHREDDED PORK

IN CAPITAL SAUCE

■ PREPARATION ■

Cut pork into matchstick-sized shreds. Mix pork with salt, cornstarch and egg white. Cut green onions into ½-inch shreds.

■ COOKING ■

Heat oil in wok or deep-fryer. When hot, add pork, separating all shreds, and stir-fry for about 2 minutes. Drain and pour off oil to use for other purposes. Meanwhile, heat 3 tablespoons oil in wok or pan. When hot, add yellow bean paste, sugar, soy sauce and sherry. Stir until smooth and glossy, then stir in blended cornstarch. Bring back to boil and add pork. Stir in green onions and sprinkle over the sesame oil.

■ SERVING ■

Serve on crispy rice flour noodles. If liked, wrap spoonfuls of pork and rice in lettuce leaves to eat with fingers.

★★

Cooking time: about 6 minutes

Serves: 4-6

Cooking method: stir-fry, p.42

Easy to prepare

Goes well with other dishes for family or party meals

Illustrated opposite

Yellow bean paste, stir-fried in oil with sugar and soy sauce, etc, is often referred to as Capital sauce as it is very popular in Peking.

---

12 oz boneless pork loin

½ teaspoon salt

3 tablespoons cornstarch

1 egg white

2 green onions

Vegetable oil for deep-frying

Capital sauce:

3 tablespoons vegetable oil

1½ tablespoons yellow bean paste

1 tablespoon sugar

½ tablespoon dark soy sauce

1 tablespoon dry sherry

½ tablespoon cornstarch blended with 2 tablespoons water

1 teaspoon sesame oil

1⅓ cups glutinous rice

2 tablespoons dried shrimp

1 lb ground pork

1 teaspoon salt

1½ tablespoons finely chopped onion

1 tablespoon finely chopped fresh ginger root

1 tablespoon light soy sauce

1 egg

2 tablespoons cornstarch

PEARL-STUDDED PORK BALLS

★ ★ ★ ★

Cooking time: 25 minutes

Serves: 4–6

Cooking method: steam, p.49

Takes time to prepare

Serve with a party meal

Illustrated on p.184

■ PREPARATION ■

Soak rice in cold water to cover for at least 8 hours. Drain well. Soak dried shrimp in hot water to cover for 25 minutes. Drain and finely chop. Place pork in bowl and add dried shrimp, salt, onion, ginger, soy sauce, egg and 1½ tablespoons water. Combine thoroughly. Mix soaked rice with cornstarch. Form pork mixture into even-sized balls and wet each ball lightly with water. Roll balls in rice mixture and pat on lightly to get an even covering.

■ COOKING ■

Arrange balls on steaming tray in steamer and steam vigorously for about 25 minutes.

■ SERVING ■

Serve on a heated dish and accompany with either a good quality soy sauce, tomato sauce or other mixed dip sauces (see page 211)

---

4 medium dried Chinese mushrooms

¼ cup dried shrimp

2 green onions

2 slices fresh ginger root

2 water chestnuts

1 lb ground pork

1½ tablespoons dry sherry

2 eggs

½ teaspoon MSG (optional)

1 teaspoon salt

Pepper to taste

Vegetable oil for deep-frying

CRISPY MEAT BALLS

★ ★ ★

Cooking time: 5 minutes per batch

Serves: 6–7

Cooking method: deep-fry, p.45

Fairly quick and easy to prepare

A good starter for a party meal

While the meat balls in the Pearl-Studded Pork Balls are soft due to being steamed, these are crisp and crunchy as they are deep-fried. Crispy Meat Balls are smaller and suitable for accompanying drinks but they are also good served with boiled rice.

■ PREPARATION ■

Soak dried mushrooms and dried shrimp separately in hot water to cover for 25 minutes. Drain. Discard tough mushroom stalks and chop caps roughly. Chop shrimp, green onions, ginger and water chestnuts. Mix pork, mushrooms, shrimp, ginger, green onions, water chestnuts, sherry, eggs, monosodium glutamate, if using, salt and pepper in large bowl. Combine thoroughly, then form into small balls.

■ COOKING ■

Heat oil in wok or deep-fryer. When hot, add meat balls, in 1-2 batches, and fry over medium heat for about 5 minutes until golden brown. Drain.

LONG-STEAMED PORK HOCK

★ ★ ★ ★

Cooking time:
about 2¾ hours

Serves: 8–10

Cooking methods:
simmer, deep-fry
p.45 and steam p.49

Lengthy cooking

**Impressive dish for
a party meal**

■ PREPARATION ■

Bring large pan of water to boil. Add pork hock and boil for about 5 minutes, then remove and drain. Rub skin and flesh with dark soy sauce. Heat oil in wok or deep-fryer. When hot, fry pork for about 5 minutes. Drain.

■ COOKING ■

Place pork hock in flameproof casserole and add light soy sauce, ginger, stock, salt, sugar and star anise. Bring to boil and simmer for about 5 minutes. Turn hock over and put on lid. Place casserole into a steamer, and cook for 2½ hours, turning hock over every 30 minutes.

■ SERVING ■

Serve the hock in a heated deep bowl with the sauce poured over the top. If liked, stir-fry about 1 lb spinach, then arrange it around the hock. A knife may be used to carve off the meat into bite-sized pieces but usually the meat is tender enough to remove with a pair of chopsticks.

1 pork hock with skin on, about 5 lb before boning; ask the butcher to remove the bone
2 tablespoons dark soy sauce
Vegetable oil for deep-frying
¼ cup light soy sauce
3–4 slices fresh ginger root
2½ cups good stock (see page 56)
½ teaspoon salt
3 tablespoons sugar
3 pieces star anise

DEEP-FRIED CRISPY PORK ROLLS

★ ★ ★ ★

Cooking time:
6–8 minutes

Serves: 4–6

Cooking method:
deep-fry, p.45

**A useful 'hot
starter'**

■ PREPARATION ■

Cut pork into thin slices (about 3 × 2-inches) and beat several times with meat bat or rolling pin. Mix salt, flour, sherry, monosodium glutamate, if using, and egg in bowl. Toss meat in this mixture. Cut green onions into 3-inch sections. Roll one slice of pork around 2 pieces of green onion. Secure each roll with a toothpick, then coat in breadcrumbs.

■ COOKING ■

Heat oil in wok or deep-fryer. When hot, add pork rolls, one at a time, and fry over medium heat for about 6 minutes until golden brown. Drain.

■ SERVING ■

Cut each roll on the slant into 1-inch sections and arrange on lettuce leaves. These slices of pork may be served with a tomato sauce or with a 'salt and pepper' mixture (see page 93).

1½ lb boneless pork loin
1 teaspoon salt
2 tablespoons flour
1 tablespoon dry sherry
½ teaspoon MSG (optional)
1 egg
4 green onions
1 cup dry breadcrumbs
Vegetable oil for deep-frying
6 crisp lettuce leaves

1½lb meaty pork spareribs

1½ teaspoons salt

Pepper to taste

Vegetable oil for deep-frying

Sauce:

2 teaspoons chopped fresh ginger root

2 teaspoons chopped garlic

3 tablespoons yellow bean paste

2 teaspoons sugar

2 tablespoons good stock (see page 56)

1½ tablespoons dark soy sauce

2 tablespoons dry sherry

1½ tablespoons hoisin sauce

1 tablespoon cornstarch blended with 2 tablespoons stock

CAPITAL SPARERIBS

▉ PREPARATION ▉

Chop spareribs into 1–1½-inch pieces. Place in large pan of water and bring to boil. Simmer for 2 minutes, then drain. Sprinkle with salt and pepper.

▉ COOKING ▉

Heat oil in wok or deep-fryer. When hot, fry spareribs over medium heat for about 8 minutes. Drain thoroughly, pour away oil and save for further frying. Heat 2 tablespoons oil in wok or pan. When hot, stir in ginger and garlic for about 15 seconds. Stir in yellow bean paste and sugar. Add stock, soy sauce, sherry and hoisin sauce and stir until smooth. Bring to boil, return spareribs to sauce and simmer for about 1 minute. Pour on blended cornstarch and stir until sauce thickens.

▉ SERVING ▉

Capital Spareribs can be used as a hot starter in a multi-course meal.

★★

Cooking time: about 18 minutes

Serves: 5–6

Cooking method: deep-fry, p.45

Easy to prepare and cook

Serve as a starter

Illustrated on p.188

1½–2 lb pork shoulder or fresh pork sides

1¼ cups good stock (see page 56)

1½ tablespoons sugar

¼ cup soy sauce

SOY-BRAISED PORK – LONG COOKED VERSION

▉ PREPARATION ▉

Cut pork through skin into 1 × 1½ × 2-inch pieces.

▉ COOKING ▉

Bring 5 cups water to boil in flameproof casserole. Blanch pork for 3 minutes. Pour away water. Add stock, sugar and soy sauce to casserole and bring to boil. Cover and place casserole in preheated oven at 200°C, 400°F for 15 minutes. Remove lid and stir contents. Cover and cook for another 15 minutes, then stir again. Add a little more liquid if sauce seems too thick. Reduce oven temperature to 180°C, 350°F and continue to cook for a further 1½ hours.

Note: For extra flavor, add 3–4 slices fresh ginger root at the beginning of cooking and 4–5 tablespoons rice wine when the contents are stirred for the second time. Dried squid and hot Sichuan pickles can also be used to flavor this dish.

★★

Cooking time: 2–2¼ hours

Serves: 4–6

Cooking method: braise

Easy to prepare – lengthy cooking time

Excellent with rice and vegetable dishes for family meals

Illustrated on p.188

WHITE-COOKED SLICED PORK

★★

Cooking time: 45 minutes, plus cooling time

Serves: 4-6

Cooking method: simmer

Easy to prepare

3 lb pork shoulder or fresh pork sides

1 tablespoon salt

4 slices fresh ginger root

■ PREPARATION AND COOKING ■

Bring 5 pints water to boil in heavy saucepan or flameproof casserole. Place pork in pan and add salt and ginger. Cover and simmer gently for 45 minutes. Remove pork from pan and cool for 2-3 hours. When cold, cut meat into thin slices, measuring 2 × 3 inches.

■ SERVING ■

Arrange slices overlapping in serving dish. Accompany with various simple dips such as: soy sauce, soy paste, chili oil, sesame oil, chopped green onions, shredded fresh ginger root, crushed garlic, vinegar, dry sherry.

SWEET AND SOUR PORK

★★★★

Cooking time: about 8 minutes

Serves: 4-6

Cooking methods: deep-fry p.45 and stir-fry p.42

Famous dish to serve as part of multi-course meal

2 lb lean and fat pork

Cornstarch for coating

2 slices of canned pineapple or bamboo shoot

1 small green pepper

1 small red pepper

Vegetable oil for deep-frying

Batter:

3 tablespoons cornstarch

3 tablespoons self-rising flour

1 teaspoon salt

1 egg

Sweet and Sour Sauce:

2 tablespoons sugar

3 tablespoons vinegar

3 tablespoons tomato paste

3 tablespoons orange juice

1½ tablespoons soy sauce

1½ tablespoons cornstarch blended with ¼ cup water

■ PREPARATION ■

Cut pork into 1-inch pieces and coat in cornstarch. Coarsely chop pineapple or bamboo shoot, green and red peppers. Mix cornstarch, flour, salt and egg into smooth batter. Mix sauce ingredients together until smooth. Add pork pieces to batter and coat evenly.

■ COOKING ■

Heat oil in wok or deep-fryer. When hot, fry battered pork pieces for 3½ minutes. Remove and drain. Heat 2 tablespoons oil in another wok or skillet. When hot, stir-fry pineapple and peppers for a few seconds. Add the sauce and stir over medium heat until the sauce thickens and becomes translucent. Transfer fried pork to wok or pan containing sweet and sour sauce. Stir and turn pork in sauce over medium heat for 1 minute.

See pages 43-44 for step-by-step instructions.

BEEF

Interest in beef as a food is growing in China as the population gradually becomes more mobile and the impact of Western taste spreads, but as yet it is still only eaten by a minority. The Chinese Muslims, for example, who inhabit the great cattle-raising regions of Manchuria and the area north-west of Sinkiang, eat beef to the exclusion of pork, the consumption of which is forbidden by their religion. The majority of Chinese keep oxen, cows and buffalo in twos and threes as work animals, not for their meat or as a source of dairy products, which few Chinese consume.

To a Chinese palate, beef tastes a trifle gamey and takes some getting used to. It can be cooked in the same way as pork, but it toughens more rapidly when subjected to heat and is not suitable for medium-length cooking: ie, 10-20 minutes. The majority of Chinese beef dishes are usually either very quickly stir-fried or cooked for a lengthy period by long simmering, long steaming or long red cooking.

---

1 lb beef steak (rump, top round or sirloin)
2-3 lambs' kidneys
½ teaspoon salt
Pepper to taste
1½ tablespoons cornstarch
1 egg white
12 small button mushrooms or 4 oz canned, drained straw mushrooms
2 oz canned, whole, drained bamboo shoots
¼ cup vegetable oil
3 slices fresh ginger root
1 tablespoon shortening or lard
¼ cup frozen peas
6 oz jumbo shrimp
1½ tablespoons light soy sauce
1 tablespoon oyster sauce
2 tablespoons good stock (see page 56)
1 tablespoon dry sherry
1 teaspoon sesame oil

STIR-FRIED DICED BEEF

WITH KIDNEYS, SHRIMP AND MUSHROOMS

■ PREPARATION ■

Cut beef into small cubes. Clean, then cut smooth surface of each kidney with criss-cross pattern. Cut kidneys into similar-sized cubes as beef. Rub beef and kidney with salt and pepper. Toss evenly in cornstarch and coat in egg white. Cut button mushrooms in half or drain straw mushrooms. Cut bamboo shoots into cubes of similar size to beef. Chop shrimp, if liked.

■ COOKING ■

Heat vegetable oil in wok or skillet. When hot, stir-fry beef, kidney and ginger over high heat for 1½ minutes, then drain, discarding ginger. Add fat to pan. When hot, stir-fry peas, shrimp, mushrooms and bamboo shoots over high heat for 1 minute. Stir in soy sauce, oyster sauce, stock and sherry and cook for 30 seconds. Return beef and kidneys to pan and stir-fry for another 30 seconds. Sprinkle on sesame oil.

■ SERVING ■

An unusual savory dish suitable for nibbling as an accompaniment to wine, or to eat with rice as a main course dish.

★ ★ ★

Cooking time: about 8 minutes

Serves: 6-7

Cooking method: stir-fry, p.42

Fairly quick to prepare

Goes well with most dishes on a Chinese menu

Score kidneys p.39

★ ★ ★

Cooking time: about 10 minutes

Serves: 4–6

Cooking methods: deep-fry p.45 and stir-fry p.42

Quite easy to prepare

Good with most savory and vegetable dishes

STIR-FRIED BEEF WITH CELERY

■ PREPARATION ■

Using very sharp knife, cut beef into thin slices, then cut again into matchstick-sized shreds. Place in bowl and mix with salt, cornstarch and egg white. Cut celery into similar-sized shreds as beef. Cut green onions into 2-inch sections. Finely shred chilies, discarding seeds. Shred ginger.

■ COOKING ■

Heat oil in wok or deep-fryer. When hot, fry beef for 2 minutes. Remove and drain off excess oil. Reserve oil to use for other purposes. Heat wok or skillet with 1 tablespoon of reserved oil. When hot, stir-fry ginger, chili, peppercorns, green onions and celery for 1 minute. Add bean paste, sugar, soy sauce, sherry and stock and stir together over high heat for 30 seconds. Return beef to pan and stir-fry for 30 seconds.

■ SERVING ■

Transfer to heated dish. To serve, place a small amount of beef and celery on a lettuce leaf or pancake, roll up and eat.

8 oz round steak
1 teaspoon salt
2 tablespoons cornstarch
1 egg white
4 sticks celery
2 green onions
2 fresh chilies
Vegetable oil for deep-frying
2 slices fresh ginger root
1 teaspoon pounded Sichuan peppercorns
1½ tablespoons yellow bean paste
½ tablespoon sugar
1 tablespoon soy sauce
1 tablespoon dry sherry
2 tablespoons good stock (see page 56)
12 iceberg lettuce leaves or 12 Peking duck pancakes (see page 178)

★ ★

Cooking time: about 5–6 minutes

Serves: 4–6

Cooking method: stir-fry, p.42

Easy to prepare

Serve with rice. Complements most savory dishes

QUICK STIR-FRIED BEEF WITH TOMATOES

This is a very popular beef dish in the summer in Peking where there is a profusion of tomatoes.

■ PREPARATION ■

Cut beef into thin slices and rub evenly with salt and pepper. Toss in cornstarch and coat in egg white. Cut each tomato into quarters. Shred ginger. Peel and thinly slice onions.

■ COOKING ■

Heat oil in wok or skillet. When hot, quickly spread beef slices evenly over surface of skillet and then stir-fry quickly over high heat for 1 minute. Remove and set aside. Add fat to pan. When hot, stir-fry ginger, onions and tomatoes for about 30 seconds. Add soy sauce and sherry, return beef to skillet and stir-fry all ingredients for 30 seconds.

1 lb beef steak, eg rump, filet or sirloin
1 teaspoon salt
pepper to taste
2 tablespoons cornstarch
1 egg white
5 medium tomatoes
3 slices fresh ginger root
2 medium onions
¼ cup vegetable oil
1 tablespoon shortening or lard
1 tablespoon soy sauce
1 tablespoon dry sherry

1 large sheet bean curd skin
8 oz beef tenderloin
½ teaspoon salt
Pepper to taste
1 tablespoon cornstarch
1 large ripe mango
2 slices fresh ginger root
1 tablespoon oyster sauce
½ tablespoon light soy sauce
2 teaspoons sugar
1 egg, beaten
Vegetable oil for deep-frying
6 tablespoons hoisin sauce
12 iceberg lettuce leaves

MANGO BEEF

This is a departure from traditional Chinese cooking of beef, probably influenced by the cuisine of the South Seas, Singapore, Malaysia, Thailand, Vietnam and the Philippines.

■ PREPARATION ■

Soak bean curd skin in hot water for 10 minutes. Cut beef into 12 pieces and rub with salt and pepper. Toss in cornstarch. Slice the mango flesh into 12 pieces. Shred ginger. Place few pieces of ginger over top of beef, then brush beef with oyster sauce, soy sauce and sprinkle with sugar. Cover with piece of mango. Cut bean curd sheet into 12 pieces and use to wrap up tightly each parcel of mango, ginger and beef. Seal bean curd firmly with beaten egg.

■ COOKING ■

Heat oil in wok or deep-fryer. When hot, fry beef and mango parcels in batches for 2 minutes, then turn and fry for a further minute. Drain and keep the parcels warm as you fry the others.

■ SERVING ■

Heap parcels on heated dish. Serve with spoonful of hoisin sauce and wrap in lettuce leaf.

★★★★

Cooking time: about 3 minutes per batch

Serves: 4–6

Cooking method: deep-fry, p.45

Needs care and patience to make 'parcels'

An interesting dish to combine with others

1 lb beef steak (rump, top round or sirloin)
1 teaspoon salt
1½ tablespoons cornstarch
1 egg white
3 slices fresh ginger root
3 leeks, about 8 oz
¼ cup vegetable oil
2 tablespoons shortening or lard
1 tablespoon light soy sauce
2 tablespoons good stock (see page 56)
1 tablespoon prepared English mustard
2 teaspoons red chili oil

MUSTARD AND RED CHILI OIL BEEF WITH LEEKS

■ PREPARATION ■

Cut beef into very thin slices and rub with salt. Toss in cornstarch and coat in egg white. Shred ginger. Clean leeks thoroughly and cut slantwise into 1-inch pieces.

■ COOKING ■

Heat vegetable oil in wok or skillet. When hot, fry half ginger for 30 seconds to flavor oil. Add leeks and stir-fry for 1½ minutes. Remove and set aside. Add fat to pan. When hot, stir-fry beef for 1½ minutes. Add soy sauce and remaining ginger, then return leeks and stock to the pan. Toss together for another 30 seconds.

■ SERVING ■

Transfer to heated serving dish. Trickle mustard and red oil evenly over dish.

★★

Cooking time: about 10 minutes

Serves: 4–6

Cooking method: stir-fry, p.42

Quick and easy to make

A spicy dish that goes well with lighter dishes

Score kidneys, p.39

★★

Cooking time:
5–6 minutes

Serves: 4–6

Cooking method:
stir-fry, p.42

Quick and easy to prepare

Complements most savory and vegetable dishes

Illustrated on p.188

QUICK-FRIED SHREDDED BEEF WITH GINGER AND ONIONS

1 lb beef steak, eg rump or filet
1 teaspoon salt
Pepper to taste
1½ tablespoons cornstarch
1 egg white
3 medium onions
3 slices fresh ginger root
¼ cup vegetable oil
2 tablespoons shortening or lard
2 tablespoons soy sauce
1 tablespoon sugar
3 tablespoons good stock (see page 56)
1½ tablespoons dry sherry
2 teaspoons cornstarch blended with 2 tablespoons water

■ PREPARATION ■

Using a very sharp knife, cut beef into thin slices, then cut again into matchstick-sized shreds. Sprinkle with salt and pepper. Toss in 1½ tablespoons cornstarch and coat in egg white. Peel and thinly slice onions. Shred ginger.

■ COOKING ■

Heat oil in wok or skillet. When hot, stir-fry beef over high heat for 1½ minutes. Remove and set aside. Add fat to pan. When hot, stir-fry ginger and onions over high heat for 1½ minutes. Add soy sauce, sugar and stock and stir together for 30 seconds. Return beef, add sherry and blended cornstarch and continue to stir-fry for 30 seconds.

★★★

Cooking time:
10 minutes

Serves: 4–6

Cooking method:
stir-fry, p.42

Easy to prepare

Serve with more lightly spiced dishes

Illustrated on p.188

SLICED BEEF IN BLACK BEAN AND CHILI SAUCE

1 lb beef steak (rump, top round or sirloin)
¼ teaspoon salt
Pepper to taste
2 tablespoons cornstarch
1 egg white
¼ cup vegetable oil

Sauce:
1 medium onion
2 dried chilies
1 small red pepper
1 small green pepper
1½ tablespoons salted black beans
1 tablespoon shortening or lard
3 tablespoons good stock (see page 56)
1 tablespoon dry sherry
1 tablespoon soy sauce
½ tablespoon cornstarch blended with 2 tablespoons water

■ PREPARATION ■

Cut beef into thin slices and rub evenly with salt and pepper. Toss in cornstarch and coat in egg white. Peel and thinly slice onion. Finely chop chilies. Cut red and green peppers into 1-inch pieces. Soak black beans in 4 tablespoons cold water for 3 minutes, then drain.

■ COOKING ■

Heat oil in wok or skillet. When hot, stir-fry beef over high heat for 1 minute. Remove and set aside. Add fat to the pan. When hot, stir-fry onion, black beans, chilies and peppers. Mash softened black beans with metal spoon against edge of wok or pan. Stir in stock, sherry and soy sauce over high heat. Return beef to pan and mix well. Finally, add blended cornstarch to thicken sauce. Stir all ingredients for further 30 seconds.

3 medium onions

1 lb round steak

1 teaspoon salt

¼ teaspoon white pepper

1½ tablespoons light soy sauce

1½ tablespoons dark soy sauce

½ tablespoon cornstarch blended with 1 tablespoon water

5 tablespoons vegetable oil

2 teaspoons sugar

2 tablespoons dry sherry

QUICK-FRIED SHREDDED BEEF WITH ONIONS

■ PREPARATION ■

Peel and very thinly slice onions. Thinly slice beef, then cut into shreds. Add salt, pepper, half of the soy sauces, cornstarch and 1 tablespoon oil to the beef; mix thoroughly.

■ COOKING ■

Heat remaining oil in wok or skillet. When hot, stir-fry onions for 1 minute. Push them to side of wok or pan and pour in beef. Turn beef and stir-fry for about 15 seconds. Sprinkle over sugar, remaining soy sauces and sherry. When boiling, bring onions in from side of pan and turn together with beef. Turn and mix them over high heat. The whole process should not last more than 1½ minutes after the beef has been added to the pan (the purpose is to keep the beef lightly cooked while strongly impregnated with the onion flavor).

Note: This dish is not suitable for reheating or keeping hot for long periods.

★★★

Cooking time: about 5 minutes

Serves: 4–6

Cooking method: stir-fry, p.42

Quick to prepare

Goes well with most dishes

1¾ lb beef steak (rump, top round or sirloin)

2 slices fresh ginger root

1½ tablespoons soy sauce

1½ tablespoons hoisin sauce

1 tablespoon Worcestershire sauce

½ teaspoon salt

1½ teaspoons lightly pounded Sichuan peppercorns

1 green pepper

5 tablespoons vegetable oil

SICHUAN PEPPERED BEEF MEDALLIONS

■ PREPARATION ■

Cut beef at an angle into ⅙-inch thickness, then trim into medallion round shapes. Finely chop ginger. Mix soy, hoisin and Worcestershire sauces together and use as marinade for beef. Stir salt, peppercorns and ginger into marinade and leave beef to season for about 30 minutes. Turn beef over and marinate for further 30 minutes. Cut peppers into 1-inch squares.

COOKING

Heat oil in wok or skillet. When hot, add beef pieces and space them evenly on surface of pan. Cook for 2 minutes, then turn them over and fry for another minute. Add pepper and pour in any leftover marinade. Stir-fry for 30 seconds.

★★★

Cooking time: about 6 minutes, plus marinating time

Serves: 4–6

Cooking methods: shallow-fry and stir-fry, p.42

Quick to cook

Rather spicy, so best served with lighter, and less seasoned dishes

CANTONESE STIR-FRIED BEEF IN OYSTER SAUCE

★★

Cooking time: about 8 minutes

Serves: 4–6

Cooking method: stir-fry, p.42

Easy to prepare

Accompany with other savory and vegetable dishes

Illustrated on p.213

▣ PREPARATION ▣

Cut beef into thin strips and mix with salt and pepper. Toss in cornstarch and coat in egg white. Shred ginger. Cut each snow pea slantwise in half or cut green onions slantwise in 1½-inch sections.

▣ COOKING ▣

Heat oil in wok or skillet. When hot, fry ginger in oil to flavor. Add beef and stir-fry over high heat for about 1 minute. Remove and set aside. Add fat to pan. When hot, stir-fry snow peas or green onions for 1–2 minutes. Add stock and soy sauce and continue to stir-fry for 30 seconds. Return beef to pan, add oyster sauce and sherry and stir-fry over high heat for 30 seconds.

1 lb beef steak, (rump, top round or sirloin)
1 teaspoon salt
Pepper to taste
2 tablespoons cornstarch
1 egg white
3 slices fresh ginger root
4 oz (1 cup) trimmed snow pea pods or 3–4 green onions
¼ cup vegetable oil
1 teaspoon shortening or lard
1½ tablespoons good stock (see page 56)
1 tablespoon soy sauce
1½ tablespoons oyster sauce
1 tablespoon dry sherry

SICHUAN HOT CRISPY-FRIED SHREDDED BEEF

★★★★

Cooking time: about 15 minutes

Serves: 4–6

Cooking methods: deep-fry p.45 and stir-fry p.42

Care required in timing the cooking

A spicy dish, excellent with rice

Illustrated on p.188

PREPARATION

Using a very sharp knife, cut beef into thin slices, then cut again into matchstick-sized shreds. Whisk eggs, salt and cornstarch to make batter. Add shredded beef and coat evenly. Cut carrots and ginger into similar-sized shreds as beef. Divide each green onion into quarters lengthways, then cut into 1½-inch sections. Coarsely chop garlic. Shred chilies, discarding seeds.

▣ COOKING ▣

Heat oil in wok or deep-fryer. When hot, fry beef, stirring to keep shreds separate, for 4 minutes. Remove with perforated spoon and set aside. Reheat oil, then fry beef again to ensure it is crispy. Drain beef on paper towels. Reserve oil from wok to use for other purposes. Heat wok or skillet with 1 tablespoon of the reserved oil. When hot, stir-fry carrots, green onion, garlic, ginger and chilies over medium heat for 2½ minutes. Add sugar, soy sauce, vinegar and finally beef. Turn ingredients around quickly over high heat for 15 seconds.

1 lb beef (rump, top round or sirloin)
3 eggs
1 teaspoon salt
1 cup cornstarch
Vegetable oil for deep-frying
Sauce:
3 medium carrots
4 slices fresh ginger root
3 green onions
3 garlic cloves
2 fresh chilies
1 dried chili
2 tablespoons sugar
1½ tablespoons soy sauce
3 tablespoons vinegar

LAMB

Lamb is not eaten as often as beef in China. Indeed, the southern Chinese, especially the Cantonese, abhor mutton. Peking, on the other hand, has been called the 'Mutton Capital' and from Peking westwards, along the length of the old silk route, lamb and mutton are eaten almost exclusively. These meats are invariably cooked with quantities of strong-tasting vegetables, such as garlic, ginger, onion and leeks. Half of the restaurants in Peking reek of the smell of these vegetables being cooked and fried with the meat. The natives of Peking find the smell very inviting, but the majority of southerners would retreat a mile!

12 oz leg of lamb
2 green onions
2 slices fresh ginger root
3 garlic cloves
4½ tablespoons soy sauce
¾ tablespoon yellow bean paste
7 tablespoons vegetable oil
Pepper to taste
3 tablespoons dry sherry
12 oz lambs' liver
3 lambs' kidneys
1½ tablespoons sesame oil

TRIPLE LAMB QUICK FRY

■ PREPARATION ■

Cut lamb meat into thin slices or cubes. Coarsely shred green onions. Coarsley chop ginger and garlic. Place lamb in bowl with 1½ tablespoons of soy sauce, yellow bean paste, 1 teaspoon oil, pepper to taste, 1 tablespoon sherry and green onions. Marinate for about 30 minutes. Cut liver as lamb and place in another bowl with 1½ tablespoons soy sauce, 1 tablespoon sherry, 1 teaspoon oil, half the ginger and garlic. Cut each kidney into 4 pieces and score smooth side with a criss-cross pattern, if liked. Marinate in another bowl with 1½ tablespoons soy sauce, 1 tablespoon sherry, 1 teaspoon oil and the remaining ginger. Marinate three types of lamb for 30 minutes.

■ COOKING ■

Heat 3 tablespoons oil in wok or skillet. When hot, stir-fry marinated leg of lamb over high heat for 1½ minutes. Remove and set aside. Reheat wok or skillet with 1½ tablespoons oil. When hot, stir-fry marinated liver over high heat for 1½ minutes. Remove and set aside. Finally, heat remaining oil in wok or skillet. When hot, stir-fry kidneys over high heat for 1 minute, then push them to side of skillet. Add sesame oil and return lamb meat and liver to pan. Mix together with kidneys and stir-fry for another 30 seconds. Serve immediately.

Note: As can be seen from the above timing, it is very important that nothing is overcooked or undercooked. Therefore, make sure that all the ingredients are prepared before you commence cooking.

★ ★ ★ ★

Cooking time: about 6 minutes, plus marinating time

Serves: 6–7

Cooking method: multiple stir-fry, p.42

Requires care in cooking

Suitable for a family or party dinner

★★

Cooking time: about 1¼ hours

Serves: 6-7

Cooking methods: stir-fry p.42 and long simmer

Easy to prepare

A main meal to be served with plenty of rice

RED-COOKED LAMB

Like most Chinese meats and poultry, lamb can be cooked with soy sauce. With lamb, less sugar is required than with pork, but much more ginger is added.

PREPARATION

Cut lamb into 1-inch pieces. Parboil lamb in pan of water for 3-4 minutes, then drain.

COOKING

Heat oil in wok or flameproof casserole. When hot, stir-fry ginger for about 2 minutes to flavor oil. Add lamb and turn it in seasoned oil for 3-4 minutes. Add stock, soy sauce, sugar, yellow bean paste, sherry and pepper. Bring to boil and simmer gently for 1 hour, stirring occasionally. Serve directly from wok or casserole at table.

1½-2lb shoulder or leg of lamb

3 tablespoons vegetable oil

5-6 slices fresh ginger root

2 cups good stock (see page 56)

¼ cup soy sauce

1 teaspoon sugar

1½ tablespoons yellow bean paste

¼ cup dry sherry

Pepper to taste

★★★

Cooking time: about 1¾ hours

Serves: 6-7

Cooking methods: stir-fry p.42 and long simmer

Serve as Red-cooked Lamb

VARIATION

LONG-BRAISED RED-COOKED LAMB WITH CHINESE MUSHROOMS AND CHESTNUTS

This is a slightly fancier version of Red-Cooked Lamb, which with the addition of extra ingredients requires longer cooking. It is a dish for those who like rich, savory food.

Soak 10-12 medium dried Chinese mushrooms in hot water to cover for 15 minutes. Discard tough stalks. Boil 6oz chestnuts for 15 minutes, then remove skins. Add mushrooms and chestnuts to lamb casserole at start of cooking. Increase stock to 2½ cups and soy sauce to 5 tablespoons. Cook for 1½ hours. As with previous recipe, the dish should be served directly from the casserole, and the diners help themselves. An ideal dish to accompany it is steamed buns (see page 240).

1 lb lean lamb, lightly frozen

½ teaspoon salt

½ cup vegetable oil

8 oz young leeks

1 tablespoon soy sauce

1 tablespoon yellow bean paste

1½ tablespoons dry sherry or rice wine

1½ tablespoons good stock (see page 56)

¼ teaspoon pepper

1 tablespoon wine vinegar

2 tablespoons cornstarch blended with 2 tablespoons water

1½ teaspoons sesame oil

2 tablespoons finely chopped garlic

QUICK STIR-FRIED LAMB IN GARLIC SAUCE

■ PREPARATION ■

Cut lamb into very thin slices, about 2½ × 1½ inches. Place meat in bowl and marinate with salt and 2 tablespoons oil. Leave to season for 30 minutes.

Cut leeks slantwise into 1-inch sections and wash thoroughly. Mix together soy sauce, yellow bean paste, sherry, stock, pepper, vinegar, blended cornstarch and sesame oil. Put aside for later use.

■ COOKING ■

Heat remaining 6 tablespoons oil in wok or skillet. When very hot, stir-fry garlic, then lamb quickly over high heat for 20 seconds. Drain away any excess oil. Add leeks and stir-fry quickly for 15 seconds. Pour in soy sauce mixture and continue to stir-fry ingredients over high heat for 15 seconds. Serve immediately.

Note: The success of the dish depends largely on the use of high heat and stir-frying with speed. The action produces a dish with a very Pekingese flavor.

★★
Cooking time: about 4–6 minutes, plus marinating time

Serves: 4–6

Cooking method: stir-fry, p.42

Quick to cook

Complements most Chinese dishes

1½ lb leg of lamb

8 oz pork skin

2 green onions

3 garlic cloves

3 slices fresh ginger root

1½ teaspoons salt

Pepper to taste

2½ cups good stock (see page 56)

3 tablespoons white wine

1 tablespoon light soy sauce

¼ teaspoon MSG (optional)

Dip sauce:

¼ cup soy sauce

1 tablespoon finely chopped fresh ginger root

1 tablespoon finely chopped garlic

1 tablespoon finely chopped green onions

PEKING JELLY OF LAMB

This is a traditional Peking dish often used for eating with congee (rice gruel) or as an hors d'oeuvre item.

■ PREPARATION ■

Cut lamb into 1½ × 1 × 1-inch pieces. Cut pork skin into smaller pieces. Parboil lamb and pork skin in pan of water for 2 minutes, then drain. Cut green onions into 1-inch sections, keeping green and white pieces separate. Thinly slice garlic. Shred ginger.

■ COOKING ■

Place pork skin on the bottom of heavy casserole and cover with lamb. Add salt, pepper, white part of two green onions and ginger. Pour in stock and about 1¼ cups water to cover the contents and bring to the boil. Reduce heat to low, cover and simmer for 1¼ hours. Cool, then place in refrigerator to encourage setting.

Contents should be set after 3 hours. Remove casserole

★★★★
Cooking time: 1½ hours, plus setting time

Serves: 6–8

Cooking method: long simmer

Rather time-consuming to prepare

A good hors d'oeuvre or picnic dish

from refrigerator and peel away pork fat and skin. Heat briefly to melt jelly and then stir in wine, soy sauce, monosodium glutamate, if using, garlic and green parts of green onions. Pour lamb mixture into rectangular mold or dish (about $10 \times 4 \times 3$ inches) and leave in refrigerator to set again. Mix dip sauce ingredients together.

■ SERVING ■

Turn mold out on to a serving dish and cut into ¼-inch slices. Serve with dip sauce.

★ ★ ★

Cooking time: about 10 minutes

Serves: 4–6

Cooking method: stir-fry, p.42

Fairly easy to prepare

Combines well with other Chinese dishes

STIR-FRIED LAMB AND LIVER

WITH BAMBOO SHOOTS, PEAS, LOTUS SEEDS AND GARLIC

■ PREPARATION ■

Soak dried mushrooms, if using, in hot water to cover for 25 minutes. Drain and discard tough stalks. Cut lamb into small cubes. Cut liver into similar-sized cubes. Rub salt into lamb and liver. Toss in cornstarch. Coat in egg white. Cut bamboo shoots into cubes. Thinly slice the garlic. Blanch lotus seeds in pan of boiling water for 3 minutes, then drain.

■ COOKING ■

Heat 3 tablespoons of oil in wok or skillet. When hot, stir-fry lamb cubes over high heat for 1 minute. Remove and set aside. Heat remaining oil in wok or skillet. When hot, stir-fry cubed liver for 1 minute. Remove and set aside. Melt shortening or lard in the skillet. When hot, stir in garlic for 10 seconds, then add bamboo shoots, peas, lotus seeds and mushrooms. Stir-fry over high heat for 2 minutes. Add stock, soy sauce and sherry and continue to stir and turn for 1 minute. Return lamb cubes and liver to pan and stir-fry gently for 1 minute.

---

2 oz dried Chinese mushrooms or canned straw mushrooms, drained

12 oz leg of lamb

8 oz lamb liver

1 teaspoon salt

1½ tablespoons cornstarch

1 egg white

3 oz canned whole bamboo shoots, drained

4 garlic cloves

¼ cup lotus seeds

¼ cup vegetable oil

1½ tablespoons shortening or lard

¾ cup green peas

3 tablespoons good stock (see page 56)

1½ tablespoons light soy sauce

1½ tablespoons dry sherry

3 lb leg of lamb

4 slices fresh ginger root

4 garlic cloves

2 teaspoons salt

¼ teaspoon pepper

3 tablespoons vinegar

Vegetable oil for deep-frying

Batter:

1 egg

¼ cup cornstarch

2 tablespoons self-rising flour

Dip sauce:

3 tablespoons sea salt

1½ tablespoons pounded Sichuan peppercorns

½ cup Peking Duck sauce (see page 178)

½ cup wine vinegar mixed with 2 tablespoons shredded fresh ginger root

MUSLIM DEEP-FRIED SIMMERED LAMB

■ PREPARATION ■

Cut lamb into 2½ × ½-inch strips. Parboil in pan of water for 3 minutes, then drain.

■ COOKING ■

Place lamb pieces in bottom of heavy pan. Add ginger, garlic, salt, pepper and vinegar. Bring to boil, reduce heat and simmer gently for 45 minutes or until sauce has been completely absorbed. Remove lamb from casserole and leave until cold. Whisk the batter ingredients in a mixing bowl. Use to coat each piece of lamb. Heat oil in wok or deep-fryer. When hot, fry lamb pieces for about 3 minutes.

To make dip sauce, heat salt and peppercorns in small, dry skillet over medium heat for 1½ minutes, stirring continuously. Divide into 2 small bowls. Add half the duck sauce and ginger-flavored vinegar to each bowl.

■ SERVING ■

Arrange lamb on heated serving dish. Accompany with dip sauce.

★★★

Cooking time: about 1¼ hours

Serves: 4–6

Cooking methods: simmer and deep-fry, p.45

Not too difficult to prepare

Adds variety to menus of mostly stir-fried dishes

1½ lb leg of lamb

½ teaspoon salt

Pepper to taste

½ tablespoon yellow bean paste

1 tablespoon soy sauce

1 tablespoon hoisin sauce

1½ tablespoons dry sherry

2 medium onions

6 slices fresh ginger root

2 green onions

2-3 garlic cloves

¼ cup vegetable oil

MARINATED LAMB
WITH ONION AND GINGER

■ PREPARATION ■

Cut lamb into 2 × 1 × ¼-inch thick slices. Sprinkle and rub with salt and pepper. Mix yellow bean paste, soy sauce, hoisin sauce and sherry together. Add this marinade to lamb and leave to season for 30 minutes. Peel and thinly slice onions. Shred ginger. Cut green onions into 1-inch sections. Coarsely chop garlic.

■ COOKING ■

Heat oil in skillet or wok. When hot, stir-fry onion and ginger over high heat for 45 seconds, then push them to sides of skillet. Spread out marinated slices of lamb in one layer at center of skillet and fry over high heat for 1¼ minutes on each side. Sprinkle with green onions and garlic. Bring in onions and ginger from sides of skillet and stir-fry for 1 minute.

★★★

Cooking time: about 6 minutes, plus seasoning time

Serves: 4–6

Cooking methods: shallow-fry and stir-fry, p.42

Quick to cook

Combines well with most Chinese dishes

Steamed Ground Rice and Pork in Lotus Leaves (*above*), a full of flavor, long steamed dish; recipe page 190.

Quick-fried Shredded Lamb and Leeks (*left*), accompany with a dip sauce of your choice; recipe page 210.

4–5 lb neck of lamb

3 medium onions

2 dried chilies

4 slices of fresh ginger root

4 garlic cloves

7½ cups water

3 teaspoons salt

Dip sauce:

9 tablespoons soy sauce

2 tablespoons finely
　chopped garlic

2 tablespoons finely
　chopped fresh ginger
　root

2 tablespoons finely
　chopped green onions

2 tablespoons finely
　chopped fresh coriander
　(cilantro)

1½ tablespoons prepared
　English mustard

1½ tablespoons wine vinegar

3 tablespoons dry sherry

1 tablespoon sesame oil

1 tablespoon vegetable oil

MUSLIM LONG-SIMMERED LAMB

(OF THE LUNG FU SAI TEMPLE, PEKING)

As the lamb is cooked quite simply, the character of the dish comes largely from the sauce into which the lamb is dipped before eating.

■ PREPARATION ■

Cut lamb into 2 × 1 × ¼-inch thick slices. Parboil in pan of water for 3 minutes, then drain. Peel and slice onions. Shred chilies, discarding seeds. Shred ginger. Crush garlic.

■ COOKING ■

Place lamb in heavy flameproof casserole. Add water, salt, onion, ginger, garlic and chili. Bring to boil, reduce heat and simmer slowly for 3 hours, turning the contents every 30 minutes. Add more water if the sauce becomes too thick. Meanwhile, mix dip sauce ingredients together.

■ SERVING ■

Serve casserole at the table. The diners eat the lamb with the dip sauce and steamed buns (see page 240), which can be used to sandwich the meat after dipping in the sauce.

★★

Cooking time:
3 hours

Serves: 8–10

Cooking method:
long simmer

Easy to prepare
and lengthy
cooking time

Normally eaten
without
accompaniment

---

8 oz leg of lamb

1 teaspoon salt

Pepper to taste

3 slices fresh ginger root

8 oz young leeks

5 oz cellophane or ribbon
　noodles

2 teaspoons dried shrimp

3 tablespoons vegetable oil

1¼ cups good stock (see
　page 56)

½ chicken bouillon cube

2 tablespoons light soy sauce

1½ tablespoons dry sherry

1½ tablespoons vinegar

1 teaspoon sesame oil

QUICK-FRIED SHREDDED LAMB AND LEEKS

■ PREPARATION ■

Cut lamb into matchstick-size shreds and sprinkle with salt and pepper. Cut ginger into similar shreds. Wash leeks thoroughly and shred them. Soak noodles in hot water for about 5 minutes, then drain. Cover the dried shrimp in boiling water and soak for 10 minutes, then drain.

■ COOKING ■

Heat oil in wok or skillet. When hot, stir-fry ginger and leeks over high heat for 1 minute. Add lamb and continue to stir-fry for 1 minute. Pour in stock and add crumbled bouillon cube, soy sauce, sherry, shrimp and vinegar. Bring to boil, stirring. Simmer for 5 minutes, then add noodles and simmer for further 5 minutes. Sprinkle with sesame oil.

★★

Cooking time:
15 minutes

Serves: 4–6

Cooking methods:
stir-fry p.42 and
simmer

Easy to prepare

Excellent just with
rice

Illustrated on p.209

★ ★ ★ ★

Cooking and eating time: about 2 hours

Serves: 4-6

Cooking method: at table, in hot pot

Fairly time-consuming

A dish to be eaten without accompaniment

Illustrated on p.180

PEKING MONGOLIAN HOT POT

This dish was introduced into Peking in the 17th century. It consists entirely of wafer-thin slices of lamb which diners cook themselves by immersing them in boiling stock in a hot pot (fondue) at the table. For southerners this seems a primitive version of a hot pot, for in the south many different types of food are cooked in a hot pot, often including various kinds of seafood, different types of meat and vegetables. These all contribute to the flavor of the stock in the pot. In Peking they seem to prefer a purity of flavor and only cook lamb. To cook this dish you will need a conventional Peking hot pot, made of brass and heated with charcoal, or an electric wok or an electric skillet, capacity $7\frac{1}{2}$-10 cups (see page 11).

■ PREPARATION ■

Thinly slice partially frozen lamb with razor sharp knife and lay slices on saucers for each diner. The slices must be wafer thin or they will take too long to cook and will be tough. Shred green onions and cut into $1\frac{1}{2}$-inch sections. Clean and trim cabbage. Cut into 2-inch pieces and place in 1-2 bowls. Blanch noodles in pan of boiling water for 3 minutes, then rinse under cold, running water. Arrange in 2 bowls. Make the 3 types of dip sauce and place each one in a small bowl on the table within easy reach of the diners.

■ COOKING AND SERVING ■

Bring 7 cups of stock to boil in hot pot. Add salt, half green onions and half ginger to pot. After 15 seconds diners can start cooking and eating. Each diner picks up 2-3 slices of lamb in his chopsticks and dips them into the boiling stock for a few minutes to cook the lamb. Then the meat goes into the beaten egg and then into one of the dip sauces before being eaten.

After a few rounds of lamb have been eaten, each person may cook some noodles and cabbage in the stock. Unlike the meat, these are left to cook for a few minutes in the stock. After about half the food has been cooked, the host may add more stock to the pot, or add all the remaining ingredients and bring to the boil for about 4 minutes; the food will have formed a savory soup to be drunk.

4-5 lb lean lamb, lightly frozen

3 green onions

1 small Chinese white cabbage

1 lb wheat flour noodles

4 oz cellophane noodles

9-10 cups good stock (see page 56) or water

$1\frac{1}{2}$ teaspoons salt

1 fresh egg, beaten and placed in a bowl in front of each diner

4 slices fresh ginger root

Dip sauce 1:

$\frac{2}{3}$ cup soy sauce

2 tablespoons finely chopped green onions

1 tablespoon finely chopped garlic

1 tablespoon vegetable oil

Dip sauce 2:

$\frac{1}{2}$ cup wine vinegar

2 tablespoons finely shredded fresh root ginger

Dip sauce 3:

6 tablespoons sesame paste or peanut butter

2 tablespoons sesame oil

2 tablespoons water

1 tablespoon soy sauce

1 tablespoon chili sauce

Mongolian Barbecue of Lamb (*above*), an entertaining dish to be served in pancakes with cucumber, green onions and sauce; recipe page 215. Long-steamed Wine-soaked Lamb with Tangerine Peel and Turnips (*left*), the lamb cooking liquid provides a delicious winey soup; recipe page 214. Cantonese Stir-fried Beef in Oyster Sauce (*right*), snow peas make a good alternative to green onions recipe page 203.

6 medium dried Chinese mushrooms

1 tablespoon dried shrimp

6 oz cellophane noodles

2 slices fresh ginger root

2 cloves garlic

2 green onions

3½ tablespoons vegetable oil

1 tablespoon shortening or lard

1 tablespoon drained, canned chopped winter pickles or snow pickles

8 oz ground lamb

2 tablespoons light soy sauce

1 tablespoon oyster sauce

1½ teaspoons red chili oil

¼ cup good stock (see page 56)

1 teaspoon sesame oil

'ANTS CLIMBING UP TREES'

(STIR-FRIED LAMB WITH CELLOPHANE NOODLES)

This recipe is so called because the finished dish of ground lamb with cellophane noodles is reminiscent of ants (lamb) climbing up trees (noodles). Although this dish is usually cooked with ground pork, ground lamb is equally good and some say even better.

■ PREPARATION ■

Soak dried mushrooms and shrimp separately in hot water to cover for 25 minutes. Drain and discard tough mushroom stalks. Finely chop shrimp and mushroom caps. Cut noodles into 3-inch sections and soak in water to cover for 5 minutes. Drain. Shred ginger. Crush garlic. Coarsely chop green onions.

■ COOKING ■

Heat vegetable oil in wok or skillet. When hot, stir-fry shrimp, mushrooms and ginger over high heat for 30 seconds. Add shortening or lard and garlic, half green onions, pickles and stir them around before adding ground lamb. Stir-fry for about 2 minutes, then lower heat and simmer for 3 minutes. Add noodles. Sprinkle them with soy sauce, oyster sauce, chili oil and stock and remaining green onions. Toss all ingredients together and sprinkle with sesame oil.

★★★

Cooking time: 15 minutes

Serves: 4–6

Cooking methods: stir-fry p.42 and simmer

Quite easy to prepare

Goes well with most other Chinese dishes

1½ lb lamb

12 oz turnips

1 dried tangerine peel

2 cups dry white wine

⅔ cup dry sherry

1¼ cups water

5 slices fresh ginger root

1½ teaspoons salt

LONG-STEAMED WINE-SOAKED LAMB

WITH TANGERINE PEEL AND TURNIPS

■ PREPARATION ■

Cut lamb into 1-inch cubes. Cut turnips similarly. Parboil lamb and turnips in pan of water for about 3 minutes, then drain. Soak tangerine peel in hot water for 5 minutes, then drain and break into small pieces.

■ COOKING ■

Put lamb and turnip into large, heavy flameproof casserole with wine, sherry, water, ginger, salt and tangerine peel. Bring to boil, then place casserole, covered, in steamer and steam for 3 hours. If you do not have a large enough steamer, it is possible to cook the dish by placing the casserole into a pan containing about 2 inches water (a roasting pan will do) and then double boil the casserole over medium heat for the same amount of time.

★★

Cooking time: 3 hours

Serves: 7–8

Cooking method: steam, p.49

Easy to prepare – lengthy cooking time

Serve with plenty of rice to mop up the soup

Illustrated on p.212

■ SERVING ■

This dish is brought to the table and diners serve themselves. The soup in which the lamb and turnips are cooked is quite clear, extremely savory and somewhat winey. It is an extremely good soup to drink after every mouthful of rice at a meal.

★★★★

Cooking time: about 2 hours, plus marinating time

Serves: 5-6

Cooking methods: steam p.49 and deep-fry p.45

Time and care needed in preparation

A main meal to eat unaccompanied

Illustrated on p.212

MONGOLIAN BARBECUE OF LAMB

Lamb is often eaten on the Steppes of Mongolia where it is sometimes barbecued over a big smoldering fire. This dish is a favorite among diners in my restaurant, where it is cooked in the following way.

■ PREPARATION ■

Cut lamb along the grain into 6 long strips. Shred ginger and green onions. Mix with peppercorns and salt and use to rub over lamb. Mix soy sauce, yellow bean paste, hoisin sauce, five spice powder and sherry and place in a bowl with lamb. Marinate for 1-2 hours.

■ COOKING ■

Pack seasoned lamb strips in a heatproof bowl, cover top with foil. Place in steamer and steam for about 2 hours or place bowl in pan containing 2 inches of water and simmer for 2 hours. Remove from bowl and leave to cool until required. When required, heat oil in wok or deep-fryer. When hot, fry lamb for 4 minutes.

■ SERVING ■

Place lamb on chopping board and chop into bite-sized pieces while still hot. Serve dish in same way as Peking Duck. Spoon some duck sauce onto a pancake or lettuce leaf, then place on a few slices lamb, followed by a little cucumber and green onion shreds. Form into a roll and turn up at the end so nothing falls out, then eat.

3-4 lb leg of lamb

4 slices of fresh ginger root

5 green onions

1 tablespoon pounded Sichuan peppercorns

1 tablespoon salt

3 tablespoons soy sauce

1½ tablespoons yellow bean paste

1½ tablespoons hoisin sauce

¼ teaspoon five spice powder

2 tablespoons dry sherry

Vegetable oil for deep-frying

Wrapping and eating:

12 Peking Duck pancakes (see page 178) or lettuce leaves

2 small bowls of Peking Duck sauce (see page 178)

3 saucers matchstick-sized pieces of cucumber

3 saucers shredded green onions

DESSERTS

Frying Peking 'Toffee Apples' (*left*); recipe page 252.
Chinese Gooseberry Salad with Mandarin and Lotus
Seeds (*above*); recipe page 223.

甜
品

DESSERTS
Desserts are not part and parcel of a normal Chinese meal, hence the scarcity of desserts on the menus of most Chinese restaurants. Most restaurant chefs concentrate on meats and savories and tend to regard sweets as little more than confectionery. On the other hand, most Chinese banquets and party menus would include one or two sweet courses, which are sandwiched between the progression of numerous savory courses.

It should not be assumed from this that Chinese sweets, cakes and confectioneries are limited in range. If you went to a Chinese market you would find stalls overflowing with bon bons, dried fruits and cakes which would do credit to the best confectionery shops in the West.

1¼ lb glutinous rice
5 tablespoons shortening or lard
6 tablespoons sugar
¼ cup nuts, eg almonds, walnuts, chestnuts or lotus seeds (optional)
6 tablespoons candied and dried fruits, eg ginger, cherries, angelica, mixed candied fruits, or dried lichee, or raisins or pitted date pieces
½ cup sweet bean paste

EIGHT TREASURE PUDDING

The candied fruits provide the colorful pattern on this steamed pudding.

■ PREPARATION ■
Wash rice and place in saucepan. Cover with ½-inch water. Bring to boil and simmer gently for 11-12 minutes. Add half shortening and all sugar, turn and stir until well mixed. Grease sides of a large heatproof basin or bowl heavily with remaining shortening (shortening must be cold). Stick nuts and candied or dried fruits of your choice in a pattern on sides of basin in shortening, arranging remainder at bottom of basin. Place layer of sweetened rice in basin, then spread a thinner layer of sweet bean paste on top of rice. Repeat layers, finishing with a rice layer. Cover basin with foil, leaving a little room for expansion.

■ COOKING ■
Place basin into steamer and steam steadily for 1 hour 10 minutes, until cooked.

■ SERVING ■
Invert the basin on to a large round heated serving dish to turn out the pudding. Decorate with extra candied fruits etc, if liked.

★★★★

Cooking time: about 1¼ hours
Serves: 6–8
Cooking method: steam, p.49
Requires patience to prepare
Good dessert for Western palate
Illustrated on p.220

ALMOND 'TEA'

This is a sweet hot dessert drink, which we Chinese enjoy drinking slowly after a multi-course savory meal.

■ PREPARATION ■

Grind almonds and rice in blender or food processor. Add 2½ cups water and blend until smooth. Add sugar, almond extract and another 1¼ cups water. Stir together until well blended.

■ COOKING ■

Transfer almond mixture to heavy-based pan and slowly bring to boil, stirring. Simmer very gently for 10 minutes, stirring constantly. Add milk and blended cornstarch. Continue to cook and stir for further 5 minutes.

■ SERVING ■

Serve in small bowls, in small quantities at a time, as it is likely to be very hot.

★★

Cooking time:
20-25 minutes

Serves: 5-6

Cooking method:
simmer

Easy to make

Ideal after multi-
course meal

1¼ cups blanched almonds

⅔ cup long grain rice

¼ cup sugar

1 teaspoon almond extract

6 tablespoons milk

1½ tablespoons cornstarch
blended with
3 tablespoons water

PEARS IN HONEY SAUCE

■ PREPARATION ■

Peel pears, leaving stalks and a little surrounding skin. Blend honey with liqueur, 1 tablespoon of sugar and 2 tablespoons water.

■ COOKING ■

Stand pears in flat-bottomed pan and barely cover with water. Bring slowly to boil. Add remaining sugar and simmer gently for 20 minutes. Refrigerate pears with a quarter of the sugar water for 2 hours, discarding remaining sugar water.

■ SERVING ■

Stand each pear in small bowl. Spoon over a little sugar water, then pour about 2 tablespoons of honey sauce over each pear. Chill for another 30 minutes before serving.

★★★

Cooking time:
25 minutes, plus
chilling time

Serves: 6

Cooking method:
simmer

Quite easy to make

Refreshing dessert

Illustrated on p.221

---

6 firm, ripe pears

¼ cup runny honey

¼ cup sweet liqueur, eg
Chinese Rose Dew,
kirsch, cherry brandy,
crème de menthe

¼ cup sugar

8 oz canned water chestnuts, drained

¾-1 cup sugar

1½ cups water chestnut flour

¼ cup corn oil

3 tablespoons vegetable oil

WATER CHESTNUT 'CAKE'

These cakes are quite unique in texture. They have the appearance and feel of rubbery slices of firm jelly, but you will experience a crunchy sensation when you bite through the shreds of water chestnut in the jelly.

■ PREPARATION ■
Cut water chestnuts into matchstick-sized shreds.

■ COOKING ■
Place water chestnuts in saucepan, and add sugar and 2 cups water. Bring to boil. Stir in water chestnut flour and add another 1¾ cups water. Stir and mix well, then simmer for 5 minutes. Add corn oil, stir and bring once more to boil. Reduce heat to very low and simmer gently for 5 minutes. Pour mixture into a square cake pan or jelly roll pan. Place pan in steamer and steam for 30 minutes. Remove from steamer and leave to cool.

When cold, the 'cake' is like firm jelly with streaks of water chestnut inside. Cut into square pieces about the thickness of bread slices. Heat vegetable oil in skillet. When hot, fry each slice of chestnut 'cake' for 2½ minutes on each side. Serve hot or cold.

★ ★ ★

Cooking time: about 1 hour

Serves: 5-6

Cooking methods: simmer, steam p.49 and shallow-fry

Usually served as a dim sum item

---

1 recipe Almond 'Tea' (see page 219)

1 tablespoon unflavored gelatin

⅔ cup evaporated milk

ALMOND JUNKET

■ PREPARATION AND COOKING ■
Repeat Almond 'Tea' recipe until almond mixture is brought to the boil. Meanwhile, sprinkle gelatin over a bowl containing 5-6 tablespoons water. Place bowl in pan of hot water to dissolve gelatin. Instead of adding 1¼ cups water, stir in dissolved gelatin. Bring slowly to boil, stirring constantly. Simmer very gently for 10 minutes. Mix in evaporated milk. Simmer for further 5 minutes, stirring. Pour almond mixture into square deep-sided dish. Leave to cool for 30 minutes, then chill in refrigerator.

■ SERVING ■
After 1½-2 hours, the mixture will be set. Cut the junket into squares, triangular wedges or diamond shapes. They can be served on their own, mixed with other jellies or added to a fruit salad. Their distinctive appeal lies in their nutty flavor.

★ ★ ★

Cooking time: about 30 minutes, plus cooling and chilling time

Serves: 5-6

Cooking method: simmer

Delicious with fruit

Illustrated on p.220

★ ★ ★ ★

Cooking time: about 5–6 min per batch, plus firming time

Serves: 6–7

Cooking method: simmer

Time-consuming to make

Traditional dessert at Chinese New Year

YUAN HSAIO OR NEW YEAR DUMPLINGS

These dumplings came to be served as New Year dumplings because they are smooth, round and full – symbolic of good fortune. However, they are also deceptive because each has a heart of sesame paste and very hot sugar which is often twice as hot as the exterior of the dumplings and the liquid in which they are served. Therefore, give them time to cool a little before eating.

■ PREPARATION ■

Add 1¼ cups water to rice flour. Mix and squeeze with your hand into a rough dough. Add more water slowly and gradually until dough is smooth and does not flake in the hand as you knead and mix. Form and roll it into a long 18-inch sausage. Cut into 18 pieces and press each piece of dough into a round.

Heat oil in pan. When hot, pour it over sesame paste. Stir it in until paste becomes soft and pasty. Add sugar and red bean paste. Stir until well blended. Place mixture in refrigerator for 30 minutes to become firm. Divide filling into 18 pieces. Place each piece of filling on a dough round. Fold it over to wrap filling completely, then roll into a ball.

■ COOKING ■

Heat 6 cups water in large saucepan. Add dumplings to boiling water, a few at a time. Bring to boil and simmer over medium heat for 5-6 minutes when dumplings will rise to top. Remove dumplings with slotted spoon.

■ SERVING ■

Divide the dumplings between 6 bowls and cover with the cooking water.

Dough skin:

1 cup glutinous rice flour

Filling:

1½ tablespoons vegetable oil

1½ tablespoons sesame paste or peanut butter

1½ tablespoons sugar

3 tablespoons sweet red bean paste

★

Preparation time: 8 minutes

Serves: 4–6

Easy to prepare

Illustrated on p.217

CHINESE GOOSEBERRY SALAD
WITH MANDARIN AND LOTUS SEEDS

■ PREPARATION ■

Drain lotus seeds and mandarin orange segments, reserving orange juice. Peel Chinese gooseberries and slice the flesh. Place lotus seeds, mandarin segments and Chinese gooseberry slices in a serving dish. Spoon over reserved juice and mix together gently.

8-10 oz can lotus seeds

8 oz can mandarin oranges

2-3 Chinese gooseberries

223

DIM SUM

Wontons, see pages 230–231, can be deep-fried (*left*);
see also page 238. Lotus Leaf Savory Rice (*above*); recipe page 70.

點
心

DIM SUM

Dim sum are Chinese snacks or 'small eats' which are consumed between meals. The Chinese tradition of eating dim sum is becoming increasingly popular both at home and abroad. So widespread is the popularity of these snacks that institutions have grown up which serve only or mainly dim sum. Indeed, a good proportion of the large Chinese Cantonese restaurants in Western cities such as London, New York, Toronto, San Francisco and Los Angeles serve dim sum throughout the day until dusk. Dim sum are generally served from heated trolleys, which are pushed through the restaurant so the customer may choose what he likes.

They are rarely eaten with rice, and consist mainly of crispy deep-fried items which Westerners take to readily, or steamed items which are often served in steam baskets. These latter are picturesque and succulent, and are thought to constitute healthy eating.

In the warmer south, dim sum are prepared and eaten in tea houses and small restaurants and even outdoors rather than at home. In north China, which has severe weather during a good part of the year, and where people eat out much less often, the preparation and eating of dim sum remains largely a domestic activity. There the whole family, from the very old to the very young, will gather together and make dim sum (mostly steamed or poached dumplings or Chiaotzus and steamed and stuffed buns or Bao tzus) by the hundred. Domestic dim sum take the place of a full-scale meal and are usually prepared and eaten during festivals and holidays when there are more hands available.

There are scores of different dim sum, many of them fancy, but the main line consists of no more than a score of items. Northern dim sum are less well known in the West than those from the south, there being many more Cantonese restaurants abroad. The southern Cantonese dim sum are undoubtedly daintier and require more skill to make than those from the north. For practical reasons we shall confine ourselves to those dim sum which can be readily made at home.

Peking Kuo–Tieh dumplings are fun to make for a celebration meal. The same dumplings can be simmered, then drained and eaten with a spicy sauce (Red Chili Oil Dumplings), but these are steamed and then shallow-fried.

1 After mixing the flour with boiling then cold water, the dough is gathered with the hand.

For recipe see
**Peking Kuo–tieh
Dumplings, p. 241**

For recipe see
**Red Chili Oil
Dumplings, p. 268**

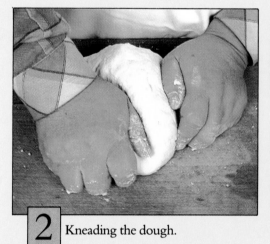

2 Kneading the dough.

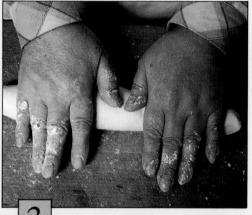

3 Rolling the dough into a sausage shape before cutting it into small pieces.

4 Flouring the pieces of dough.

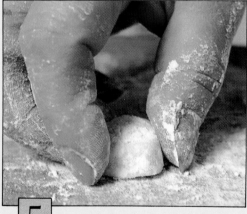

5 Forming the pieces into rounds.

6 Flattening the balls of dough.

7 Rolling out each round of dough.

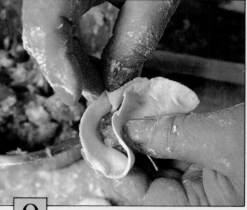

8 Filling the center of each round.

9 Folding over the dough and pinching the edges firmly to seal.

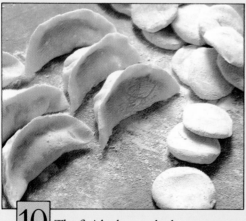

10 The finished uncooked dumplings and flattened dough.

11 Shallow-frying the dumplings.

Steamed buns and dumplings are an important part of northern Chinese cooking and are a popular breakfast or snack sold at roadside stalls for people going to work.

Stuffed wontons are easy to make because wonton skins are sold ready-made at many good Chinese food stores. But whether you buy or make the skins, fried or steamed wontons make a tasty snack. Alternatively, wontons can be simmered for a delicious addition to soup.

To filling 20 wonton skins:

3–4 oz ground pork

⅓ cup ground shrimp

2 tablespoons chopped
    green onion

Salt and pepper

1 tablespoon rice wine

1 tablespoon finely chopped
    fresh ginger root

Allow about 4 wontons per person

1 Adding rice wine to the stuffing mixture.

2 Adding ginger to the mixture.

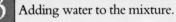

3 Adding water to the mixture.

4 Stirring well to form an evenly flavored mixture.

5 Filling the center of the wonton skins. (Allow about 1 teaspoon of filling per wonton.)

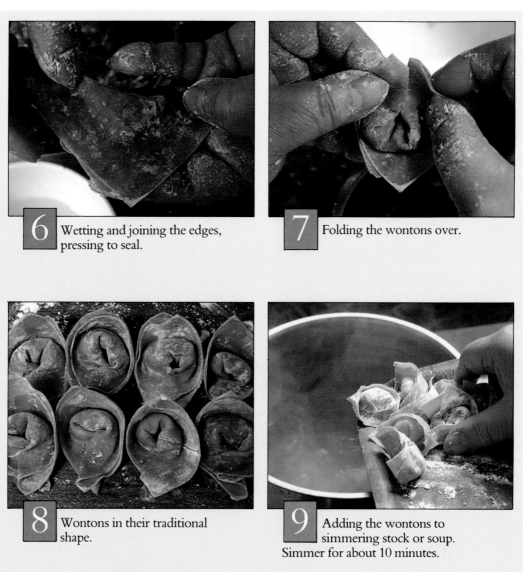

6 Wetting and joining the edges, pressing to seal.

7 Folding the wontons over.

Deep–fried Crispy Wontons are illustrated on p. 238

Wonton Soup is illustrated on p. 234

8 Wontons in their traditional shape.

9 Adding the wontons to simmering stock or soup. Simmer for about 10 minutes.

The final cooked wontons.

Dough skin wrappers:

1 egg

2 cups all-purpose flour

1/2 teaspoon salt

1/2 cup water

Cornstarch

SPRING ROLL WRAPPERS

★★★
Preparation time:
about 30 minutes,
plus resting time

Spring roll wrappers or pancakes are generally available at the majority of major Chinese supermarkets, but they can also be easily made at home. Spring roll wrappers can vary greatly in size. The daintier, smaller ones are no more than 3 inches long, while some can reach 10 inches in length.

▦ PREPARATION ▦

Lightly beat egg. Sift flour and salt into large bowl. Make a well in the center and mix beaten egg and water into the flour. Stir with a wooden spoon to form smooth dough. Place dough on floured board and knead for 10 minutes or until smooth. Cover with damp cloth and leave to rest for about 30 minutes. Roll dough into 12-inch sausage, then cut into 1½-inch pieces. Dust with cornstarch and flatten with palm of hand. Roll as thinly as possible, then trim to 6 × 7-inch rectangles. Dust with cornstarch and stack.

1¾ cups sliced lean pork or chicken meat

2 slices fresh ginger root

3 oz canned bamboo shoots

8 medium-sized dried Chinese mushrooms

2 green onions

3 tablespoons vegetable oil

1 teaspoon salt

2 tablespoons soy sauce

1½ cups bean sprouts

1 tablespoon cornstarch blended with 2 tablespoons water

Beaten egg for sealing

Vegetable oil for deep-frying

SPRING ROLL FILLINGS

★★★★
Cooking time:
45 minutes for
filling,
3¾–4½ minutes per
batch of spring
rolls

Serves: 6–8

Cooking methods:
stir-fry p.42 and
deep-fry p.45

Fairly easy to
make with practice

Useful side dish
with soy-based dip
sauce

Illustrated on
pp.235 and 266

Almost any mixture of meat and vegetables can be used as fillings for spring rolls. They need to be shredded and quickly stir-fried, then left to cool before wrapping in the pancakes as fillings. The most popular ingredients for fillings are the following.

▦ PREPARATION ▦

Cut pork or chicken into matchstick-sized shreds. Cut ginger and bamboo shoots into similar or finer shreds. Soak dried mushrooms in hot water to cover for 25 minutes. Drain and discard tough stalks. Cut mushroom caps into fine shreds. Divide green onions lengthwise in half then cut into ½-inch sections.

▦ COOKING ▦

Heat 3 tablespoons of oil in wok or skillet. When hot, stir-fry ginger, salt, mushrooms and shredded meat over high heat for 1¼ minutes. Add all other ingredients, except cornstarch, and stir-fry for 1 minute. Pour in blended cornstarch, stir and turn for another 30 seconds. Remove from heat and leave to cool.

▦ FILLING THE PANCAKES ▦

Take 2 tablespoons of filling and spread across each pancake just below center. Fold pancake up from bottom by raising lower corner to fold over filling. Roll filling over once, and bring in 2 corners from side to overlap each other. Finally, fold top flap down, sealing with little beaten egg. Stack spring rolls as you make them, placing them so that weight of pancake rests on flap that has just been sealed.

■ COOKING THE PANCAKES ■

Fry pancakes soon after they have been made, otherwise they may become soggy. Heat oil in wok or deep-fryer. When hot, fry not more than 5-6 pancakes at one time for 3¾-4½ minutes until golden brown and crispy. Once fried, they can be kept crisp in oven for up to 30 minutes. Or store them in refrigerator for a day after an initial frying of 2½ minutes, then refry them for 3 minutes when required.

■ SESAME SHRIMP ON TOAST ■

★ ★ ★ ★

Cooking time: about 4 minutes per batch

Serves: 7-8

Cooking method: deep-fry, p.45

Quite easy to make

Excellent party starter

Illustrated on p.239

1 cup shrimp, fresh or frozen, shelled
¼ cup pork fat
1 teaspoon salt
Pepper to taste
½ teaspoon ground ginger
1 tablespoon dry sherry or white wine
1½ tablespoons finely chopped green onion
1 egg white
2 teaspoons cornstarch
6 slices bread
⅔ cup sesame seeds
Vegetable oil for deep-frying

These toasts make an excellent starter and can be used as canapés for a cocktail party.

■ PREPARATION ■

Chop and mix shrimp and pork fat into a paste in a bowl. Add salt, pepper, ginger, sherry or wine, green onion, egg white and cornstarch. Mix together thoroughly. Spread mixture very thickly on top of slices of bread. Spread sesame seeds evenly over surface of large plate or small tray. Place each piece of bread, spread-side down, on sesame seeds. Press gently so that each slice has a good coating of seeds.

■ COOKING ■

Heat oil in wok or deep-fryer. When hot, fry slices of bread, spread-side down (only 2-3 slices of bread can be fried at a time) for 2½ minutes. Turn over and fry for further 1½ minutes. Drain on paper towels.

■ SERVING ■

When all slices of bread have been fried and drained, place each piece of bread on chopping board, cut off and discard crusts. Cut slices into 6 rectangular pieces (the size of fish fingers) or into 4 triangles. Arrange them on heated serving dish and serve hot.

Steamed buns (*above*), a
tempting savory snack.
Wonton Soup (*left*),
wonton-making needs
practice to perfect; recipe
page 231.
Spring Rolls (*right*), serve
these famous deep–fried
savory rolls as a snack or as
part of a multi–course
meal; recipe page 232.

12 quails' eggs, drained if necessary
1½ cups shrimp, fresh or frozen, shelled
¼ cup pork fat
2 egg whites
1 teaspoon salt
¼ teaspoon pepper
¼ teaspoon MSG (optional)
1 tablespoon cornstarch
1 teaspoon dry sherry
½ teaspoon sesame oil
1 teaspoon finely chopped green onion
6 slices thin white bread
1½ tablespoons finely chopped carrot
1½ tablespoons finely chopped cilantro leaves
Vegetable oil for deep-frying

QUAILS' EGGS ON SHRIMP TOASTS

This is a more elaborate version of the popular Sesame Shrimp on Toast. They make very attractive and appealing canapé at any cocktail party.

■ PREPARATION ■

Place eggs in pan of water. Bring to boil and simmer for 4 minutes. Drain and plunge into cold water. Chop shrimp and pork fat together to form smooth paste. Place them in bowl and add egg whites, salt, pepper, monosodium glutamate, if using, cornstarch, sherry, sesame oil and green onion. Mix together until smooth. Shell quails' eggs and cut in half lengthwise. Spread each piece of bread evenly with shrimp mixture, then cut each slice of bread into 4 pieces. Press half a quail's egg into mixture and pinch of chopped carrot at one end and chopped cilantro at the other end.

■ COOKING ■

Heat oil in wok or deep-fryer. When hot, lower slices of bread, in batches, shrimp-side down, into oil. Fry for 1½ minutes, then turn over gently and fry for a further minute. Turn them once again and fry for another 15 seconds. Remove and drain on paper towels.

★★★★

Cooking time: about 3 minutes per batch

Serves: 6–8

Cooking method: deep-fry, p.45

A little time-consuming to prepare

Use good quality soy, or soy, chili and ketchup as a dip sauce

Attractive canapé

½ oz dry yeast
1¼ cups warm water
1 teaspoon sugar
3½ cups self-rising flour
Filling:
6 dried Chinese mushrooms
1 lb ground pork
2 tablespoons light soy sauce
1 teaspoon salt
1 teaspoon sugar
½ teaspoon pepper
¼ teaspoon MSG (optional)
2 tablespoons water
1 Chinese white cabbage
2 teaspoons sesame oil

BAO TZU STEAMED BUNS

■ PREPARATION ■

Mix yeast with 4 tablespoons warm water and sugar. Leave until frothy; about 10 minutes. Sift flour into large bowl. Make well in center. Pour in yeast mixture with remaining 1 cup warm water. Mix and knead dough. Leave in a warm place until dough doubles in size. Knead well, then leave to rise until about half size again.

For filling, soak dried mushrooms in hot water to cover for 25 minutes. Drain and discard tough stalks. Chop mushroom caps into ¼-inch pieces. Put ground pork in a large bowl. Add soy sauce. Mix together half salt, sugar, pepper, monosodium glutamate, if using, and water. Add to meat mixture. Wash cabbage and blanch whole in a saucepan of boiling water for 30 seconds. Squeeze cabbage dry and cut into small pieces. Mix mushrooms

★★★★

Cooking time: 12 minutes

Serves: 10–12

Cooking method: steam, p.49

Fairly easy to make with practice

Tasty snack

Illustrated on p.266

and cabbage together with remaining salt, 2 teaspoons sesame oil and then mix with ground pork.

Divide dough into 28–30 balls. Roll each ball into 3-inch flat rounds. Put 1 tablespoon meat filling on each round. Gather up edges. Pinch dough together to enclose filling.

■ COOKING ■

Put buns in a steamer on greased paper, about 1-inch apart. Steam for 12 minutes.

★ ★ ★ ★

**Cooking time:
12 minutes**

Serves: 10–12

**Cooking method:
steam, p.49**

**Fairly easy to
make with practice**

Eat as snack

BAO TZU STEAMED BUNS

STUFFED WITH SWEET BEAN PASTE

½ oz dry yeast

1¼ cups warm water

1 teaspoon sugar

3½ cups self-rising flour

Sweet bean paste

■ PREPARATION ■

Mix yeast with 4 tablespoons warm water and sugar. Leave until frothy, about 10 minutes. Sift flour into large bowl. Make well in center. Pour in yeast mixture with remaining 1 cup warm water. Mix and knead dough. Leave in a warm place until dough doubles in size. Knead well, then leave to rise until about half size again.

Take a piece of dough (about 2–3 tablespoons), punch down and knead again for a few minutes. Form it into a cup or shell. Stuff each bun with 2 teaspoons sweet bean paste. Gather up dough to enclose filling. Leave to prove for 15–20 minutes.

■ COOKING ■

Place buns in a steamer on greased paper, 1-inch apart. Steam for 12 minutes.

237

Crispy Wontons (*above*). Wontons (page 231)
can be deep-fried for 2½–3 minutes and served
with a dip sauce or Sweet and sour sauce, found
on page 197.
Steamed Siu Mai (*above right*), steamed
dumplings filled with a savory mixture of
shrimp, pork and vegetables; recipe page 240.
Peking Kuo-tieh Steamed and Sautéed
Dumplings (*center right*), a Northern dim sum
dumpling filled with a pork mixture; recipe
page 241.
Sesame Shrimp on Toast (*below right*), serve as a
sumptuous starter or as part of a buffet spread;
recipe page 233.

1½ cups boiling water

2 cups cold water

1 teaspoon dry yeast

1 tablespoon sugar

4 cups self-rising flour

3 tablespoons vegetable oil

LOTUS LEAF SHAPED STEAMED BUNS

■ PREPARATION ■

Mix the boiling water with cold water. Sprinkle over the yeast and stir in ½ teaspoon of the sugar. Cover and stand for 3 minutes until the yeast froths. (If the bubbling does not take place, discard and start again with new yeast.) Sift the flour into a large bowl and gradually stir in yeast mixture with 1 tablespoon of the vegetable oil and the rest of the sugar to form a soft dough. Knead until the texture becomes elastic. Leave the dough in a warm draughtfree place for 2-3 hours until the dough doubles in size. Punch down dough to reduce it to the original size. Cover with a damp cloth and leave for another 20-30 minutes. When risen, turn out the dough and knead again. Roll into a 1½-inch thick roll. Cut the dough into 1-inch sections, roll these into a ball and flatten with hand.

With a rolling pin, roll the dough into 3-inch rounds. Brush oil on half of the top. Fold the other half over and score a criss-cross pattern over the top. Pinch in slightly around the edge at intervals to form shape of lotus leaf.

■ COOKING ■

Place buns in a heatproof dish in a steamer and steam over high for 6 minutes.

★ ★ ★ ★

Cooking time: 6 minutes

Serves: 5-6

Cooking method: steam, p.49

Fairly easy to make after practice

Ideal accompaniment to rich meaty dishes with lots of sauce

---

6 dried Chinese mushrooms

2 drained, canned bamboo shoots

⅔ cup shrimp, fresh or frozen, shelled

1 green onion

2 eggs

12 oz ground pork

2 tablespoons peas

½ teaspoon salt

Pinch of MSG (optional)

Pinch of white pepper

½ teaspoon sugar

2 tablespoons vegetable oil

2 tablespoons cornstarch

1 teaspoon sesame oil

4 oz wonton skins

STEAMED SIU MAI

■ PREPARATION ■

Soak dried mushrooms in hot water to cover for 25 minutes. Drain and discard tough stalks. Chop mushroom caps. Finely chop bamboo shoots, shrimp and green onion. Lightly beat eggs. Mix pork, mushrooms, bamboo shoots, shrimp, peas and egg together in bowl. Add salt, green onion, monosodium glutamate, if using, white pepper, sugar, vegetable oil, cornstarch and sesame oil and combine thoroughly. Place 1¼ teaspoons of meat and vegetable mixture in the center of a wonton skin. Gather up edges to form a kind of 'flower pot' with an open top.

■ COOKING ■

Place dumplings in steamer. Steam for 10-11 minutes. Serve very hot.

★ ★ ★ ★ ★

Cooking time: 10-11 minutes

Serves: 6-7

Cooking method: steam, p.49

Time-consuming to make

Serve with soy-based dip as starter or side dish

Illustrated on p.239

★ ★ ★ ★

Cooking time:
about 20 minutes

Serves: 8-10

Cooking method:
part fry and part
steam, p.49

**Requires practice
to perfect**

**Traditionally
served with dip of
fresh grated ginger
root with vinegar**

Illustrated on p.239

■ PEKING KUO-TIEH STEAMED AND SAUTEED DUMPLINGS ■

Both this and Red Chili Oil Dumplings (see page 268) are Northern dim sum. The ingredients used for Kuo-Tieh Dumplings are the same, the only differences being the dip sauce and the way in which the dumplings are cooked.

■ PREPARATION ■

Sift flour in bowl and mix in boiling water. Leave for 5 minutes. Add cold water, then knead well.

For the stuffing, finely chop ginger and green onions. Grind pork and shrimp together. Add ginger, green onions, salt, soy sauce, sugar and 1 tablespoon water. Mix together well. Finely chop Chinese cabbage and season lightly with salt, pepper and monosodium glutamate, if using. Add to pork mixture, combining well.

Form dough into long roll and then cut off about thirty 1-inch pieces. Roll each piece into a flat pancake and then place teaspoon of pork stuffing in center. Fold pancake in half to form half circle and seal edges. Repeat process until all ingredients are used.

■ COOKING ■

Heat 3 tablespoons vegetable oil in wok or skillet over medium heat. When hot, tilt pan so that the surface is evenly coated in oil. Arrange dumplings evenly over the surface and fry over high heat for 2½ minutes, until the bases of the dumplings are brown. Pour 2½ cups hot water down side of pan. Cover and continue to cook over high heat until almost all the water has evaporated. Add 2 tablespoons hot vegetable oil down side of pan. Lower heat and continue to cook, covered, until all water has evaporated. Remove from heat. Use a metal spatula to gently loosen dumplings from bottom of pan. Place a large serving dish face-down over the dumplings. Quickly turn pan and dumplings over on to the dish, so that the brown side of the dumplings is face upwards.

■ SERVING ■

Transfer the dumplings to a heated serving plate and keep warm while you prepare the dip sauce. Mix all the dip sauce ingredients together and pour over the dumplings.

Dough skin:

3 cups all-purpose flour

2½ cups boiling water

5 tablespoons cold water

Stuffing:

2 slices fresh ginger root

2 green onions

1 cup diced lean pork

¾ cup shrimp, fresh or frozen, shelled

1 teaspoon salt

1 tablespoon light soy sauce

1 teaspoon sugar

8 oz Chinese white cabbage

Pinch of pepper

Pinch of MSG (optional)

5 tablespoons vegetable oil

Dip sauce:

2 tablespoons shredded fresh ginger root

5 tablespoons vinegar

2 tablespoons soy sauce (optional)

REGIONAL CUISINE

Green Onion Pancakes – chef's version; recipe page 250.

地區性烹飪法

Regional Cuisine

CHINA IS ABOUT the same size as the continental United States, and may be divided into four regions: Peking, Shanghai, Sichuan and Canton. As you will see, each region has its own distinctive ways of cooking, so that dishes from Shanghai are as different from those of Sichuan as Coney Island hot dogs are from the Creole cooking of Louisiana.

■ PEKING AND THE NORTH ■

Peking is to China what Paris is to France: the many cultural threads of the country are drawn to the capital. All the various provincial styles of cooking are represented in Peking though the most common dishes have drawn their inspiration locally. These use regional produce and seem to reflect local culinary traditions and the harsh northern climate.

The huge numbers of sheep kept in the region have had a far greater influence on local cooking than dishes from the emperor's palace, so it is not surprising that the Chinese have nicknamed Peking 'Mutton City'. Mutton and lamb and the extensive use of ginger, leeks, garlic, and green onions give northern cooking a stronger, more robust character than in the rest of the country. The meals also seem heavier because steamed wheat buns, noodles and Chinese pancakes are served more often than rice. These substantial fillers are eaten as side dishes, seasoned with sauce, or are served with the many local slowly simmered or braised dishes to mop up the richly flavored sauces.

There are fewer fresh vegetables in Peking and the surrounding area, especially in the winter months, than in the warmer regions to the south, though huge crops of the familiar Chinese, or Tientsin, cabbage are grown as they keep well through the winter. To make up for the lack of variety, there is a comparatively greater use made of pickled and preserved vegetables.

Northern China was once overrun by Tartar hordes from nearby Mongolia, then ruled for many years by Mongolian emperors such as Genghis and Kublai Kahn. Their influence on northern cooking can be seen in the local preference for less sophisticated foods such as roasted and barbecued meat dipped in strong-tasting sauces and condiments. Even when stir-frying the huge, delicately flavored shrimp caught off the Shantung coast, thick savory soy paste is favored over lighter seasonings.

The region's two most famous dishes, Peking Duck and Mongolian Hot Pot, also originated from the Tartars. Though its skin is crispy and the meat is juicy, the duck is simply cooked, then rolled up in a pancake with a piquant sauce and crunchy vegetables. For Mongolian Hot Pot, thinly sliced lamb is cooked at the table in boiling stock sometimes containing noodles and cabbage. The meat is dipped into

THE REGIONS
OF CHINA

NEI MONGOL
(INNER MONGOLIA)

JILIN

Tonghua
Shenyang

LIAONING

GOBI DESERT

Peking

PO
HAI

Luda

Huhhot

Yellow R.

Yantai

ORDOS
DESERT

Tianjin

Weihai

GANSU

Shijiazhuang

HEBEI

Qingdao

YELLOW
SEA

EAST
CHINA
SEA

PACIFIC OCEAN

Yinchuan

Dezhou

SHANXI

Jinan

NINGXIA
HUIZU

SHANDONG

Grand
Canal

JIANGSU

Great Wall

Taiyuan

Fen
He R.

Weishan

Yangzhou

Xining

Fenyang

Kaifeng

Gaoyou

Pukow

Lanzhou

Zhengzhou

Hongze

Zhenjiang
Suzhou

Fengxiang

Wei R.

Luoyang

Huai R

Shanghai

Xi'an

HENAN

Chao

Hefei

Nanjing

Tai

Hangzhou
Shaoxing

SHAANXI

HUBEI

Yangtse R.

Qimen

Jinhua

BASIN OF SICHUAN

Yangtse

Wuhan

Jiujiang

Jingdezhen

ZHEIJIANG

Min R.

Jialing R.

SICHUAN

Gorges
Dongting

LU SHAN

Poyang

Chengdu

Tuo R.

Nanchang

WUYI
MOUNTAINS

Fuzhou

Chonqing

Changsha

JIANGXI

FUJIAN

TAIWAN

HUNAN

Quanzhou

GUIZHOU

Hengyang

Longyan

Renhuai

Dong'an

Xiamen

Xuanwei

Guiyang

NAN LING

Zhangzhou

Guilin

Chao'an

Shantou

Kunming

Liuzhou

Bei
Jiang

Dong Jiang

Dian Chi

GUANGXI
ZHUANGZU

Huizhou

YUNNAN

Xi
Jiang
(Pearl R.)

HONG KONG

Puer

Nanning

Guangzhou (Canton)

GUANGDONG

Haikou

HAINAN

SOUTH CHINA
SEA

COOKERY SCHOOLS

Northern/Peking

Peking

Shandong

Eastern/Shanghai

Shanghai

Huaiyang

Suzhe

Hangzhou

Fukien

Western/ Sichuan

Sichuan

Southern/Canton

Guangzhou (Canton)

Dong Jiang

Shantou

one of several strong sauces and afterwards the richly flavored stock is shared as soup
to end the hearty one-dish meal.

■ SHANGHAI AND THE EAST ■

Shanghai, the gateway to eastern China, is one of the largest cities in the world and
centuries ago was the first seaport opened to traders from the West. This made the
area one of the most affluent in China. Situated along with the other main cities of the
region on the Yangtze River delta where China's great river flows into the East
China Sea, Shanghai also marks the boundary between north and south China.

The lush region is very fertile and the climate is temperate with mild seasons. This
seems to be reflected in the nature of eastern cooking, which is full of fresh-water
produce and the bounty of abundant rice harvests. The many rivers, streams and
ponds provide fish and shellfish in plenty. A wide range of vegetables thrive on the
intensively irrigated land as well as millions of ducks which are reared every year.
There are also many pig and poultry farms. These foods are tender, their flavors are

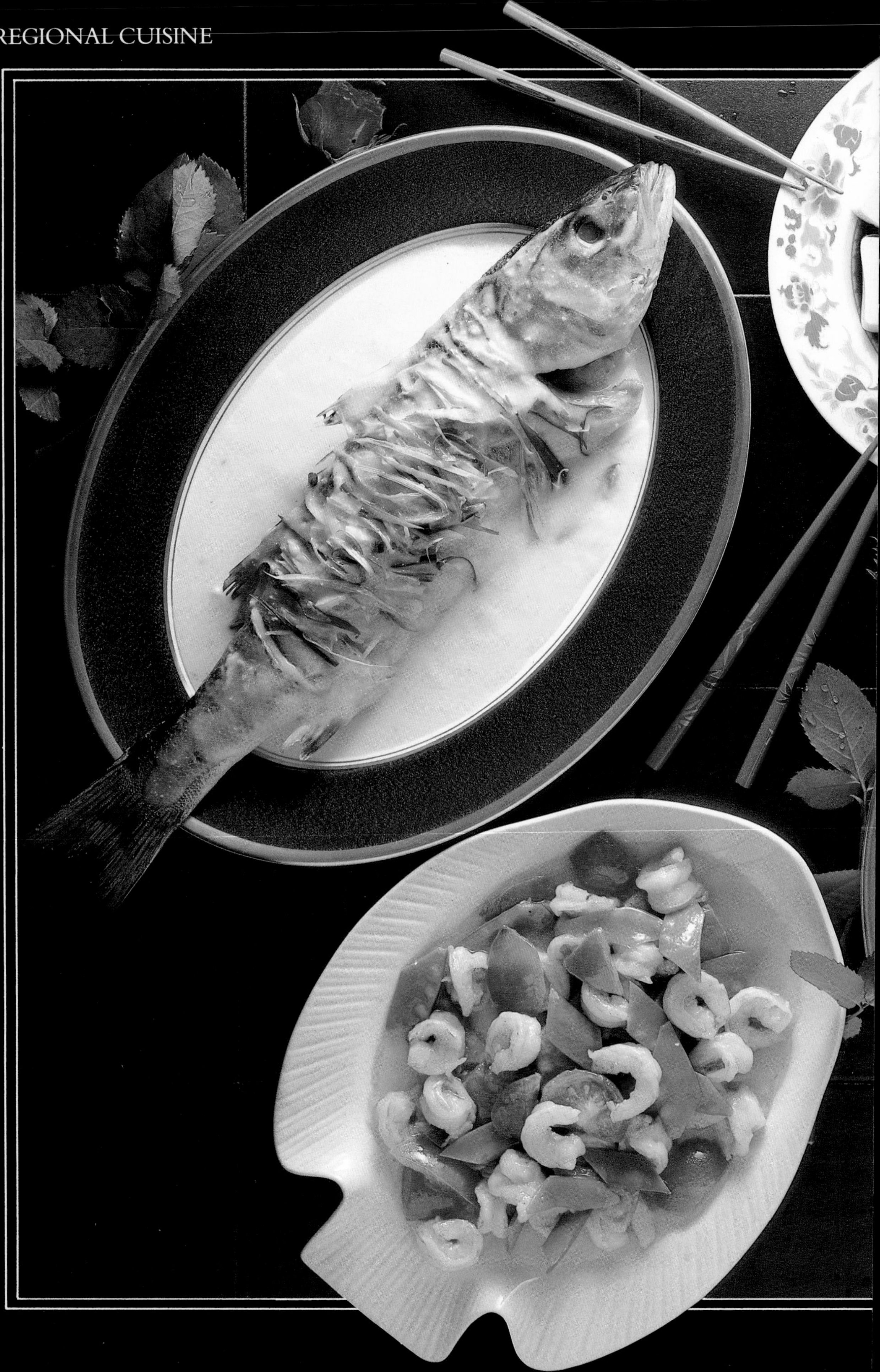

A colorful and varied selection of dishes from the Shanghai region, which covers a wide range of cooking techniques from succulent long-steamed pork hock and steamed whole fish with garnish and savory white sauce to quick, lightly stir-fried dishes such as shrimp and tomato wedges with snow pea sections, and bean curd with chopped shrimp.

地
區
性
烹
飪
法

delicate, so the seasonings used with them are mild.

This does not mean that the cooking is simple or unsophisticated. Generally speaking, Shanghai and eastern Chinese dishes are slightly sweet and rich both in the amount of fat and in the variety and quality of other ingredients used. They are also known for their elaborate presentation.

As in northern China, steamed wheat buns and plain noodles are widely eaten here. The buns, however, are smaller, with delicate stuffings such as crab eggs, young bamboo shoots or ground pork with aspic. The region's enormous rice crop is not wasted, for much of it is used in vinegar and in wine. China's finest rice vinegar is a dark aromatic one called Chinkiang after the town in which the vinegar is made. It, as well as rice wine, is produced in great quantity. Known as 'yellow wine' because of its pale golden color, the most famous one in China, Shaoshing, comes from a town of that name just south of the Yangtze River. Rice wine is naturally used in many local dishes such as those red-braised, a cooking method whereby fish, meat or poultry cooks slowly in a mixture of rice wine and dark soy sauce until the mixture reduces and can be served spooned over rice and noodles.

◼ SICHUAN AND THE WEST ◼

Known as the rice bowl of China, Sichuan and the other fertile provinces of the western part of the country are over a thousand miles from the sea and surrounded by high mountains and deep river valleys. This is the home of well over one hundred million people who, due to their geographical location and reasonably prosperous peasant background, have produced dishes with a remarkably sophisticated range of flavors. Fresh foods such as pork, river fish and vegetables are combined with smoked, pickled and dried ingredients, while in the same dish sour, sweet and salty flavors are carefully balanced with chilies.

◼

One of the most common sights along the Yangtze River is the transplanting of rice from the nursery to the paddy field, which is always done by hand. By comparison, running a market stall seems positively tranquil, especially between sales.

The chili-hot aspect of Sichuan, Hunan and other western Chinese food is the one that is best known to people outside China. Fresh and dried chilies are used by the people of western China both for health and a good table. Much of the year the weather is extremely humid and the people believe that perspiring wards off illness. They also believe that instead of burning the taste buds, chili stimulates them to be more sensitive to a full range of flavors and after-tastes.

The winter in this part of China is mild, so cultivation is possible all year long. Besides rice, wheat, corn, citrus fruit and Sichuan peppercorns are major crops. Mushrooms, cloud ears and other fungi, both wild and cultivated, as well as bamboo grow in great profusion on the largely agricultural, well irrigated land.

As the western provinces were so isolated from the busy sea and river trade carried on in the rest of China, preserving locally produced food in the humid climate became essential. The smoking, pickling, spicing and drying that of necessity went on gave a strong flavor to ingredients used in many of their dishes. Perhaps for this reason the western Chinese palate became appreciative of the more pungently flavored vegetables such as onions, garlic, fresh ginger, green onions, chilies and peppers as well as nutty aromatic ones such as sesame oil, sesame seeds and sesame butter and peanuts. When used in conjunction with salty soy bean products such as soy sauce, soy paste, bean curd cheese and black beans, these ingredients produce the characteristic piquant spiciness characteristic of many western Chinese dishes. The Chinese outside this region have understandably adopted the best of them so that now, even in the West, people can enjoy the pleasure of western Chinese cooking.

■ CANTON AND THE SOUTH ■

As far as food is concerned, the Cantonese are easily the most indulgent people in China. They and the other southern Chinese live in a semi-tropical region where the soil is so fertile that two rice crops a year are grown and people can also engage in small-scale fruit and fish farming. A great variety of green leafy vegetables are grown and meat is readily available from a large selection of reared animals, including pigs, cattle and poultry.

Fresh seafood is an enormously important element in their cooking as the south has the longest coastline of any region in China. All along the coast vast quantities of fish and shellfish are brought in including shrimp, scallops, crabs, eels, and crayfish as well as more exotic delicacies such as abalone, sea cucumber, shark – and shark's fin. Probably it is such variety that has inspired southern Chinese cooks to incorporate seafood flavors through oyster sauce, shrimp sauce and shrimp paste into meat and even vegetable dishes. This juxtaposition of flavors creates highly savory dishes and clever cooks are not beyond introducing meats such as shredded chicken into basically seafood dishes.

That being said, southern Chinese dishes generally are not highly seasoned. Endlessly creative, the cooks aim at cooking very fresh foods together to bring out the best in each of them, adding only a few condiments to enhance the mixture. The Cantonese are especially partial to stir-frying.

Egg rather than plain noodles are used in many dishes, but rice is eaten at every meal including the variously-flavored soft rice stew, congee, usually served for breakfast. Served with plain boiled rice are an enormous number of meat and vegetable dishes, usually three or four at both lunch and dinner. Even so, the greedy southern Chinese make time and room for tea and savory snacks called dim sum. These are pastry tidbits stuffed with meat, seafood and vegetable mixtures, then sautéed, deep-fried or steamed.

3 large green onions

3 cups all-purpose flour

1¼ cups boiling water

⅓ cup shortening or lard

5 tablespoons cold water

1¼ tablespoons large-grained sea salt

GREEN ONION PANCAKES

★★★★
Cooking time:
5 minutes each

Serves: 5–6 (makes 10)

Cooking method:
shallow-fry

Needs practice to perfect

A good starter

Illustrated on p.243

These pancakes, often included as a Northern dim sum item, are more aromatic and tasty than one would imagine. They are normally eaten on their own, or they can be eaten to supplement other savory dishes. The strong presence of onion and the occasional sharpness of the sea salt grains in the crispy dough give them an unexpectedly simple appeal.

■ PREPARATION ■

Coarsely chop green onions. Sift flour into large bowl. Slowly add boiling water and 1 tablespoon of fat. Stir with fork or pair of chopsticks for 3 minutes. Mix in cold water and knead for 2 minutes. Leave dough to stand for 30 minutes. Form and roll dough into long roll and cut into 10 equal sections. Roll each piece into a ball and press the ball into a flat pancake. Sprinkle pancake evenly with salt and chopped green onion. Fold it up from the sides to form a ball, then press again into a pancake.

■ COOKING AND SERVING ■

Heat remaining fat in wok or skillet. When hot, spread pancakes evenly over pan and fry over low heat for 2½ minutes on either side, until golden brown.

⅔ cup shredded lean pork

4 medium dried Chinese mushrooms

2 tablespoons wood ears

3 stalks golden needles (tiger lily buds)

3 green onions

4 eggs

5 tablespoons vegetable oil

2½ tablespoons light soy sauce

½ teaspoon sugar

2½ tablespoons good stock (see page 56)

1 tablespoon dry sherry

1 teaspoon sesame oil

EGG FLOWER PORK – MU SHU ROU

★★★
Cooking time:
about 6–8 minutes

Serves: 4–6

Cooking method:
stir-fry, p.42

Quick to cook

Illustrated opposite

This dish is often used as a pancake filling, and served like Peking Duck (see page 178).

■ PREPARATION ■

Cut pork into matchstick-size shreds. Soak dried mushrooms and wood ears in hot water to cover for 25 minutes. Drain, discard tough stalks, then cut mushroom caps into similar-sized shreds as pork. Cut golden needles and green onion into 1-inch sections. Beat eggs lightly with fork.

■ COOKING ■

When cooking this dish, it is best to use 2 woks or skillets – one small and one large. Heat 2 tablespoons of oil in larger pan. When hot, stir-fry mushrooms and pork for 1½ minutes. Add wood ears, green onions and golden needles. Stir together for 1 minute, then add soy sauce, sugar and stock. Toss together for another minute,

continued page 252

remove from heat. Heat remaining vegetable oil in smaller pan and pour in beaten eggs. Heat steadily over low heat until set and then stir to break up eggs into ½-inch pieces. Transfer eggs to larger pan and reheat. Sprinkle on sherry and sesame oil. Stir and turn over high heat for a few seconds and serve.

PEKING SLICED FISH IN 'STANDARD SAUCE'

■ PREPARATION ■
Cut fish into 2 × 1-inch slices. Rub with salt. Dust with cornstarch. Coat with egg white. Shred ginger. Cut green onions into ½-inch shreds.

■ COOKING ■
Heat oil in wok or deep-fryer until very hot. Remove from heat and leave to cool for 30 seconds. Add fish slices, one by one, to oil and fry for 1 minute. Return pan to heat and fry for 1 minute. Remove fish and drain. Heat shortening in wok or skillet. When hot, stir-fry ginger and green onion for few seconds. Add soy sauce, vinegar, sugar, stock, wine or sherry and crumbled bouillon cube. Mix well. Finally, stir in blended cornstarch and bring to boil. Add fish to sauce and spread slices out. Baste a few times with sauce.

■ SERVING ■
Transfer fish to heated dish. Pour sauce over.

PEKING SPUN SUGAR 'TOFFEE APPLES'

This is an infinitely more refined version of the Toffee Apple than those often encountered at funfairs.

■ PREPARATION ■
Mix flour with water and beaten egg. Beat to smooth batter. Peel and core apples. Cut each apple into 5-6 equal pieces. For sugar coating, heat sugar and oil in small saucepan. Stir continuously until sugar has melted and blended with oil. Keep hot. Dip apple pieces in batter, then sprinkle with sesame seeds.

Ingredients (first recipe):

1¼ lb white fish fillets, eg sole, flounder, carp, halibut etc.

1½ teaspoons salt

2 tablespoons cornstarch

1 egg white

Vegetable oil for deep-frying

Sauce:

3 slices fresh ginger root

2 green onions

2 tablespoons shortening or lard

2 tablespoons light soy sauce

1½ tablespoons wine vinegar

1 teaspoon sugar

3 tablespoons good stock (see page 56)

2 tablespoons rice wine or dry sherry

½ chicken bouillon cube

½ tablespoon cornstarch blended with 1½ tablespoons water

★★★
Cooking time: about 10 minutes
Serves: 5-6
Cooking methods: deep-fry p.45 and stir-fry p.42
Quite easy to prepare
Goes well with most other Chinese dishes

Ingredients (second recipe):

5 medium cooking (tart) apples

2 tablespoons sesame seeds

Batter:

1 cup all-purpose flour

½ cup cold water

1 egg

Vegetable oil for deep-frying

Sugar coating:

1 cup sugar

2 tablespoons vegetable oil

★★★★★
Cooking time: 2½ minutes per batch
Serves: 6-8
Cooking method: deep-fry, p.45
Needs practice to perfect
One of the few Chinese desserts easily acceptable to Western palates
Illustrated on p.254

■ COOKING ■

Heat oil in wok or deep-fryer. Fry battered apple pieces in batches for 2½ minutes. Drain. When all apple pieces have been fried and drained, add 2-3 pieces at a time to hot sugar coating. Pull them out one at a time with a pair of wooden chopsticks, then dip quickly into bowl of ice-cold water. Retrieve immediately and set aside. (This makes sugar coating brittle, and prevents batter from becoming soggy.) Repeat with all the apple pieces.

■ SERVING ■

Either divide toffee apples into individual dishes, as in the West, or pile them on to a large serving dish from which diners may help themselves.

RIVAL OF CRAB
(OR SAI PAN HSIA)

★★★

Cooking time: about 20 minutes

Serves: 5-6

Cooking method: stir-fry, p.42

Interesting and fairly easy to prepare

Good as part of a multi-dish meal

This recipe is said to have been a favorite of the Empress Dowager. Whenever she requested a dish of crab in the winter, which was unavailable in the North at this time of year due to the severity of the weather, she was presented with this dish instead.

■ PREPARATION ■

Cut fish into cubes. Sprinkle and rub with salt. Beat eggs with fork in bowl for 10 seconds. Beat 1 egg yolk with 1 tablespoon water for 6-7 seconds. Beat remaining egg yolk with tomato paste for 6-7 seconds in separate bowl. Finely chop ginger. Cut green onion into ¼-inch shreds. Mix sauce ingredients together until smooth.

■ COOKING ■

Heat shortening and oil in wok or skillet. When hot, stir-fry ginger and green onion over medium heat for 15 seconds. Add fish cubes, turn and gently stir them quickly for 30 seconds. Stir in beaten eggs and mix with fish. When eggs are about to set, pour or drop in yolk and water mixture, then sprinkle over yolk and tomato paste mixture. Scramble lightly and turn contents over. Add sauce mixture and continue to turn and scramble gently and lightly for 1½ minutes. Transfer mixture to heated dish.

½ lb white fish

1½ teaspoons salt

4 eggs

2 egg yolks

1 tablespoon water

1¼ tablespoons tomato paste

2 slices fresh ginger root

1 green onion

2 tablespoons shortening or lard

1½ tablespoons vegetable oil

Sauce:

1 tablespoon cornstarch

¼ cup good stock (see page 56)

1 tablespoon shrimp sauce

½ tablespoon oyster sauce

1 teaspoon salt

2 tablespoons dry sherry or white wine

Peking 'Toffee Apples' (*left*), apple pieces coated in a brittle sugar coating; recipe page 252.

Quick Fry of Three Sea Flavors (*above right*), shrimp, scallop and squid are the three flavors; recipe page 260.

Multi-colored Shrimp Balls (*below right*), coated in crumbled noodles, shredded cabbage and carrot, serve this attractive party dish on a bed of cucumber slices; recipe page 256.

2 slices fresh ginger root

1⅓ cups shrimp, fresh or frozen, shelled

¼ cup pork fat

2 egg whites

½ teaspoon salt

Pepper to taste

2 tablespoons cornstarch

1 teaspoon dry sherry or white wine

½ teaspoon sesame oil

2 leaves green cabbage

1 carrot

2 radishes (optional)

2 oz rice flour noodles

Vegetable oil for deep-frying

■ MULTI-COLORED SHRIMP BALLS

★★★★

Cooking time: 2½–3 minutes per batch

Serves: 5–6

Cooking method: deep-fry, p.45

Good as a light attractive starter

Illustrated on p.255

■ PREPARATION ■

Finely chop ginger. Finely chop shrimp with pork fat. Place mixture in bowl. Add egg whites, salt, pepper, cornstarch, ginger, sherry or wine and sesame oil. Mix thoroughly. Shred cabbage finely. Finely chop carrot. Peel radishes, if using, and chop red skin.

Heat oil in wok or deep-fryer. When hot, add rice flour noodles; they will puff immediately. Remove and drain. Crumble noodles and mix with cabbage, carrot and radish. Spread mixture over a large dish or tray.

Form pork fat and shrimp paste into small balls, using about 2–3 teaspoons of mixture at a time. Roll them over finely chopped vegetable and noodle mixture to take on multi-colored coating.

■ COOKING ■

Reheat oil in wok or deep-fryer. When hot, gently fry shrimp balls in batches for 2½–3 minutes until cooked through and crispy. Drain.

½ lb spring greens or green cabbage

2 teaspoons salt

4–5 tablespoons vegetable oil

2 eggs

2 green onions

1 lb cooked rice (see page 68)

2 tablespoons chopped ham

¼ teaspoon MSG (optional)

SHANGHAI EMERALD FRIED RICE

★★★

Cooking time: about 8 minutes

Serves: 4–6

Cooking method: stir-fry, p.42

Quite easy to prepare

Serve with other savory dishes for an informal meal

Illustrated on p.258

■ PREPARATION ■

Wash and finely shred cabbage. Sprinkle with 1½ teaspoons of salt. Toss and leave to season for 10 minutes. Squeeze dry. Heat 1½ tablespoons of oil in wok or pan. When hot, stir-fry cabbage for 30 seconds. Remove from pan. Add 1 tablespoon oil to wok or pan. When hot, add beaten eggs to form a thin pancake. As soon as egg sets, remove from pan and chop. Chop green onions.

■ COOKING ■

Heat 2–3 tablespoons oil in wok or saucepan. When hot, stir-fry green onion for few seconds. Add rice and stir with green onion. Reduce heat to low, stir and turn until rice is heated through. Add cabbage, most of egg and ham. Stir and mix them together well. Sprinkle with monosodium glutamate, if using, and remaining salt. Stir and turn once more, then sprinkle with remaining egg.

★★★

Cooking time:
about 5–6 minutes

Serves: 5–6

Cooking methods:
deep-fry p.45 and
stir-fry p.42

Quick to cook

**Serve with any
combination of
dishes**

Illustrated on p.259

STIR-FRIED CHICKEN WITH BABY CORN

ON CRISPY NOODLES

■ PREPARATION ■

Cut chicken into ¼-inch cubes or shred. Rub with salt.
Dust with cornstarch. Coat with egg white. Chop each
baby corn into halves or quarters. Dice bamboo shoots.
Mix all sauce ingredients together in bowl.

■ COOKING ■

Heat oil in wok or deep-fryer. When hot, add rice
noodles; they will puff up immediately. Remove and
drain. Place and press level on large heated serving dish.
Pour away oil to use for other purposes, leaving 4
tablespoons. Reheat wok or pan. When hot, stir-fry
chicken for 30 seconds. Add ham, bamboo shoots, corn,
peas and mushrooms and stir-fry over medium heat for 1
minute. Pour in sauce, stir and turn together for about 30
seconds until boiling and thickened.

■ SERVING ■

Pour chicken and corn mixture over crispy noodles.

½ lb chicken breast meat

½ teaspoon salt

1 tablespoon cornstarch

½ egg white

6 baby corns

¼ lb canned bamboo shoots,
diced

Vegetable oil for deep-
frying

2 oz rice flour noodles

½ cup diced cooked cured
ham (optional)

3 tablespoons peas

1 cup button mushrooms

Sauce:

1 teaspoon salt

Pepper to taste

½ tablespoon light soy sauce

¼ cup good stock (see page
56)

½ teaspoon sugar

2 tablespoons dry sherry or
white wine

1 tablespoon cornstarch
blended with 3
tablespoons water

上海和東方

257

Crab Meat with Cream of
Chinese Cabbage (*above
left*), a light dish to serve as
part of a multi-dish meal;
recipe page 96.
Shanghai Emerald Fried
Rice (*below left*), a simple
yet useful rice dish
garnished with chopped
egg; recipe page 256.
Stir-fried Chicken with
Baby Corn on Crispy
Noodles (*above*), a colorful
main course dish; recipe
page 257.

259

4–6 large shrimp, fresh or
frozen, shelled

6 medium-sized scallops

3–4 oz squid

1½ teaspoons salt

Pepper to taste

6 tablespoons vegetable oil

2 slices fresh ginger root

1 medium-sized fresh green
chili

2 green onions

2 garlic cloves

1 carrot

1 stalk celery

2 tablespoons good stock
(see page 56)

1 tablespoon light soy sauce

2 tablespoons Chinese wine-
lee paste

1 teaspoon sesame oil

QUICK FRY OF THREE SEA FLAVORS

If wine-lee paste is unavailable, use 1½ tablespoons dry sherry and ½ tablespoon brandy mixed with 1 teaspoon cornstarch.

■ PREPARATION ■

Cut each shrimp into 3 sections and scallops in half. Clean squid under cold running water and score it with criss-cross cuts ½-inch apart, then cut it into similar-sized pieces as the shrimp sections. Sprinkle on salt, pepper and 1½ teaspoons of vegetable oil. Finely shred ginger and chili, discarding seeds. Cut green onions into ½-inch shreds. Finely chop garlic. Thinly slice carrot and celery.

■ COOKING ■

Heat 4 tablespoons of oil in wok or skillet. When hot, stir-fry shrimp, scallops and squid over high heat for 1½ minutes. Remove with slotted spoon. Pour in remaining oil, reheat and add ginger, garlic, green onions, carrot, celery and chili. Stir-fry quickly over high heat for 30 seconds, then pour in stock, soy sauce and wine-lee paste. When boiling, return three sea flavors and stir together for about 1 minute. Sprinkle over sesame oil.

★★★

Cooking time:
5–6 minutes

Serves: 4–6

Cooking method:
stir-fry, p.42

Scoring squid, p.41

Quick to cook

Illustrated on p.255

上
海
和
東
方

★★

Cooking time:
1 hour 20 minutes

Serves: 5-6

Cooking method:
simmer

Easy to prepare
but requires time
to cook

Serve the soup at
the beginning or in
the middle of a
Chinese meal

The spareribs can
be eaten as a
supplementary
main course

CHINESE MUSHROOM SOUP WITH SPARERIBS

■ PREPARATION ■

Cut spareribs into individual ribs, then chop into 2-inch lengths. Parboil them for 3 minutes in a saucepan of boiling water. Drain. Soak dried mushrooms in hot water to cover for 25 minutes. Drain and discard tough stalks. Cut half quantity of mushroom caps in half. Shred ginger.

■ COOKING ■

Place spareribs and ginger in a heavy saucepan or casserole. Add 3¾ cups water. Bring to boil and simmer for 5 minutes, skimming away any scum. Reduce heat, then add salt, pepper and soy sauce and simmer gently for 45 minutes. Stir in mushrooms, stock and crumbled bouillon cubes. Continue to cook gently for 30 minutes.

■ SERVING ■

Serve soup in a tureen. It is customary in China for diners to ladle out the soup to drink from their own rice bowls, then to pick out spareribs and eat, first dipping them into a dip sauce (soy sauce mixed with a little chili and sesame oil).

2½ lb pork spareribs
12 large or medium dried Chinese mushrooms
2 slices fresh ginger root
1 teaspoon salt
Pepper to taste
1 tablespoon light soy sauce
2½ cups good stock (see page 56)
1½ chicken bouillon cubes

Pork Balls
Chrysanthemum Style
(*above*), coated in strips of
egg omelet; recipe page
269.
Red–cooked Oxtail (*left*)
for special occasions cut
the carrots attractively;
recipe page 268.
Bang Bang Chicken
(*right*), an easy to make
starter or main dish; recipe
page 265.

1¼ cups vegetable oil

2 oz rice flour noodles

Milk mixture:

6 egg whites

1¼ cups milk

¼ cup unsweetened
  evaporated milk

1¼ tablespoons cornstarch

½ teaspoon salt

Pepper to taste

Scant ½ cup crab meat

Garnish:

1½ tablespoons chopped
  ham

1½ tablespoons cilantro
  leaves

FRIED 'MILK' WITH CRAB MEAT ON CRISPY NOODLES

■ PREPARATION ■

Beat egg whites with a fork in a bowl for 20 seconds. Add milk, evaporated milk, cornstarch, salt and pepper. Beat together until smooth.

■ COOKING ■

Heat oil in wok or skillet. When hot, continue heating for 10 seconds over medium heat. Drop rice flour noodles into hot oil. Noodles will crisp and froth up into great mass. Remove noodles immediately on to absorbent kitchen paper to drain. Pour away oil to use for other purposes, except 2 tablespoons. Reheat wok or pan. When hot, stir-fry crab meat for 30 seconds, breaking it up into smaller pieces and shreds. Pour in milk and egg white mixture. Turn and stir slowly, scraping up continuously from bottom, until mixture thickens and sets.

■ SERVING ■

Spread crispy noodles on base of a heated serving dish. Pour crab mixture over noodles. Sprinkle with chopped ham and cilantro.

★★★

Cooking time:
about 10 minutes

Serves: 5–6

Cooking methods:
deep-fry p.45 and
stir-fry p.42

Combines well in a
multi-course meal

1½ lb pork shoulder or fresh
  pork sides

1 medium onion

2 red or green peppers

2 dried chilies

2 green onions

¼ cup vegetable oil

Sauce:

2½ tablespoons dark soy
  sauce

1½ tablespoons light soy
  sauce

1½ tablespoons hoisin sauce

2 tablespoons good stock
  (see page 56)

1½ tablespoons tomato
  paste

1½ tablespoons chili sauce

1½ tablespoons sugar

■ SICHUAN DOUBLE ■ COOKED PORK

■ PREPARATION ■

Place pork in large saucepan of water. Bring to boil and simmer for 30 minutes. Leave pork to cool in water for another 30 minutes. Remove, drain and slice pork very thinly. Peel and thinly slice onion. Cut peppers into pieces. Seed and shred chilies. Cut green onions into 2 inch sections.

■ COOKING ■

Heat oil in wok or skillet. When hot, stir-fry onion for about 1 minute. Add pork and stir-fry for 2 minutes. Stir in sauce ingredients. Bring to boil, add peppers, green onions and chilies and stir for another 2 minutes.

★★★

Cooking time:
35 minutes, plus
cooling time

Serves: 4–6

Cooking methods:
simmer and stir-
fry, p.42

A spicy dish that
goes well with rice
and vegetable
dishes

Illustrated on p.188

BANG BANG CHICKEN

★★★★

Cooking time:
35 minutes, plus cooling time

Serves: 8–10 (as a starter)

Cooking method: simmer

Quite easy to make

An excellent cold starter

Illustrated on p.263

1 medium cucumber
3 lb chicken
3 slices fresh ginger root
3 teaspoons salt
Sauce:
5 tablespoons peanut butter
2½ tablespoons sesame oil
2 teaspoons sugar
1 teaspoon salt
¼ cup good stock (see page 56)
1½ tablespoons red chili oil

■ PREPARATION ■

Scrape cucumber and cut into large matchstick-size shreds. Mix all sauce ingredients together in a bowl, except red chili oil, until well blended.

■ COOKING ■

Place chicken in saucepan of water with ginger and salt. Bring to boil, cover and simmer for 35 minutes. Allow chicken to cool in water for 45 minutes. Remove chicken and drain well. Place on chopping board and chop off wings and legs, leaving body. Chop body into 2 pieces. Hit each piece of chicken several times with back or side of chopper to loosen meat. Remove meat from bones or carcass and cut into large matchstick-size shreds.

■ SERVING ■

Arrange shredded cucumber on base of large serving dish. Pile shredded chicken on top. Pour sauce over chicken and sprinkle with red chili oil. Alternatively, serve on bed of shredded lettuce and green onion.

TRIPE, SQUID AND PEA SOUP

★★★

Cooking time:
about 2½ hours, including cooking tripe

Serves: 4–6

Cooking method: simmer

Takes time to prepare

A soup of character served in the Chinese or Western style

½ lb dried squid
3 teaspoons salt
3 slices fresh ginger root
¾–1 lb tripe (pork or beef)
2 cups green peas
3¾ cups good stock (see page 56)
1 chicken bouillon cube
1½ tablespoons cornstarch blended with ¼ cup water
Salt and pepper to taste
1 teaspoon sesame oil

The presence of shredded tripe and dried squid in this green-colored soup gives it an unmistakably Chinese flavor.

■ PREPARATION ■

Soak dried squid in warm water to cover for 3 hours. Place salt and ginger in saucepan with 5 cups water. Bring to boil and add tripe. Simmer for 1½ hours. Drain tripe and squid then cut into matchstick-size shreds. Purée peas in a blender.

■ COOKING ■

Place squid in saucepan with 1¼ cups boiling water. Simmer until liquid in pan has been reduced by half, about 15 minutes. Add tripe and stock and simmer gently for 30 minutes. Add pea purée and crumbled bouillon cube. Heat and stir gently for 10 minutes. Add blended cornstarch and salt and pepper to taste. Stir in sesame oil. Continue to cook for 2 minutes, stirring.

Red Chili Oil Dumplings
(*left*), a good starter or
snack served with a hot
spicy dip sauce; recipe page
268.
Bao Tzu Steamed Buns
(*center*), a savory or sweet
filled steamed dim sum;
recipe page 236.
Mini Spring Rolls (*right*),
these delicious savories can
be made in all sizes; recipe
page 232.

Hainan Chicken Rice
(*above*), a useful family
dish; recipe page 272.

Dough skin:

3 cups all-purpose flour

2½ cups boiling water

5 tablespoons cold water

Stuffing:

2 slices fresh ginger root

2 green onions

1 cup diced lean pork

¾ cup shrimp, fresh or frozen, shelled

1 teaspoon salt

1 tablespoon light soy sauce

1 teaspoon sugar

8 oz Chinese white cabbage

Pinch of pepper

Pinch of MSG (optional)

Dip sauce:

2 tablespoons red chili oil

1 tablespoon soy sauce

1 tablespoon finely chopped garlic

1 tablespoon finely chopped green onion

RED CHILI OIL DUMPLINGS

These dumplings make a good starter to a multi-course meal or they can be eaten on their own as a snack. The hot spicy dip sauce adds considerable zest to the dish.

■ PREPARATION ■

Sift flour in bowl and mix in boiling water. Leave for 5 minutes. Add cold water, then knead well.

For the stuffing, finely chop ginger and green onions. Grind pork and shrimp together. Add ginger, green onions, salt, soy sauce, sugar and 1 tablespoon water. Mix together well. Finely chop Chinese cabbage and season lightly with salt, pepper and monosodium glutamate, if using. Add to pork mixture, combining well.

Form dough into long roll and then cut off about thirty 1-inch pieces. Roll each piece into a flat pancake and then place teaspoon of pork stuffing in center. Fold pancake in half to form half circle and seal edges. Repeat process until all ingredients are used.

■ COOKING ■

Bring large saucepan of water to boil and add dumplings, 6 at a time. Simmer over medium heat for 5 minutes, then drain.

■ SERVING ■

Transfer the dumplings to a heated serving plate and keep warm while you prepare the dip sauce. Mix all the dip sauce ingredients together and pour over the dumplings.

★★★★

Cooking time: about 25 minutes

Serves: 8–10 (makes 30)

Cooking method: poach

Dumplings take time to make

A good starter dish

Illustrated on p.266

To prepare dumplings, see pp.227–228

---

2 garlic cloves

5–6 lb oxtail (ask butcher to cut into sections)

2–3 young carrots

3 slices fresh ginger root

1 teaspoon salt

6 tablespoons soy sauce

1½ tablespoons hoisin sauce

¼ cup dry sherry

⅔ cup good stock (see page 56)

2 teaspoons sugar

2 tablespoons peas (optional)

RED-COOKED OXTAIL

■ PREPARATION ■

Crush garlic. Clean oxtail. Cut carrots slantwise into ¼-inch slices. Blanch oxtail for 3–4 minutes in a pan of boiling water. Drain and place in heavy saucepan or flameproof casserole with garlic, ginger, salt, soy sauce, hoisin sauce and carrots. Add 3¾ cups water.

■ COOKING ■

Bring contents of pan to boil, cover and simmer very gently for 1½ hours. Turn contents every 30 minutes. Add sherry, stock and sugar and continue to simmer gently for further 1 hour, turning contents after 30

★★

Cooking time: about 2½ hours

Serves: 4–6

Cooking method: simmer

Easy to prepare, lengthy cooking

Illustrated on p.262

minutes. Add peas 10 minutes before end of cooking time. (If cooked in oven, cook at 150°C, 300°F for 3 hours.)

★ ★ ★ ★

Cooking time:
about 8 minutes

Serves: 5–6

Cooking method:
deep-fry, p.45

Take time to
prepare

Serve with a party
meal

Illustrated on p.262

PORK BALLS CHRYSANTHEMUM STYLE

■ PREPARATION ■

Soak dried Chinese mushrooms in hot water to cover for 25 minutes. Drain and discard tough stalks. Finely chop mushroom caps. Finely chop ginger, shrimp and green onion. Place ground pork in bowl and add ginger, shrimp and green onion. Place ground pork in bowl and add ginger, shrimp, green onion, cornstarch, mushroom, salt, pepper, monosodium glutamate, if using, and egg white. Mix together until smooth and then make into small meat balls. Beat eggs. Heat 3 tablespoons oil in flat-bottomed pan. When hot, pour in quarter of beaten egg and make thin omelet. Repeat this process 3 more times with rest of egg. Cut 4 egg omelets into fine strips. Spread out egg strips and then roll meat balls in them. Press egg strips on to the balls firmly.

■ COOKING ■

Heat oil in wok or deep-fryer. When hot, gently fry the meat balls, in 2 batches if necessary, for about 4 minutes or until brown and crisp. Drain.

■ SERVING ■

Serve the pork balls on bed of shredded lettuce surrounded by orange slices; for a party, surround with chrysanthemum flowers.

4 medium dried Chinese mushrooms

2 slices fresh ginger root

½ cup shrimp, fresh or frozen, shelled

1 green onion

8 oz ground pork

¼ cup cornstarch

1½ teaspoons salt

Pepper to taste

½ teaspoon MSG (optional)

1 egg white

4 eggs

Vegetable oil for deep-frying

地
區
性
烹
飪
法

Ho–Fen Noodles with
Beef in Black Bean Sauce
(*above*), a substantial dish
with a rich flavored sauce;
recipe page 273.
Cha Siu Roast Pork (*above
right*), marinated, roasted
pork with carrot flower
garnish; recipe page 274.
Crab Meat Soup (*below
right*), a light soup with
crab meat, bean curd and
spinach or lettuce; recipe
page 275.

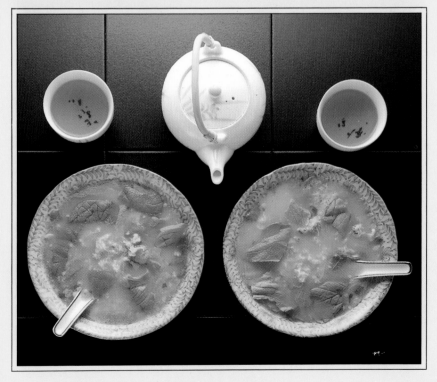

3¼–3¾ lb chicken

2 teaspoons salt

Pepper to taste

1 lb long grain rice

2 medium onions

12 oz broccoli or spring greens

⅔ cup green peas (optional)

2 chicken bouillon cubes

1½ teaspoons sesame oil

Sauce:

3 green onions

4 garlic cloves

¼ cup good soy sauce

1 tablespoon red chili oil

HAINAN CHICKEN RICE

This is a useful family dish which can be eaten on its own by a family or party of 4-6 people without the need for it to be supplemented, as is usual in China, by at least 2-3 other dishes.

★ ★ ★ ★

Cooking time:
about 1¼ hours

Serves: 4–6

Cooking method:
simmer

Useful family dish
to be eaten
unaccompanied

Illustrated on p.267

■ PREPARATION ■

Chop chicken through bones into 30 large bite-size pieces. Rub with salt and pepper. Wash and measure rice. Place in saucepan and add an equal amount of water. Bring to boil, cover, reduce heat and simmer for 5-6 minutes. Remove from heat and leave rice to cook and absorb all water, covered, for 10 minutes. Thinly slice onions. Chop broccoli into 2-inch pieces or finely shred spring greens. Finely chop green onions and garlic.

■ COOKING ■

Place chicken pieces in large saucepan of boiling water and blanch for 3 minutes. Drain and place them in large heavy saucepan or flameproof casserole. Pour in 7½ cups of water and add onions. Bring to boil, reduce heat and simmer gently for 45 minutes. Add broccoli or spring greens, peas, if using, and crumbled bouillon cubes to pan and simmer for 5 minutes. Remove chicken pieces and vegetables and put aside. Pour three-fifths of stock into a separate saucepan (to use as soup for diners). Add partially cooked rice to remaining chicken stock in the heavy pan or casserole. Place over low to medium heat and cook gently for 10–15 minutes until rice has absorbed all stock. Just before end of cooking time, arrange chicken pieces and vegetables on top.

■ SERVING ■

Heat stock in the saucepan. Adjust seasonings, and sprinkle with half the chopped green onion and sesame oil. Mix ingredients for sauce together and pour it over chicken in casserole. Divide and serve in as many small bowls as there are diners.

★ ★ ★

Cooking time:
about 12 minutes

Serves: 5-6

Cooking methods:
simmer, and stir-
fry, p.42

**Quite easy to
prepare**

**Excellent as part of
a multi-dish meal
for hearty
appetites**

Illustrated on p.270

■ HO-FEN NOODLES WITH BEEF IN BLACK BEAN SAUCE ■

Ho-Fen noodles are flat ribbon rice flour noodles. If unavailable use any rice flour noodles.

■ PREPARATION ■

Place noodles in saucepan of boiling water and simmer for 3–4 minutes. Drain and rinse under cold running water to keep separate. Thinly slice onions. Cut ginger into thin shreds. Soak black beans in water to cover for 5 minutes. Drain and coarsely chop. Cut beef into thin $1\frac{1}{2} \times \frac{1}{2}$-inch pieces. Dust and rub with cornstarch. Coat with egg white. Slice red pepper. Crush garlic. Cut green onions into 2-inch sections.

■ COOKING ■

Heat oil in wok or skillet. When hot, stir-fry onion, ginger and garlic over medium heat for 3–4 minutes until onions are soft. Push them to sides of pan. Add beef to center of pan and stir-fry for 1 minute. Push to side of pan. Add 3 tablespoons shortening to center of wok or skillet. When melted, add black beans and stir and mash them into shortening. Add soy sauce, oyster sauce, chili sauce and stock. Stir together until sauce boils. Add blended cornstarch and stir to thicken, mixing sauce well. Bring onion and beef into center of pan and mix with sauce. Remove half beef mixture from wok or skillet and put aside. Add noodles to wok, then turn and mix with beef mixture.

■ SERVING ■

Transfer well coated noodles to a heated serving dish. Heat remaining shortening in wok or pan. When hot, stir-fry red pepper and green onion over high heat for 30 seconds. Return reserved beef mixture, stir and mix well, for 30 seconds. Spoon over noodles. Alternatively, serve beef mixture on plain noodles.

¾ lb Ho-Fen rice flour noodles
2 medium onions
2 slices fresh ginger root
1 lb lean beef, such as rump or top round
1½ tablespoons cornstarch
1 egg white
1 medium to large red pepper
2 garlic cloves
3 green onions
4 tablespoons vegetable oil

Sauce:

⅓ cup shortening or lard
1½ tablespoons salted black beans
2 tablespoons soy sauce
1½ tablespoons oyster sauce
1½ tablespoons chili sauce
¼ cup good stock (see page 56)
1½ tablespoons cornstarch blended with 3 tablespoons water

2 lb boneless pork loin

Marinade:

2 tablespoons dark soy sauce

1 tablespoon yellow bean paste

1 tablespoon hoisin sauce

1 tablespoon oyster sauce

1 tablespoon sugar

1½ tablespoons vegetable oil

1 tablespoon red bean curd cheese

Garnish:

carrot flowers

---

2 lb pork spareribs

6 medium plums

1 tablespoon salted black beans

3 teaspoons sugar

2½ tablespoons soy sauce

1½ tablespoons oyster sauce

1 tablespoon vegetable oil

CHA SIU ROAST PORK

This special way of rapidly roasting marinated meat, practiced mainly by the southern Cantonese, can be applied to all kinds of good cuts of meat.

■ PREPARATION ■

Cut pork into 2 strips, about 2–2½ inches thick and 6–7 inches long. Mix ingredients for the marinade in large bowl. Add 2 pieces of pork and rub thoroughly with marinade. Leave to marinate for 30 minutes.

■ COOKING ■

Place 2 strips of pork on wire rack over roasting tin filled with 1½-inch of water to catch drips. Place in preheated oven at 220°C, 425°F and roast for 7–8 minutes. Reduce oven temperature to 180°C, 350°F (to avoid burning) and roast for another 12–13 minutes. By this time meat will be coated with the dark marinade.

■ SERVING ■

Remove the pork and cut across the grain into ½-inch thick slices. The distinguishing feature of pork so rapidly roasted is that each slice of pork has a dark rim of well cooked pork with even darker encrustation of marinade, surrounding a center of lighter cooked pork. The contrast between the well cooked and lighter cooked meat not only provides visual appeal but also an appetizing difference in flavor. Serve Cha Siu pork in overlapping slices on a bed of lightly stir-fried vegetables – bean sprouts or spinach.

★★

Cooking time: about 20 minutes, plus marinating time

Serves: 6–8

Cooking method: roast

Simple to prepare

Serve with vegetables and stir-fry dishes at a family meal or dinner party

Illustrated on p.271

STEAMED SPARERIBS WITH PLUMS

■ PREPARATION ■

Chop spareribs into 1-inch sections. Pit plums and cut each in half. Soak black beans in hot water for 5 minutes. Drain. Place all ingredients in a heatproof dish. Turn and mix thoroughly.

■ COOKING ■

Cover dish well with foil. Place in a steamer and steam vigorously for 1 hour.

★★

Cooking time: 1 hour

Serves: 4–6

Cooking method: steam, p.49

Easy to prepare

Serve with any combination of dishes

SOY CHICKEN IN AROMATIC OIL

■ PREPARATION ■

Chop chicken through bones into 20–24 bite-size pieces. Place in flameproof casserole. Thinly slice onions. Coarsely chop garlic. Shred ginger. Cut green onions into ½-inch shreds.

■ COOKING ■

For aromatic oil, heat shortening and oil in small saucepan or skillet. When hot, stir-fry sliced onion, ginger, garlic, peppercorns and star anise for 4–5 minutes. Pour seasoned oil through a sieve over chicken pieces. Place casserole over medium heat and stir-fry chicken pieces in the aromatic oil for 4–5 minutes. Add stock, soy sauce, salt and sugar. Bring to boil, then cook over high heat for 10–12 minutes, stirring all the time, until sauce is reduced to less than one quarter. Sprinkle with green onion and sesame oil.

Ingredients
3½–4 lb chicken
2 medium onions
4 garlic cloves
4 slices fresh ginger root
2 green onions
¼ cup shortening or lard
3 tablespoons vegetable oil
¾ tablespoon pounded Sichuan peppercorns
1½ tablespoons star anise
1½ teaspoons sesame oil
Sauce:
1¼ cups good stock (see page 56) or water
3 tablespoons soy sauce
1 teaspoon salt
1 tablespoon sugar

CRAB MEAT SOUP

■ PREPARATION ■

Flake crab meat, thawing first if necessary. Coarsely chop ginger. Cut green onions into ½-inch shreds. Cut bean curd into cubes. Wash spinach, removing any tough stems and discolored leaves.

■ COOKING ■

Heat oil in wok or saucepan. When hot, stir-fry ginger and green onion for 30 seconds. Add crab meat and stir-fry for 15 seconds. Pour in stock. Add crumbled bouillon cube and salt and pepper. Bring to boil, stirring. Add spinach and bean curd. Bring contents to boil again, stirring, then simmer gently for 2 minutes. Stir in blended cornstarch and cook until thickened.

Ingredients
½ cup crab meat, fresh or frozen
2 slices fresh ginger root
2 green onions
1 cake bean curd
½ lb young spinach
2 tablespoons vegetable oil
3¾ cups good stock (see page 56)
1 chicken bouillon cube
1 teaspoon salt
Pepper to taste
2 tablespoons cornstarch blended with 5 tablespoons water

How to Choose and Order Chinese Food

WHEN CHOOSING CHINESE FOOD the average Westerner is faced with several problems. None of these is insurmountable or even difficult, given a few very simple guidelines.

The first aim of any Chinese meal is harmony and variety – in color, texture, flavor, method of cooking and food materials.

A Chinese meal is essentially a hot buffet. A group of dishes is served on the table at the same time, to be shared by everyone. Dishes are only served singly if one person is eating alone. Even at a formal banquet or dinner party, the dishes are served in groups, one after the other. Chinese hors d'oeuvres consist of four to eight dishes all served at once, for example.

▧ CHOOSING FOR A SMALL GROUP ▧
OF FOUR TO SIX PEOPLE

In China people generally eat in groups: family groups, groups of friends, groups of colleagues. And Chinese food is best eaten in this way, for only then can you enjoy a variety of dishes.

Usually you should order one more dish than there are people: four dishes for three people, five dishes for four people. It is only when you are entertaining particularly lavishly that you have two extra dishes.

It is not until you have more than five or six dishes that you should start duplicating the order of one or two particular favorites. Normally you will want to avoid overcrowding the table by duplicating dishes, and it is only when the dishes become too small to be shared by all the people around the table that you should think of doubling any order.

You should ensure variety by selecting dishes from the range of foods available. When you have ordered a chicken dish, next order a fish. When you've ordered a meat dish, then select a vegetable. If you choose a seafood dish, next pick a bean curd or tofu dish. After rice, order noodles, especially if everybody's hungry and bulky food is required.

The next thing that you should bear in mind is the method of cooking. Try to achieve as much variety as possible here also. After you've ordered a stir-fried dish, order something that has been cooked longer: a red–cooked dish or one that has been braised for a long time in a clay pot or casserole. After ordering a deep-fried crispy dish, pick a steamed dish. And after selecting a highly spiced dish, order a lightly cooked, fresh-tasting dish.

Texture is closely related to the method of cooking employed. Most deep-fried dishes are crispy. Steamed or simmered dishes are tender. But stir-fried dishes can be soft or crunchy, or a combination of both, depending on their ingredients. Try to

■
The following menu suggestions should help you select dishes that combine to produce meals that are well balanced in terms of flavor and texture. All the dishes mentioned may be found in the recipe sections in the book. The wines listed are suggestions only and are in no way obligatory. Beer, China tea or, indeed, mineral water, are equally suitable to be served as accompaniments to a Chinese meal.

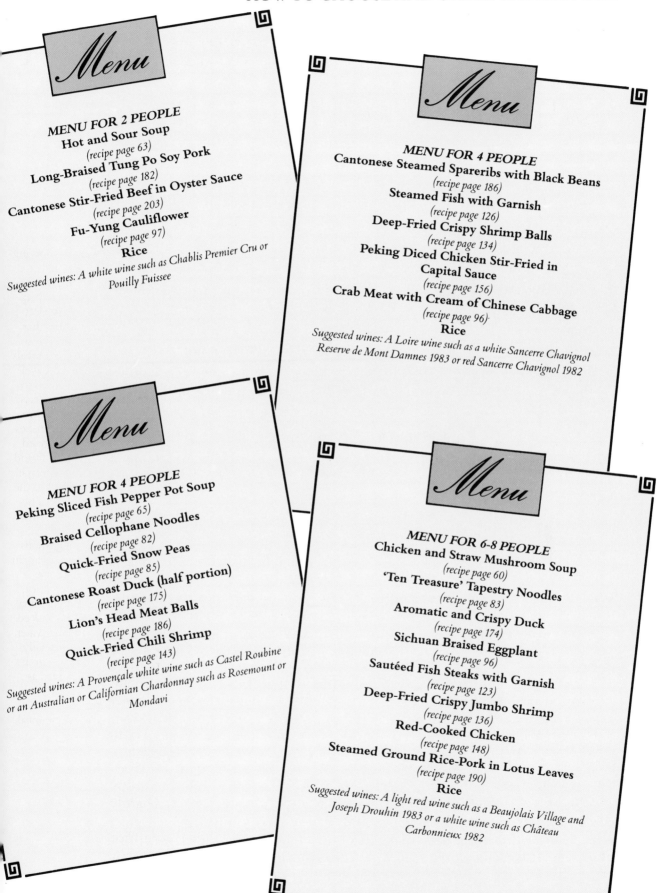

Menu

MENU FOR 2 PEOPLE
Hot and Sour Soup
(recipe page 63)
Long-Braised Tung Po Soy Pork
(recipe page 182)
Cantonese Stir-Fried Beef in Oyster Sauce
(recipe page 203)
Fu-Yung Cauliflower
(recipe page 97)
Rice
Suggested wines: A white wine such as Chablis Premier Cru or Pouilly Fuissee

Menu

MENU FOR 4 PEOPLE
Cantonese Steamed Spareribs with Black Beans
(recipe page 186)
Steamed Fish with Garnish
(recipe page 126)
Deep-Fried Crispy Shrimp Balls
(recipe page 134)
Peking Diced Chicken Stir-Fried in
Capital Sauce
(recipe page 156)
Crab Meat with Cream of Chinese Cabbage
(recipe page 96).
Rice
Suggested wines: A Loire wine such as a white Sancerre Chavignol Reserve de Mont Damnes 1983 or red Sancerre Chavignol 1982

Menu

MENU FOR 4 PEOPLE
Peking Sliced Fish Pepper Pot Soup
(recipe page 65)
Braised Cellophane Noodles
(recipe page 82)
Quick-Fried Snow Peas
(recipe page 85)
Cantonese Roast Duck (half portion)
(recipe page 175)
Lion's Head Meat Balls
(recipe page 186)
Quick-Fried Chili Shrimp
(recipe page 143)
Suggested wines: A Provençale white wine such as Castel Roubine or an Australian or Californian Chardonnay such as Rosemount or Mondavi

Menu

MENU FOR 6-8 PEOPLE
Chicken and Straw Mushroom Soup
(recipe page 60)
'Ten Treasure' Tapestry Noodles
(recipe page 83)
Aromatic and Crispy Duck
(recipe page 174)
Sichuan Braised Eggplant
(recipe page 96)
Sautéed Fish Steaks with Garnish
(recipe page 123)
Deep-Fried Crispy Jumbo Shrimp
(recipe page 136)
Red-Cooked Chicken
(recipe page 148)
Steamed Ground Rice-Pork in Lotus Leaves
(recipe page 190)
Rice
Suggested wines: A light red wine such as a Beaujolais Village and Joseph Drouhin 1983 or a white wine such as Château Carbonnieux 1982

Menu

PEKING AND THE NORTH
STARTERS
Peking 'Pomegranate' Snow-Flake Shrimp Balls
(recipe page 135)
Peking Kuo-Tieh Steamed and Sautéed Dumplings
(recipe page 241)
Peking Jelly of Lamb
(recipe page 206)
Cold Tossed Cucumber Salad
(recipe page 85)
Suggested wine: A rosé Sancerre Chavignol 1982/83

PRINCIPAL DISH
Peking Duck (with pancakes, shredded cucumber and green onion and duck sauce) *(recipe page 178)*

MAIN COURSES (SERVED WITH RICE)
Quick Stir-Fried Lamb in Garlic Sauce
(recipe page 206)
Soft-Fried Peking Sliced Fish in Wine Sauce
(recipe page 131)
Soy-Braised Pork – Long Cooked Version
(recipe page 196)
Yellow Flowing Egg (Lui Huang Dan)
(recipe page 115)
Suggested wines: A St. Emilion red like Ch la Tour Figeac Cru Classic 1976 or Gevrey Chambertin Drouhin Laroze 1980

DESSERT
Peking 'Toffee Apples'
(recipe page 252)
Suggested wine: Muscat de Beaune de Venice

Menu

SHANGHAI AND THE EAST
STARTERS
Shanghai Cold-Tossed Noodles
(recipe page 80)
Multi-Colored Shrimp Balls
(recipe page 256)
Yangtze 'Fish Salad'
(recipe page 126)
Yellow Fish Soup
(recipe page 62)
Suggested Wine: A Beaune white wine such as Clos de Mouches, Joseph Drouhin 1982/83

MAIN COURSES (SERVED WITH RICE)
Yangchow Fried Rice
(recipe page 70)
Long-Steamed Pork Hock
(recipe page 195)
Salt and Pepper Shrimp
(recipe page 138)
Shanghai Quick-Braised Chicken on the Bone
(recipe page 165)
Quick Fry of Three Sea Flavors
(recipe page 260)
Steamed Stuffed Bean Curd
(recipe page 107)
Suggested wines: A Chilean red such as Cousino Macul Antiquas Reserve 1976 or a Spanish Rioja Conde de la Salaceda Reserve 1976

DESSERT
A fresh fruit salad including melon

order as wide a variety of textures as possible.

Soups and semi-soups are essential lubricants which help wash down bulky foods. The sensation of washing a mouthful of food with a savory soup is peculiar to Chinese eating. In Western cuisine, soups and solids are rigorously segregated. But again, the incorporation of soups and semi-soups into the main meal add variety in texture.

Variety in flavor and differences in the degree of flavor and spiciness are all factors you should bear in mind when choosing dishes. Again, select as wide a range as possible.

When eating, aim for this variety too. After a meat dish you will naturally gravitate towards a seafood flavor or a vegetable dish. After a spicy dish, try a bite of a fresh, natural-tasting dish. After a hot dish, try a cold dish. After a dry dish, a soup dish. The possible sequences and combinations are almost endless.

■ CHOOSING FOR ONE ■

Occasionally you may find yourself dining alone, in which case it will not be possible to order a variety of tastes and textures. In this situation a Chinese will choose a soup and a composite rice or noodle dish which contains meat, fish or vegetables. An extra meat, fish or vegetable dish might be ordered to make a lavish meal. But for the Chinese the soup would be essential, while an American might prefer to wash the meal down with a soda, a beer or a glass of wine.

■
Four Regional Menus
These are all intended as full-scale Chinese dinners, which are usually for 8–10 people.

Menu

SICHUAN AND THE WEST
STARTERS
Bang Bang Chicken
(recipe page 265)
Red Chili Oil Dumplings
(recipe page 268)
Simple Sichuan Smoked Chicken
(recipe page 156)
Sichuan Dan Dan Noodles
(recipe page 81)
Suggested wine: The distinctive flavor of an Alsace wine such as a Gewurztraminer 1982 would go particularly well with these dishes

MAIN COURSES (SERVED WITH RICE)
Sichuan Double Cooked Pork
(recipe page 264)
Red-Cooked Oxtail
(recipe page 268)
Sichuan Braised Eggplant
(recipe page 96)
Ma Po Tofu (Bean Curd)
(recipe page 106)
Hunan Chili Squid
(recipe page 142)
Suggested wines: A red Burgundy such as Pinot Noir 1980 or a white Hermitage Rhone wine

DESSERT
Almond 'Tea'
(recipe page 219)

Menu

CANTON AND THE SOUTH
STARTERS
Cantonese Poached Shrimp with Two Dips
(recipe page 136)
Steamed Spareribs with Plums
(recipe page 274)
Deep-Fried Crab Claws
(recipe page 135)
Steamed Siu Mai
(recipe page 240)
Suggested wine: Muscadet Millenaire Marquis de Goulaine 1983

MAIN COURSES (SERVED WITH RICE)
Cha Siu Roast Pork
(recipe page 274)
Salt-Buried Baked Chicken
(recipe page 158)
Stir-Fried Spinach in Shrimp Sauce
(recipe page 89)
Cantonese Roast Duck
(recipe page 175)
Sliced Beef in Black Bean and Chili Sauce
(recipe page 201)
Rice
Suggested Wines: A red wine such Barolo Kiola reserve 1974 or if white is preferred, a Meursault 1978

DESSERT
Water Chestnut 'Cake'
(recipe page 222)
Suggested wine: Japanese plum wine

▧ CHOOSING FOR TWO ▧

In the Western world people often dine out as a couple and regularly eat with one friend or colleague. Here I recommend the selection of at least three dishes: a meat dish, a fish or seafood dish and a vegetable dish.

If that is not enough, have both a fish dish *and* a seafood dish. You will also need a rice or noodle dish and a soup—though the latter is not mandatory if you are drinking wine or beer.

In that case you may consider exchanging the soup for a starter. Try a light dish like a pancake roll, a dim sum dish or even spareribs which can be eaten Western style, with your fingers. The Chinese never eat spareribs as a main course to complement a rice or noodle dish.

If you are extra hungry, have both a rice and a noodle dish. In this case take your noodles as a simple chow mein which is fried noodles cooked with bean sprouts and shredded meat. That will satisfy the largest of appetites.

▧ CHOOSING FOR A DINNER PARTY ▧

We are dealing here with a dinner party of more than six people, otherwise refer back to the section on 'Choosing for a small group of four to six people' and add and duplicate dishes as necessary.

At a dinner party the number of dishes should exceed the number of people by three or four portions. As a result the table should appear like a grand buffet – a hot

buffet at that. There should not be less than eight to ten separate dishes served, with several of these being double or triple servings. This means that you can have whole chickens, ducks and fish, and piles of vegetables and meat-filled dumplings.

If you are employing an outside caterer for your dinner party, it may be advisable to have the dishes brought to the table in two or three stages. This will stop the table becoming too overcrowded, with too many choices at once. And unless you have a round table with a Lazy Susan not everyone will be able to sample every dish.

■ ORDERING FOR A BANQUET ■

Cold dishes and Chinese hor d'oeuvres can be arranged on the table before the guests are seated. This should then be followed by three or four hot starter dishes.

A typical large Chinese family meal, where all the dishes are shared from the center of the table

These should be in small serving dishes – not more than eight inches in diameter. They are designed to stimulate the appetite rather than satisfy it.

Between the starters and the main courses, you can have a soup served. This acts as punctuation and helps slow down the proceedings. A Chinese banquet is meant to proceed at a leisurely pace.

Following the soup will be the main courses – or the 'big dishes' as they are known in China. These may consist of whole ducks, chickens, geese, fish or lobster, along with one or two mixed dishes – like seaslugs with meatballs or stuffed mushrooms – and a large dish of glistening vegetables.

Just when the diners are beginning to feel a little full, a large dish of noodles should arrive. These are there to make sure that no one goes away hungry.

Then, when your guests are beginning to feel that the meal is almost over, a bowl of fruity or sweet soup should arrive. This is not a dessert though; it is another punctuation which heralds another series of dishes.

Groups of four to six medium-size dishes should then be served, with a small bowl of rice provided for each person. These dishes should all be fairly plain dishes with no overwhelming spices or flavorings. They are meant to settle the stomach after the spicy dishes served earlier. It is only then that a large bowl of fresh fruit should be served to mark the end of the banquet.

Naturally you will have to discuss the details of your banquet with the caterers. But if you feel that the meal outlined here is too much, eliminate the hors d'oeuvres and stop the meal after the sweet soup.

■ WESTERN WINE AND CHINESE FOOD ■

The combination of these two vast territories of epicurean delight is still very much in the exploratory stage. In China there is only one word, 'Jiu', which covers beer, wine and liquor. And in Hong Kong, Singapore and Taiwan you'll see well-heeled Chinese still at restaurant tables with several bottles of whiskey, drinking it as if it were table wine. Many believe that Scotch is a brand of British wine that should be gulped down by the tumblerful. The Chinese are either great drinkers, or they do not drink at all. So you should not set great store by their opinion of wines.

On the other hand, Western wine experts rarely have an extensive knowledge of Chinese cuisine. So far the marriage between Western wine and Chinese food is still largely virgin territory which remains to be explored by men and women of discerning palates.

In my opinion, though, there is no doubt that wine does go very well indeed with Chinese food. For some of the more elaborate menus in this chapter, I have selected several Western wines that I feel best complement the dishes being served.

281

Index

Page numbers in *italic* refer to the illustrations.

A

air-drying, 52
almond: crispy 'seaweed' with, 84
junket, *220, 222*
'tea', 219
'ants climbing up trees', 214
apple: Peking spun sugar 'toffee apples', 252-3, *254*
asparagus, sauté of four vegetables, 92, *94*

B

baby corn, 16, *24*
stir-fried chicken on crispy noodles with, 257, *259*
bacon: stir-fried Chinese omelet with onion and, 110
bamboo shoots, 16, *24*
preparation, *33*
sauté of four vegetables, 92, *94*
spring roll fillings, 232-3, *235, 266*
stir-fried lamb and liver with peas, lotus seeds, garlic and, 207
bamboo steamers, 8, *10, 49*
bang bang chicken, *263, 265*
banquets, choosing food for, 281
Bao Tzu steamed buns, 236-7, *266*
Bao Tzu steamed buns with sweet bean paste, 237
barbecue spareribs, 193
bean curd (tofu), 26, *27*, 100-7
bean curd, ham, mushroom and spinach soup, 64

braised bean curd family-style, 105
braised with mushrooms, 106-7
braised mussels with mushrooms and, *133*, 142
cold tossed, 100
with crab meat and peas, 101, *103*
with eight precious ingredients, 104
Sichuan Ma Po tofu, *102*, 106
steamed stuffed, 107
stir-fried with shrimp, 101
bean-curd cheese, 26
quick-fried spinach with, 88
stir-fried spinach in shrimp sauce, 89
bean curd skin, *18*, 26
mango beef, 200
bean sprouts, 16, *22*
with garlic and green onions, 93
spring roll fillings, 232-3 *235, 266*
beef, 198-203
beef broth tomato soup, 57
Cantonese stir-fried beef in oyster sauce, 203, *213*
chow mein, 76-7
Ho-fen noodles with beef in black bean sauce, *270 273*
mango beef, 200
mustard and red chili oil beef with leeks, 200
preparation, *38*
quick-fried shredded beef with ginger and onions, *188, 201*
quick-fried shredded beef with onions, 202
quick stir-fried beef with tomatoes, 199
Sichuan hot crispy-fried shredded beef, *188*, 203
Sichuan peppered beef medallions, 202
sliced beef in black bean and

chili sauce, *188*, 201
stir-fried with celery, 199
stir-fried diced beef with kidneys, shrimp and mushrooms, 198
stock, 57
beggars' chicken, 153
beggars' noodles, 72, *78*
black beans, salted, 26, 53
Cantonese steamed spareribs with, 186
Ho-fen noodles with beef in black bean sauce, *270, 273*
quick-fried crab in hot black bean sauce, 144
sliced beef in black bean and chili sauce, *188, 201*
steamed scallops with black bean sauce, *132*, 138
blanching, 52, 53
boiling, 53
bread: quails' eggs on shrimp toast, 236
sesame shrimp on toast, 233, *239*
broccoli: Hainan chicken rice, *267, 272*
quick-fried in oyster sauce with crab, 92
The Buddhist's delight, 88
buns: Bao Tzu steamed buns, 236-7, *266*
lotus leaf shaped steamed buns, 240
steamed, *234*

C

cabbage, Chinese flowering, 16, *22*
cabbage, Chinese white, 16, *24*
The Buddhist's delight, 88
with chilies, 87, *91*
crab meat with cream of Chinese cabbage, 96, *258*
duck carcass soup, 179

red chili oil dumplings, *227-8, 266*, 268
red-cooked, 86
salad, 87
shredding, *31*
stir-fried with Chinese mushrooms and dried shrimp, 86
white-cooked, 87
white-cooked chicken with, 162
whole chicken or duck soup, 60-1
cabbage, green: Shanghai emerald fried rice, 256, *258*
Shanghai vegetable rice, 72, *75*
cabbage, salted (pickled), 29
cakes, water chestnut, 222
Cantonese cuisine, 249, 272-5
Cantonese ginger and onion crab, *128*, 140-1
Cantonese poached shrimp with two dips, *117, 137*
Cantonese roast duck, 175
Cantonese steamed spareribs with black beans, 186
Cantonese stir-fried beef in oyster sauce, 203, *213*
capital sauce, 157, *192, 193*
capital spareribs, *188*, 196
carrot: sauté of four vegetables, 92, *94*
cashew nuts, *20*, 29
cauliflower, Fu-yung, *94*, 97
celery: cold tossed in mustard sauce, 92
stir-fried beef with, 199
stir-fried chicken and celery on rice, *150*, 152
cellophane noodles, 16, *18*, 68
see also noodles
Cha Siu roast pork, *271, 274*
chestnuts, *21*
long-braised red-cooked lamb with Chinese mushrooms and chestnuts, 205
red-cooked with Chinese

mushrooms and, 169
Chiankiang vinegar, *28, 29*
chicken, 148–67
  bang bang chicken, *263, 265*
  chicken and straw mushroom soup, 60
  with chilies and red pepper, 163
  crispy 'five spice' chicken legs, *147,* 166
  drunken chicken, 161
  Fu-yung, *154,* 167
  gold and silver rice gruel, 71, *74*
  Hainan chicken rice, *267,* 272
  hot-tossed shredded chicken in red chili oil, 158
  long-steamed lotus leaf-wrapped, 166
  melon chicken, 165, *172*
  paper-wrapped deep-fried, *151,* 152
  Peking diced chicken stir-fried in capital sauce, 157
  Peking sliced egg-battered chicken in garlic and onion sauce, 160–1
  preparation, *36–7*
  quick braised chicken with honey, 160
  red-cooked, 148
  royal concubine chicken, 156–7
  salt-buried baked chicken, 158, *159*
  Shanghai quick-braised chicken on the bone, *155,* 164
  simple Sichuan smoked chicken, 156
  simulated beggars' chicken, 153
  soy chicken in aromatic oil, 275
  spring roll fillings, 232–3, *235, 266*
  steamed chicken in aromatic ground rice, 163
  stir-fried with baby corn on crispy noodles, 257, *259*
  stir-fried chicken and celery on rice, *150,* 152
  stir-fried with garlic and cucumber, 149, *154*
  stir-fried sliced chicken with zucchini, 164
  stock, 56
  strange flavor chicken, 167
  velvet of chicken, ham and corn soup, 65
  white-cooked with Chinese white cabbage, 162
  white-cut, 149
  whole chicken soup, 60–1

chicken fat, 29, 53
chili, 16, *24*
  chicken with red pepper and, 163
  Chinese white cabbage with, 87, *91*
  dried, 14, *20*
  quick-fried chili shrimp, 143
  sliced beef in black bean and chili sauce, *188, 201*
chili oil, *28, 29*
  hot-tossed shredded chicken in red chili oil, 158
  mustard and red chili oil beef with leeks, 200
  red chili oil dumplings, *227–8, 266,* 268
chili powder, 26
chili sauce, *28*
  Hunan chili squid, 142
Chinese gooseberry salad with mandarin and lotus seeds, 223
Chinese pancakes, *176–7,* 178–9
choppers, *11,* 13, 30, *30*
chopping boards, *11,* 13
chopsticks, *10, 12,* 13
chow mein: basic, 76
  beef, 76–7
  Singapore, 77, *79*
cilantro (coriander), *20,* 26
clam: Fukien clam soup, 145
cleavers, *11,* 13, 30, *30*
cloud ears, 14
collards: crispy 'seaweed' with almonds, 84
congee, 69, 71, *74*
cooking pots, *11,* 13
coriander (cilantro), *20,* 26
corn: baby corn, 16, *24*
  stir-fried chicken on crispy noodles with, 257, *259*
  velvet of chicken, ham and corn soup, 65
cornstarch, 52
crab: bean curd with peas and, 101, *103*
  Cantonese ginger and onion crab, *128,* 140–1
  crab meat soup, *271,* 275
  crab meat with cream of Chinese cabbage, 258
  with cream of Chinese cabbage, 96
  deep-fried crab claws, 135
  fried 'milk' with crab meat on crispy noodles, 264
  Fukien crab rice, 73
  Huang-pu boatmen's egg omelet, 111
  quick-fried broccoli in oyster sauce with, 92
  quick-fried crab in hot black bean sauce, 144

crackling cream of ground fish soup, 61
crustaceans, 134–45
cucumber: bang bang chicken, *263, 265*
  cold tossed salad, 85, *90*
  hot-tossed shredded chicken in red chili oil, 158
  stir-fried chicken with garlic and, 149, *154*

D

daikon radish, *see* turnip, Chinese
dates, red, 14, *21*
desserts, 218–25
  almond junket, *220, 222*
  Chinese gooseberry salad with mandarin and lotus seeds, 223
  eight treasure pudding, 218, *220*
  pears in honey sauce, 219, *221*
  water chestnut 'cake', 222
  Yuan Hsaio (New Year dumplings), 223
dim sum, 226–41
  Bao Tzu steamed buns, 236–7, *266*
  Bao Tzu steamed buns with sweet bean paste, 237
  green onion pancakes, *243, 250*
  lotus leaf shaped steamed buns, 240
  Peking Kuo-tieh (steamed and sautéed dumplings, *227–8, 239,* 241
  quails' eggs on shrimp toast, 236
  sesame shrimp on toast, 233, *239*
  spring roll fillings, 232–3, *235, 266*
  spring roll wrappers, 232
  steamed Siu Mai, *239,* 240
  stuffed wontons, 230–1
dinner parties, choosing food for, 279–81
dips: Cantonese poached shrimp with two dips, *117,* 137
dried foods, 14–16
drinks, almond 'tea', 219
drunken chicken, 161
duck, 168–79
  aromatic and crispy, *173,* 174
  basic red-cooked, 169
  basic white-simmered, 168–9
  Cantonese roast, 175

duck carcass soup, 179
gold and silver rice gruel, 71, *74*
Kou Shoa deep-fried boneless duck, 171
lotus leaf wrapped long-steamed, 170
Peking duck, *176–7,* 178
preparation, *39*
quick-fried in soy and mustard sauce, 174–5
red-cooked with chestnuts and Chinese mushrooms, 169
white-simmered double-cooked tangerine duck, 170–1
whole duck soup, 60–1
duck fat, 53
duck's eggs, 27
dumplings: New year, 223
  Peking Kuo-tieh (steamed and sautéed dumplings), *227–8, 239,* 241
  red chili oil dumplings, *227–8, 266,* 268
  steamed Siu Mai, *239,* 240

E

egg noodles, 16, *18*
  see also noodles
egg white, 52
eggplant: deep-fried cakes, 93
  Sichuan braised, 96
eggs, 26–9, 108–17
  basic plain stir-fried omelet, 109
  basic steamed egg, 112
  egg flower pork (Mu Shu Rou), 250–2, *251*
  egg-flower soup, *59,* 63
  egg-fried rice, *48*
  egg pouches (small omelets), 114
  fancy steamed eggs, 112
  Huang-pu boatmen's egg omelet, 111
  Peking sliced egg-battered chicken in garlic and onion sauce, 160–1
  Peking sliced fish omelet, 118
  quails' eggs on shrimp toast, 236
  steamed in three colors, 114
  stir-fried Chinese omelet with onion and bacon, 110
  stir-fried Chinese omelet with tomatoes, *102,* 109
  stir-fried with oysters, 115
  stir-fried scallops with, 144

stir-fried shrimp 'soufflé', 110
yellow flowing egg (Lui
    Huang Dan), 115
eight treasure pudding, 218, 220
electric rice cookers, 13
equipment, 8–13

F

fish, 118–31
    braised whole fish in hot
        vinegar sauce, 125, 127
    crackling cream of ground
        fish soup, 61
    fish sauce, 28, 29
    Fu-yung, 119
    Peking sliced fish pepper
        pot soup, 65
    Peking sliced fish in
        'standard sauce', 252
    Peking sliced fish omelet,
        118
    poached fish balls with
        shrimp and mushrooms,
        119
    poached fish with garnish,
        130
    preparation, 40, 41
    rival of crab, 253
    sautéed fish steaks with
        garnish, 123
    soft-fried Peking sliced
        fish in wine, 131
    soy-braised sliced fish,
        123
    'squirrel' fish, 130–1
    steamed fish with garnish,
        124, 126–7
    steamed whole fish wrapped
        in lotus leaves, 121,
        122
    steaming, 49–50
    Yangtze 'fish salad', 126
five spice powder, 20, 26
    crispy five spice pork, 183
    crispy 'five spice' chicken
        legs, 147, 166
flounder: Peking sliced fish
        omelet, 118
fruit salad: Chinese
        gooseberry with mandarin
        and lotus seeds, 223
fruit, candied: eight
        treasure pudding, 218, 220
Fu-yung cauliflower, 94, 97
Fukien clam soup, 145
Fukien crab rice, 73

G

garlic, 16, 22
    bean sprouts with green
        onions and, 93
    Peking sliced egg-battered
        chicken in garlic and
        onion sauce, 160–1
    quick stir-fried lamb in
        garlic sauce, 206
    stir-fried chicken with
        cucumber and, 149, 154
    stir-fried lamb and liver
        with bamboo shoots, peas,
        lotus seeds and, 207
    stir-fried shrimp in garlic
        and tomato sauce, 145
garnishes, 35
ginger, ground, 20, 26
ginger root, 16, 22, 53
    bang bang chicken, 263, 265
    Cantonese ginger and onion
        crab, 128, 140–1
    marinated lamb with onion
        and, 208
    preparation, 32
    quick-fried shredded beef
        with onions and, 188, 201
    red-cooked lamb, 205
glutinous rice, 16, 18, 48
    eight treasure pudding, 218,
        220
    pearl-studded pork balls,
        184, 194
gold and silver rice gruel
        (congee), 71, 74
golden needles (tiger lily
        buds), 14, 21
green beans: quick fried with
        dried shrimp and pork, 90,
        97
greens: crispy 'seaweed' with
        almonds, 84
    Hainan chicken rice, 267,
        272
    Shanghai emerald fried rice,
        256, 258
ground rice: steamed chicken
        in aromatic ground rice, 163
    steamed ground rice-pork in
        lotus leaves, 190–1, 209

H

Hainan chicken rice, 267, 272
hair seaweed, 14, 21
    The Buddhist's delight, 88
    ham: bean curd, ham,
        mushroom and spinach
        soup, 64
    velvet of chicken, ham and
        corn soup, 65

herbs, 26
Ho-fen noodles with beef in
        black bean sauce, 270, 273
hoisin sauce, 28, 29, 53
honey: pears in honey sauce,
        219, 221
    quick braised chicken with,
        160
hot and sour soup, 58, 63
Huang-pu boatmen's egg
        omelet, 111
Hunan chili squid, 142
hundred year old eggs, 26, 27

I

ingredients, 14–29

J

jelly: Peking jelly of lamb,
        206–7
junket, almond, 220, 222

K

kidneys: preparation, 38–9
    stir-fried diced beef with
        kidneys, shrimp and
        mushrooms, 198
Kou Shoa deep-fried boneless
        duck, 171
kumquat, 16, 22
Kuo-tieh (steamed and
        sautéed dumplings), 227–8,
        239, 241

L

ladles, 13, 13
lamb, 204–15
    'ants climbing up trees', 214
    long-braised red-cooked
        lamb with Chinese
        mushrooms and chestnuts,
        205
    long-steamed wine-soaked
        lamb with tangerine peel
        and turnips, 212, 214–15
    Manchurian boiled and
        braised lamb noodles, 80–1
    marinated lamb with onion
        and ginger, 208

Mongolian barbecue of, 212,
        215
    Muslim deep-fried simmered
        lamb, 208
    Muslim long-simmered
        lamb, 210
    Peking jelly of lamb, 206–7
    Peking Mongolian hot pot,
        180, 211
    quick stir-fried lamb in
        garlic sauce, 206
    quick-fried shredded lamb
        and leeks, 209, 210
    red-cooked, 205
    stir-fried lamb and liver
        with bamboo shoots, peas,
        lotus seeds and garlic, 207
    triple lamb quick fry, 204
lard, 29
leek: Fukien crab rice, 73
    mustard and red chili oil
        beef with leeks, 200
    quick stir-fried lamb in garlic
        sauce, 206
    quick fried shredded
        lamb and leeks, 209, 210
lichee, 16, 22
lima beans, Yangtze stir-fried,
        85
lion's head meat balls in
        clear broth, 186–7, 192
liqueur: pears in honey sauce,
        219, 221
liver: stir-fried lamb and
        liver with bamboo shoots,
        peas, lotus seeds and garlic,
        207
lobster: Cantonese ginger and
        onion lobster, 140–1
    steamed, 139
long grain rice, 16, 18, 48
    see also rice
longon, 16, 22
lotus leaf shaped steamed buns,
        240
lotus leaves, 14, 17
    long-steamed lotus leaf-
        wrapped chicken, 166
    lotus leaf wrapped long-
        steamed duck, 170
    savory rice, 70–1, 225
    steamed ground rice-pork in,
        190–1, 209
    steamed whole fish wrapped
        in, 121, 122
lotus root, 16, 22
lotus seeds, 20, 29
    Chinese gooseberry salad
        with mandarin and, 223
    stir-fried lamb and liver
        with bamboo shoots, peas,
        garlic and, 207
Lui Huang Dan, 115

M

Madam Fei's spinach and radish salad, 89, 95
Manchurian boiled and braised lamb noodles, 80-1
mandarin orange: Chinese gooseberry salad with lotus seeds and, 223
mango beef, 200
marbled tea eggs, 26, 27
marinades, 52
  for Cha Siu roast pork, 271, 274
  marinated lamb with onion and ginger, 208
meat: preparation, 36, 38-9
  see also individual types of meat
meat balls: crispy, 194
  deep-fried crispy pork balls, 195
  lion's head meat balls in clear broth, 186-7, 192
  pearl-studded pork balls, 184, 194
  pork balls chrysanthemum style, 262, 269
Mei Kwei Lu, 29
melon chicken, 165, 172
menus, choosing, 276-81
milk: fried 'milk' with crab meat on crispy noodles, 264
Mongolian barbecue of lamb, 212, 215
Mongolian hot-pot, 11, 13
  Peking Mongolian hot pot, 180, 211
monosodium glutamate (MSG), 53
Moutai wine, 29
Mu Shu Rou (egg flower pork), 250-2, 251
multi-colored shrimp balls, 255, 256
mushrooms: poached fish balls with shrimp and, 119
  slicing, 31
  stir-fried diced beef with kidneys, shrimp and mushrooms, 198
mushrooms, Chinese dried, 14, 21
  bean curd, ham, mushroom and spinach soup, 64
  braised bean curd with, 106-7
  braised mussels with bean curd and, 133, 142
  Chinese mushroom soup with sparcribs, 261
  long-braised red-cooked lamb with Chinese mushrooms and chestnuts, 205
  red-cooked with chestnuts, and, 169

spring roll fillings, 232-3, 235, 266
steamed Siu Mai, 239, 240
stir-fried Chinese cabbage with, 86
mushrooms, straw, 24, 26
  chicken and straw mushroom soup, 60
Muslim deep-fried simmered lamb, 208
Muslim long-simmered lamb, 210
mussels: braised with bean curd and mushrooms, 133, 142
mustard: cold tossed celery in mustard sauce, 92
  mustard and red chili oil beef with leeks, 200
  quick-fried duck in soy and mustard sauce, 174-5

N

New Year dumplings, 223
noodles, 16, 18, 68, 76-83
  'ants climbing up trees', 214
  basic chow mein, 76
  beef chow mein, 76-7
  beggars' noodles, 72, 78
  braised cellophane noodles, 82, 90
  fried 'milk' with crab meat on crispy noodles, 264
  Ho-fen noodles with beef in black bean sauce, 270, 273
  Manchurian boiled and braised lamb noodles, 80-1
  Peking Ja Chiang mein noodles, 82
  Peking Mongolian hot pot, 180, 211
  Shanghai cold-tossed, 80
  Sichuan Dan Dan, 81
  stir-fried chicken with baby corn on, 257, 259
  'ten treasure' tapestry noodles, 83
  the 'Yunnan over the bridge' noodle soup, 64-5
nuts, 29
  eight treasure pudding, 218, 220

O

oils, 29
omelets: basic plain stir-fried, 109

egg pouches, 114
  Huang-pu boatmen's egg omelet, 111
  Peking sliced fish omelet, 118
  stir-fried Chinese omelet with onion and bacon, 110
  stir-fried Chinese omelet with tomatoes, 102, 109
onion: marinated lamb with ginger and, 208
  quick-fried shredded beef with, 202
  quick-fried shredded beef with ginger and, 188, 201
  stir-fried Chinese omelet with bacon and, 110
onion, green, 16, 22, 53
  bean sprouts with garlic and, 93
  Cantonese ginger and onion crab, 128, 140-1
  pancakes, 46-7, 243, 250
  Peking sliced egg-battered chicken in garlic and onion sauce, 160-1
  preparation, 34
orange: Chinese gooseberry salad with mandarin and lotus seeds, 223
oxtail, red-cooked, 262, 268-9
oyster sauce, 28, 29, 53
  Cantonese stir-fried beef in, 203, 213
  quick-fried broccoli with crab in, 92
oysters: deep-fried, 140
  stir-fried eggs with, 115

P

pancakes: Chinese, 176-7, 178-9
  green onion, 243, 250
  onion, 46-7
  spring roll fillings, 232-3, 235, 266
  spring roll wrappers, 232
paper-wrapped deep-fried chicken, 151, 152
pears in honey sauce, 219, 221
peas: bean curd with crab meat and, 101, 103
  stir-fried lamb and liver with bamboo shoots, lotus seeds, garlic and, 207
  tripe, squid and pea soup, 265
Peking cuisine, 244-5, 250-5
Peking diced chicken stir-fried in capital sauce, 157
Peking duck, 176-7, 178
Peking Ja Chiang mein noodles, 82
Peking jelly of lamb, 206-7

Peking Kuo-tieh (steamed and sautéed dumplings), 227-8, 239, 241
Peking Mongolian hot pot, 180, 211
Peking 'pomegranate' snow flake shrimp balls, 129, 135
Peking sliced egg-battered chicken in garlic and onion sauce, 160-1
Peking sliced fish in 'standard sauce', 252
Peking sliced fish pepper pot soup, 65
Peking spun sugar 'toffee apples', 252-3, 254
peppercorns, black, 53
peppercorns, Sichuan, 20, 26
  Sichuan peppered beef medallions, 202
peppers, 22, 26
  chicken with chilies and, 163
  preparation, 33
pickled mustard green, 24
pickles, 29
pine nuts, 20, 29
plum, steamed sparcribs with, 274
plum sauce, 29
pork, 182-97
  barbecue sparcribs, 193
  basic chow mein, 76
  braised bean curd family-style, 105
  Cantonese steamed sparcribs with black beans, 186
  capital sparcribs, 188, 196
  Cha Siu roast pork, 271, 274
  Chinese mushroom soup with sparcribs, 261
  crispy five spice pork, 183
  crispy meat balls, 194
  crispy skin roast pork, 183
  deep-fried crispy fingers of pork, 189, 191
  deep-fried crispy pork balls, 195
  egg flower pork (Mu Shu Rou), 250-2, 251
  lion's head meat balls in clear broth, 186-7, 192
  long-braised Tung Po soy pork, 182
  long-steamed pork hock, 195
  pearl-studded pork balls, 184, 194
  Peking Ja Chiang mein noodles, 82
  Peking Kuo-tieh (steamed and sautéed dumplings), 227-8, 239, 241
  pork balls chrysanthemum style, 262, 269
  preparation, 39
  quick fried green beans with

dried shrimp and, *90,* 97
quick-fried shredded pork in
capital sauce, *192, 193*
red chili oil dumplings,
227-8, 266, 268
Sichuan Dan Dan noodles, 81
Sichuan double cooked, *188,*
264
Sichuan Ma Po tofu, *102,* 106
Sichuan Yu-hsiang shredded
pork, *181, 190*
Singapore chow mein, 77, *79*
soy-braised (long cooked),
188, 196
spring roll fillings, 232-3,
235, 266
steamed ground pork with
Chinese sausages, *185,* 187
steamed ground rice-pork in
lotus leaves, 190-1, *209*
steamed spareribs with
plums, 274
stuffed wontons, 230-1
sweet and sour, *43,* 197
watercress and sparerib soup,
62
white-cooked sliced pork,
197
pork fat, 53
poultry, steaming, 51
see also chicken; duck

Q

quails' eggs, 26, *27*
on shrimp toast, 236

R

radish, green oriental, 16
radish, red: Madam Fei's spinach
and radish salad, 89, *95*
red chili oil, *28,* 29
hot-tossed shredded chicken
in red chili oil, 158
mustard and red chili oil beef
with leeks, 200
red chili oil dumplings,
227-8, 266, 268
red-cooked cabbage, 86
red-cooked chicken, 148
red-cooked lamb, 205
red-cooked oxtail, *262,* 268-9
red dates, 14, *21*
reducing sauces, *44*
regional cuisine, 244-75
restaurants, choosing and
ordering food in, 276-9
rice, 16, 68-73

almond 'tea', 219
basic fried, 69
egg-fried, *48*
Fukien crab rice, 73
gold and silver rice gruel
(congee), 71, *74*
Hainan chicken rice, *267,* 272
lotus leaf savory rice, 70-1,
225
plain boiled, 68
plain cooked gruel or congee,
69
preparation, 48
quick-fried shrimp in sauce
on crispy rice, 141
Shanghai emerald fried rice,
256, *258*
Shanghai vegetable rice, 72,
75
stir-fried chicken and celery
on rice, *150,* 152
Yangchow fried rice, 70, *74*
rice flour noodles, 16, *18,* 68
see also noodles
rice, glutinous, 16, *18,* 48
eight treasure pudding, 218,
220
pearl-studded pork balls,
184, 194
rice, ground: steamed chicken in
aromatic ground rice, 163
steamed ground rice-pork in
lotus leaves, 190-1, *209*
rival of crab, 253
rolling pins, 13
royal concubine chicken, 156-7

S

salads: cold tossed cucumber, 85,
90
Madam Fei's spinach and
radish, 89, *95*
watercress and water
chestnut, 86
white cabbage, 87
salt: salt and pepper shrimp, 138
salt-buried baked chicken,
158, *159*
salted eggs, 26-9
sauces, 29
black bean, *132,* 138, 144,
270, 273
black bean and chili, *188,*
201
capital, 157, *192, 193*
chili sauce, 28
garlic and onion, 160-1
hoisin sauce, *28,* 29, 53
hot vinegar, *125,* 127
mustard, 92
oyster sauce, *28,* 29, 53

reducing, *44*
shrimp, *28,* 29, 89
soy and mustard, 174-5
'standard', 252
sausages, fresh, 17
sausages, wind-dried, 14, *17*
steamed ground pork with
Chinese sausages, *185,* 187
sauté of four vegetables, 92, *94*
sautéing, 53
scallops: quick fry of three sea
flavors, *255,* 260
steamed with black bean
sauce, *132,* 138
stir-fried with egg, 144
Scotch whiskey, 281
sea bass, deep-fried and braised,
122
seafood, 134-45
seaweed, purple flat, 14, *21*
seaweed, hair, 14, *21*
The Buddhist's delight, 88
seeds, 29
sesame oil, *28,* 29, 53
sesame paste, *28,* 29
Yuan Hsaio (New Year
dumplings), 223
sesame seeds, *20,* 29
sesame shrimp on toast, 233,
239
Shanghai cold-tossed noodles,
80
Shanghai cuisine, 245-8, 256-61
Shanghai quick-braised chicken
on the bone, *155,* 164
Shanghai vegetable rice, 72, *75*
shrimp, dried, 14, *21*
quick fried green beans with
pork and, *90,* 97
Singapore chow mein, 77, *79*
stir-fried bean curd with, 101
stir-fried Chinese cabbage
with, 86
stir-fried spinach in shrimp
sauce, 89
shrimp, fresh: Cantonese
poached shrimp with two
dips, *117,* 137
deep-fried crispy jumbo
shrimp, 137
deep-fried crispy shrimp
balls, 134-5
fu-yung, 139
Huang-pu boatmen's egg
omelet, 111
multi-colored shrimp balls
255, 256
Peking Kuo-tich (steamed
and sautéed dumplings),
227-8, 239, 241
Peking 'pomegranate' snow
flake shrimp balls, *129,* 135
poached fish balls with
mushrooms and, 119
preparation, *40*

quails' eggs on shrimp toast,
236
quick fry of three sea
flavors, *255,* 260
quick-fried chili shrimp, 143
quick-fried shrimp in sauce
on crispy rice, 141
red chili oil dumplings, *227-8,*
266, 268
salt and pepper shrimp, 138
sesame shrimp on toast, 233,
239
steamed Siu Mai, *239,* 240
stir-fried diced beef with
kidneys, shrimp and
mushrooms, 198
stir-fried in garlic and
tomato sauce, 145
stir-fried 'souffle', 110
shrimp sauce, *28,* 29, 89
Sichuan braised eggplant, 96
Sichuan chili paste, 26
Sichuan cuisine, 248-9, 264-9
Sichuan Dan Dan noodles, 81
Sichuan double cooked pork,
188, 264
Sichuan hot crispy-fried
shredded beef, *188,* 203
Sichuan hot Ja Chai pickle, 29
Sichuan Ma Po tofu, *102,* 106
Sichuan peppered beef
medallions, 202
Sichuan smoked chicken, 156
Sichuan Yu-hsiang shredded
pork, *181,* 190
sieves, 13, *13*
simulated beggars' chicken, 153
Singapore Chow Mein, 77, *79*
Siu Mai, steamed, *239,* 240
snacks, *see* dim sum
snow peas, *22,* 26
quick fried, 85
sauté of four vegetables, 92
94
snow pickle, 29
sole: Peking sliced fish omelet,
118
soups, 56-65
bean curd, ham, mushroom
and spinach, 64
beef broth tomato, 57
chicken and straw
mushroom, 60
Chinese mushroom soup
with spareribs, 261
crab meat, *271,* 275
crackling cream of ground
fish, 61
duck carcass, 179
egg-flower, *59,* 63
Fukien clam, 145
hot and sour, *58,* 63
Peking sliced fish pepper pot
soup, 65
tripe, squid and pea, 265

velvet of chicken, ham and
    corn, 65
watercress and sparerib, 62
whole chicken or duck, 60-1
wonton, *234*
yellow fish, *55*, 62
the 'Yunnan over the bridge'
    noodle soup, 64-5
soy bean paste, 26
soy beans, 26
soy eggs, *27*, 29
soy sauce, *28*, 29, 53
    basic red-cooked duck, 169
    capital sauce, 157, *192*, 193
    long-braised red-cooked
        lamb with Chinese
        mushrooms and chestnuts,
        205
    long-braised Tung Po soy
        pork, 182
    quick-fried duck in soy and
        mustard sauce, 174-5
    red-cooked chicken, 148
    red-cooked lamb, 205
    red-cooked oxtail, *262*,
        268-9
    soy-braised pork (long
        cooked), *188*, 196
    soy-braised sliced fish, 123
    soy chicken in aromatic oil,
        275
sparecribs, *see* pork
spices, 26
spinach, 16, *24*
    bean curd, ham, mushroom
        and spinach soup, 64
    crab meat soup, *271*, 275
    Madam Fei's spinach and
        radish salad, 89, *95*
    quick fried with bean curd
        cheese, 88
    stir-fried in shrimp sauce, 89
spinach, water, 26
spring roll skins, 16, *18*, 232
squid: Hunan chili squid, 142
    preparation, *41*
    quick fry of three sea
        flavors, *255*, 260
    tripe, squid and pea soup, 265
'squirrel' fish, 130-1
'standard sauce', 252
star anise, *20*, 26
steamed buns, *234*
    Bao Tzu, 236-7, *266*
    lotus leaf shaped steamed
        buns, 240
steamed Siu Mai, *239*, 240
steamers, 8, *10*, 49
steaming, 49, *49-51*, 53
stir-frying, 42, *43*
stock, 56
    beef, 57
strange flavor chicken, 167
sugar, 53
sweet and sour pork, *43*, 197

sweet bean paste, 26
    Bao Tzu steamed buns with,
        237
    eight treasure pudding, 218,
        220
    Yuan Hsaio (New Year
        dumplings), 223

T

tangerine peel, 14, *21*
    long-steamed wine-soaked
        lamb with turnips and,
        212, 214-15
    white-simmered
        double-cooked
        tangerine duck, 170-1
'ten treasure' tapestry
    noodles, 83
tiger lily buds, *see* golden
    needles
toast: quails' eggs on shrimp
    toast, 236
    sesame shrimp on toast, 233,
        239
'toffee apples', 252-3, *254*
tofu, *see* bean curd
tomato: beef broth tomato
    soup, 57
    quick stir-fried beef with, 199
    stir-fried Chinese omelet
        with, *102*, 109
    stir-fried shrimp in garlic
        and tomato sauce, 145
tripe, squid and pea soup, 265
triple lamb quick fry, 204
trout: yellow fish soup, *55*,
    62
turnip, Chinese, 16, *22*
    dried, *24*
    long-steamed wine-soaked
        lamb with tangerine peel
        and, *212*, 214-15

V

vegetables, 16, 26, 84-97
velvet of chicken, ham and corn
    soup, 65
vinegar, 29, 53
    braised whole fish in hot
        vinegar sauce, *125*, 127

W

water chestnut, *24*, 26
    'cake', 222
    watercress and water
        chestnut salad, 86
water chestnut powder, 52
watercress: watercress and
    sparerib soup, 62
    watercress and water
        chestnut salad, 86
wheat flour noodles, 16, *18*,
    68
    see also noodles
whiskey, 281
white-cooked cabbage, 87
white-cooked sliced pork, 197
white-cut chicken, 149
wine, 29, 53
    choosing, 281
    drunken chicken, 161
    long-steamed wine-soaked
        lamb with tangerine peel
        and turnips, *212*, 214-15
    royal concubine chicken,
        156-7
    soft-fried Peking sliced fish
        in, 131
wine-lee paste: quick fry of
    three sea flavors, *255*, 260
winter pickle, 29
wok brushes, 8, *10*
wok scoops, 13, *13*
wok stands, 8, *10*
woks, 8, *10*, 42, 49
wontons, *238*
    skins, *18*
    soup, *234*
    stuffed, 230-1
wood ears, 16, *21*
    soft-fried Peking sliced fish
        in wine, 131

Y

Yangchow fried rice, 70, *74*
Yangtze 'fish salad', 126
Yangtze stir-fried lima beans, 85
yellow bean paste, 26, *28*
    capital sauce, 157, *192*, 193
yellow fish soup, *55*, 62
yellow flowing egg (Lui Huang
    Dan), 115
yellow rice wine, 29
Yuan Hsaio (New Year
    · dumplings), 223
The 'Yunnan over the bridge'
    noodle soup, 64-5

Z

zucchini: stir-fried sliced
    chicken with, 164

■ ACKNOWLEDGEMENTS ■

The author wishes to thank Barbara Croxford for the competence and
efficiency of her editing; Mrs D. Liang, Madam C.W. Fei and
Miss Elaine Ngaan for preparing such elegant dishes for photography;
and, the photographer, David Burch for his unstinting efforts to
make every dish an artistic creation.

The publishers wish to thank the following for the loan of china,
glassware, kitchen equipment and provisions:
Cheong-Leen Supermarkets, Tower Street, London WC2
The Reject China Shop, Beauchamp Place, London SW1
Liberty, Regent Street, London W1
David Mellor (kitchen supplies), Covent Garden, London WC2

Additional photographs were taken by Stephanie Colasanti (pages 6-7,
9, 15, 242-3, 248-9) and Michael Freeman (page 280).